CHELTENHAM TOWN
TOWN THE RISE OF THE ROBINS

'The goal' – but who scored it? Michael Duff and Jamie Victory v. Yeovil, April 1999.

CHELTENHAM
TOWN
THE RISE
OF THE ROBINS

Peter Matthews
&
Mark Halliwell

Foreword by Steve Cotterill

TEMPUS

Dedication

Peter: To my parents for developing my love of football, and to Jeanie for encouraging it to grow.

Mark: To the memory of my late father, Derek, and to Tania for all of her love and support.

First published 2002

PUBLISHED IN THE UNITED KINGDOM BY:
Tempus Publishing Ltd
The Mill, Brimscombe Port
Stroud, Gloucestershire GL5 2QG

PUBLISHED IN THE UNITED STATES OF AMERICA BY:
Tempus Publishing Inc.
2 Cumberland Street
Charleston, SC 29401

British Library Cataloguing in Publication Data.
A catalogue record for this book is available from the British Library.

ISBN 0 7524 2730 X

Typesetting and origination by Tempus Publishing.
Printed in Great Britain by Midway Colour Print, Wiltshire

Contents

Acknowledgements

The idea for this book came on the trip back from Cardiff after the play-off final in May. Both of us had independently thought about writing something about the recent successes of the club, and for both of us, the play-off victory was the moment that made us move from thought into action. We've know each other for a few years now and have always got on well, and enjoyed each other's company. Camaraderie tends to develop when you're waiting for an interview on a cold, wet away ground in the middle of winter, and it seemed sensible to pool our resources. We're mighty glad we did, having now completed the book – it was hard enough work for two people!

The plan was simple: we wanted to write the book with as much insight as we could from key people involved in the rise of Cheltenham Town. We could provide the bare facts, and a few memories, but the real colour of the book would come from those who were personally involved. Therefore, on a sunny summer's evening, we planned who we'd like to speak to. It was soon evident that our 'wish list' was too long, and, for reasons of time, needed to be focused on a few key people. The groupings were easy: players (both past and present), management and directors. We actively considered putting in interviews with supporters, but came to the conclusion that might wait for another time. In the execution of the great plan, without exception everybody has been helpful and has given freely of their time and effort – which comes as no surprise, for this is a friendly club, with no airs and graces and no need to negotiate interview fees, or liaise with agents, as some of our colleagues in the press who cover supposedly 'bigger' clubs spend their time doing.

To all those we spoke too, thanks. Particular acknowledgements are due to Paul Baker, who was very supportive of the book from an early stage (and who let Mark and me invade his house during the summer break), Steve Cotterill, who in the middle of pre-season training gave us three hours of his time one evening in Stoke and kindly wrote the foreword, and to Graham Allner, who also gave up valuable time whilst preparing for the new season. Thanks are also due to Lee Howells, who simply has an unbelievable memory of the games he's played in – it's a shame about the phone bill Lee, but many thanks!

Paul Godfrey, one of the most loyal of Cheltenham fans and now club secretary, was hugely helpful in coming up with obscure factual details needed for the writing of the book – thanks Paul. Thanks also to Spencer Feeney and Anita Syvret, editors of *The Gloucester Citizen* and *The Gloucestershire Echo* respectively, and to Antony Thompson for kindly allowing the use of pictures and match reports. To James and his colleagues at Tempus, thanks. The contract for the book was drawn up over lunchtime beers watching Germany and Ireland in the World Cup. It's good to work with a football fan as your editor, even if he does support Plymouth…

Finally, this has been a book written in our free time, whilst we kept our 'day jobs'. To our respective wives, Jeanie and Tania, thanks for your support and understanding. One day we may even persuade you to become Whaddon Road regulars.

Peter Matthews and Mark Halliwell
August 2002

Foreword

I was really pleased when I heard that Mark and Pete were writing a book about what we have achieved at Cheltenham over the last few seasons, and I'm delighted to be able to write a few words as an introduction. I consider myself really fortunate to have been manager during such a remarkable time in the club's history – firstly because of all the success we achieved, which helped raise the profile of the club, both within the town itself and within the footballing community, and secondly because of the quality of the team that I worked with – from the players and my management team through to the directors and all the others who worked so hard to achieve success.

People often ask me to tell them the secret of our success and I always give the same answer – teamwork. What we created was a group of players who were totally committed to each other and all who worked towards achieving the same thing: success for Cheltenham Town. We didn't tolerate prima donnas or players who wouldn't be part of the team ethic and, as a result, there were no cliques like you can sometimes get in football. We were also fortunate in being supported by a board of directors who are genuine football fans and who do the job for the love of the game rather any other reason, not to mention some hugely loyal supporters.

When I look back, I think my biggest contribution was, with the support of my management team, getting players to believe in themselves. Self-belief is absolutely key in football, and it was great to see individuals playing at a level that they could previously only have dreamed about. I don't think that any other team will ever go from the Dr Martens League to Division Two of the Nationwide League and have four players whose ability to adapt and improve meant that they were with the club throughout the climb – Chris Banks, Michael Duff, Lee Howells and Jamie Victory.

Talking to Mark and Pete for the book brought back some great memories. There were so many good times – from the first promotion at Burton, through to walking out at Wembley and winning the Trophy; from the night we got into the League, right the way through to Cardiff earlier this year. I suppose, though, that if I had to pick one it would be the night we won League status – born and bred in Cheltenham, I'd never thought when I was growing up that the little local team would ever get anywhere near the League, and to do it after just one full season in the Conference was incredible.

Now, of course, I've moved on, and face a different and a new challenge at Stoke. It was difficult to leave, but I know from the huge numbers of cards and messages I got from fans that people understood why I felt the time was right to go. Many of the fans who wrote said they would now look for Stoke's result as the first result after Cheltenham's – all I can say is that the first question I'll always ask after our games is how The Robins got on.

Enjoy the book!

Steve Cotterill

Prologue

Each year, for the past fifteen years, one of the authors of this book takes part in a pre-season ritual, beloved of many football fans up and down the country, namely the predictions for who will win the various divisions, from the Premiership to the Conference, who will be promoted and who will be relegated. Over the last few campaigns, the number of correct predictions has increased markedly. The simple truth behind that is that as the richer clubs get richer, at all levels of the game, football is becoming more predictable.

It is against that background that we should view the remarkable story of Cheltenham Town and their rise from the Dr Martens League – the league below the Conference (the top non-League division) – to the Division Two of the Football League. Of course, clubs have had three promotions in quick succession before: in the 1960s Northampton Town rose from the old Fourth Division to the old First Division; more famously, Wimbledon went from Southern League to the top flight of English football in under ten years, and even Cheltenham Town's new local derby opponents, Swindon Town, went from the bottom rung of the Football League to the Premiership in the relatively recent past.

Yet this is a different era for football. Nobody really believes now that a club will ever again 'do a Wimbledon' – the amount of money needed to compete means that there may now be a ceiling above which the smaller clubs cannot rise. It is this which is one of the most noteworthy aspects of the Robins' rise through the divisions. The club has gained success without spending much money, with not a penny being spent on transfer fees in the time they have been a League club and, as chairman Paul Baker admits, a wage budget that 'has been consistently in the bottom three or four of whatever league we've been in'. All of this has been achieved in a town where, as we will see, there has been only limited success in football terms in the past, and certainly nothing of any interest to the national press – had we, as local journalists, earned money for each time the national press have begun a feature on the Robins 'Cheltenham as a town is better known for its racing' we would be rich men!

The second aspect of the climb has been the continuity. Four players – Michael Duff, Jamie Victory, Lee Howells and captain Chris Banks – have been at the club throughout the five year rise. Not only is this length of service a little unusual in this day and age of players regularly changing clubs, but it is all the more worthy of comment for the fact that the nucleus of the side stayed the same as the club moved upwards. So often, once promotion is gained, new players are brought in to help the club stabilise in the better standard of football. It is to the enormous credit of the individuals concerned that so many of the side from the Dr Marten's days have been able to thrive during the rise. This continuity has been key.

And finally, perhaps most emotionally, this is partly a story of local people at their local club. In this day and age we are used to seeing football people as some sort of mercenaries. Players play for clubs they have no real affinity for, often not even in the country they were born in. Football managers come and go, and even club chairman will often fly a 'flag of convenience' – taking over control of clubs not because of their life-long support for the club involved, but for the business opportunity. The Cheltenham story is different. What other side can you remember winning a significant trophy (the play-off final at Cardiff) where the chairman, the manager and the man of the match (Paul Baker, Steve Cotterill and Martin Devaney respectively) were representing the town in which they were born. Many of the directors are Cheltonians by birth, most of the local press are too. Somehow that makes it different!

The decision to write this book was made as the authors travelled back from Cardiff on 6 May 2002 on a packed and deliriously happy train heading back to Gloucestershire. We've both grown up in the town – Peter was born there and Mark moved to the town in the late 1970s – and have both been fortunate to witness the rise at first hand from the press box, although this has been as fans first and journalists second. We hope you enjoy the book.

Further proof of the rise of Cheltenham Town – Michael Duff became the club's first full international in February 2002.

Know Your History

Automatic promotion between the Conference and the Football League was first introduced in 1987 and from then until Cheltenham Town's elevation to the League in 1999, those clubs promoted fell into one of two camps. They were either clubs relegated from the League regaining their position (a very common occurrence until the Conference became predominantly full-time in the 1990s) – for example, Lincoln, Darlington and Colchester – or they were established non-League clubs, who had been challenging at the top of the Conference table in the past – such as Scarborough (the first club to benefit from the new rule), Barnet and Macclesfield. Indeed, Macclesfield, like Kidderminster after them, had to win the Conference twice before gaining entry to the hallowed band of ninety-two League clubs as they were deprived in the first instance because of failing the stringent ground regulations that ensure that a club is ready to enter the League off the field as well as on it. What makes Cheltenham Town different is that, if we are honest, there was no real history: no years of being one of the best clubs in non-League football, and no proud history of football in the town. It is this, perhaps, that makes the story of the recent successes all the more remarkable.

The club was initially founded in 1892, but had an undistinguished start, spending its first forty years playing in local leagues in Gloucestershire, a county which then, as until the recent past, was not famed for any real interest in football – certainly not association football anyway, given the dominance of rugby union football in the area.

Things started to take off in 1932 when the club moved away from the local leagues to join the Birmingham Combination, and then in 1933/34 the only FA Cup run of note saw them knock out Carlisle United before losing to Blackpool in the third round. It was to be over sixty years before this stage of the FA Cup would be reached again.

The Cup run had, however, given the club a higher profile and in 1935 they were admitted to the foremost competition of the time in the area, the Southern League. They joined a league comprised of thirty clubs split into three sections (Eastern, Western and Central) and finished in mid-table, alongside the reserve sides of many lower division League sides. Their best player in 1936/37 was Tim Ward, who within two years was to join Derby County – where he gained England recognition.

By the time of the following season, the Southern League had reorganised and Cheltenham were in a sixteen-team division drawing on teams from as far afield as Ipswich (who won the competition) and Barry. The Robins finished eleventh and spent the last two seasons pre-war in a similar position.

The seasons immediately after the Second World War were equally consistent, with goals galore, and the star man at this time was Peter Goring, who went on to play for Arsenal in the 1950 FA Cup final. For example, in the first season before the war the Robins won two games at home 7-3 (against Bedford Town and Millwall Reserves) and went one better by beating Exeter City Reserves 8-3. On the debit side in the same season they conceded seven goals at Merthyr and six at Gravesend. A club-best sixth position in 1950/51 was followed by a disappointing eighteenth place in 1951/52, which included a 10-1 defeat at the hands of Merthyr (in fact, in the first seven post-war seasons the Robins conceded 40 goals in seven defeats in South Wales).

The eighth post-war season saw only a 2-0 defeat at Merthyr, but the Welsh club won 6-2 at Whaddon Road as Cheltenham finished in twenty-first place – their lowest placing since entering the competition. Remarkably, this nadir was to see a real rise in the Robins' fortunes as the side finished fourth in 1954/55, en route to a run of six successive top six finishes. This was the side managed by Arch Anderson, which included such favourites as goalkeeper Bill Gourlay, Sid Dunn, Peter Clelland and locally born centre-half Joe Hyde. The side finished second to Guildford City in 1955/56, and then achieved their first success in terms of silverware by beating Gravesend 4-1 on aggregate in the Southern League Cup final two years later, during a season when they scored 115 goals in the league (remarkably managing nine goals at home in a game on three occasions in the process).

After such a period of success, 1961/62 came as a rude shock. Whilst Oxford United, captained by Ron Atkinson, comfortably won the Southern League, the Robins finished bottom and were relegated from the Premier League to the First Division. Fortunately it was to be a short stay, as two years later promotion was achieved from a First Division that included clubs such as Tonbridge (also promoted), Poole Town, Canterbury City, Clacton Town and Deal Town.

The side successfully consolidated their position back in the Premier League, and then had their best season for several years as the 1960s came to an end, as they finished fourth in 1967/68 with the results including an 8-2 home win against Yeovil. Hopes of another successful season the following year were raised by an FA Cup run which took them to the first round and a home tie with Watford, who were to win the (old) Second Division Championship that year. However, the Hornets won 4-0, and although the side battled through to the Southern League Cup final for the second time in their history, they were well beaten on aggregate by Cambridge United. Worse was to follow in the league, when the side finished twenty-first and were relegated on goal difference, the team missing the scoring of Joe Gadston, who moved to Bristol Rovers, and then Ronnie Radford who moved to Newport County (en route to FA Cup folklore with Hereford United).

Two undistinguished years followed in the First Division before the league reorganised itself into First Division (North) and First Division (South). Unsurprisingly, the Robins were placed in the Northern section, and this is where one of the authors of this book entered the scene, with childhood memories of the Robins trying, and narrowly failing, to gain promotion for what seemed like seasons on end, in a similar way to the near misses of the early 1990s. In fact, the record books show a total of five near misses with three successive third place finishes (when the top two were promoted), followed by a sixth and a fifth place, before promotion was finally achieved in 1976/77 behind runaway champions Worcester City (a stabbing at the ground during the 1-0 defeat at Whaddon Road to the men from St Georges Lane leading to a temporary ban on one of the authors being allowed to attend home games by himself). At last, under Dennis Allen's management, the Robins were back in the Southern League Premier Division.

The side survived the first two seasons, but then for 1979/80 a new national non-League competition, called the Alliance Premier League was created. The Robins missed out having not finished in the top half – the condition for entry into the new league – and finished instead in what was now the Southern League Midland Division in twenty-first place, heralding a run of what was arguably some of the most depressing seasons in the club's history. Indeed, in 1982/83, when the Southern League Premier Division was reformed, Cheltenham did not make the cut, and spent the season playing in the new Southern League Midland Division, effectively the third rung of non-League football, and the lowest level at which the club had played since admission to the Southern League in 1935. By this time they were the longest serving club in the entire Southern League.

The club were to only spend one season at this level, however, and this was the beginning of the revival of the club's fortunes that would be so spectacularly be ignited by the arrival of Steve Cotterill fifteen years later. Under the management of Alan Wood, the side won the division, by one point, from Sutton Coldfield Town, and they also had a great cup run in the Southern League Cup before losing to Alvechurch in the semi-finals. This was the year of Paul Tester on the wing, with Dave Lewis supplying the goals in the centre, and some evidence of the latent potential for football in the town came when nearly 2,500 attended the crucial promotion battle with local rivals Forest Green Rovers.

Consolidation was achieved in the first season back in the Premier League when John Murphy took over from Alan Wood, and this was followed by a first ever Southern League Championship the following year. The team benefited from an influx of Swindon Town players: Ray Baverstock, Kevin Baddeley, Brian Hughes and Steve Abbley all played during the season. The team won the title on the last day when they beat Alvechurch 2-1 at Whaddon Road in front of just under 2,000 fans. Also playing a role was a certain striker by the name of Steve Cotterill, who made his debut during the championship campaign, aged eighteen.

The Robins were now in the top division of non-League football, the old Alliance Premier (now called the Gola League), playing the top part-time teams in the country. They faced some old adversaries from the Southern League, but also many clubs they had only previously met during cup competitions such as the FA Trophy. It was a significant step up in class, but during their seven seasons in the division (which later became the GM Vauxhall Conference) the club more than held their own, with relegation in 1991/92 being an unpleasant shock after having never previously finished lower than sixteenth.

In truth, Cheltenham never really threatened at any stage to challenge for a League position once this possibility was created by the decision to introduce automatic promotion to the Football League in 1987. Their best year was probably 1989/90, when they gained much national media publicity by the signing of former Scotland international, and current TV pundit, Andy Gray, and climbed up to third by December before a drop in form – instigated by eventual champions Darlington's 1-0 win at Whaddon Road – saw them end up in the more familiar placing of eleventh.

The Conference years were very entertaining for fans, not just because of the quality of sides seen at Whaddon Road, but also because, for the first time since the early

1970s, there were FA Cup runs of note, with two appearances in the first round proper in three years. The first of these took them to Molineux, home of Wolverhampton Wanderers, who were then beginning their climb from the old Fourth Division. Brett Angell, who was to later that season be transferred to Derby County, gave the Robins the lead, but the side were outdone by a hat-trick from a man who was to later be a full England international – Steve Bull.

An even better performance followed in 1990 when a magnificent team effort saw a narrow defeat at Birmingham City's St Andrews ground – intense second half pressure failing to bring about a deserved equaliser from one of the best performances ever seen from a Cheltenham side.

Another cup run came in the first season after relegation, as The Robins reached the second round for the first time since the 1930s. The unlikely venue of St Albans saw history made as the side came back from a one-goal deficit to win 2-1, Jon Purdie scoring the winner. That took them through to a home second round tie with AFC Bournemouth. After a goal by Peter Shearer (ironically a former Robins player) gave Bournemouth the lead, Christer Warren's second-half equaliser took the sides back down to Dean Court for a replay which resulted in a 3-0 defeat.

Those cup exploits were some consolation for a frustrating first season back in the Southern League, or Beazer Homes League, as it was now called. Promotion back to the Conference could only be achieved by a top place finish, and the Robins finished second behind champions Dover Athletic. Not even the goals of Jimmy Smith, who finished as top scorer in the division, nor the first Cheltenham appearances of a certain Bob Bloomer, could enable them to catch the Kent club. Further second places in 1993/94 and 1994/95 were equally disappointing, as first Farnborough and then Hednesford proved too strong. Then, in 1995/96, promotion was denied them by a club who were to feature strongly in the Cheltenham story – the newly formed Rushden & Diamonds, who finished no fewer than twenty points ahead of the third-placed Robins.

So, in four seasons, the side had finished second three times and third once, and the struggle to gain promotion was starting to resemble the battles to get out of the old First Division (North) twenty years previously. Something had to change…

1

In the Beginning
1996/97

Think back to the summer of 1996. This was the year that 'football came home' as England narrowly failed to get to the final of Euro '96 – Gazza's goal, Seaman's penalty saves, Southgate's penalty miss. Doesn't really seem that long ago does it?

Meanwhile, in Gloucestershire, a group of semi-professional footballers were getting ready for a new season, looking to finally escape from the Southern League after their three runners-up spots and one third placing in the previous four years. Cheltenham Town, under the management of Chris Robinson and the chairmanship of Arthur Hayward, were hoping for the top spot that would guarantee them promotion. This was to be Arthur Hayward's last season as chairman, after a long spell at the helm of the club:

I joined the board back in the early 1980s having moved to the area from Kent, and very soon found myself chairman because the rest of the board resigned! This was back in the 1982/83 season when we won promotion to the Southern League Premier under Alan Wood. Unfortunately things didn't go so well the following season, so we had to ask Alan to leave, and we then appointed John Murphy, which I think was really the beginning of the success story of Cheltenham Town – even though it was a long time ago – John did a really great job for us.

One of his fellow directors was Paul Baker, who would take over as chairman of the club:

I was born in Cheltenham, and I've always supported Cheltenham Town going back to the days of Roger Thorndale, Alec Carson, Alan Jefferies and that era of players. I've got great memories of Cheltenham Town and going to some memorable grounds – on the supporters coaches to Merthyr Tydfil, where I helped carry the kit off once, Dunstable and those types of places. It's been fantastic. If you can't play for, or manage, your local team, what better than to be a director. What's been great for me is being able to make a difference because I believe that we have made a difference at this club, and the impact this has had on the town generally, the morale of the town, the local economy, and bringing a real feel-good factor to the town in the last five years.

The then chairman recalls his feelings at the start of the season:

Well to be honest once we had been relegated from the Conference into the Southern League we thought it would be relatively easy to get back with our background, but

Exterior of Cheltenham Town Football Club.

as everyone knows there was always one team better than us so we ended up missing out. We kept thinking though at the start of every season that this would be our year. The other issue we had was off the field because back then the financial criteria for getting into the Conference were really strict – so not only did you have to win the league, more importantly you also had to have a sound club financially, which could be difficult to prove.

Lee Howells, Cheltenham Town's longest serving player, remembers the view of the squad:

At the start of the season we all thought we'd do well, but to be honest we felt that if we had one or two more players we might win it. Things were very different back then – we all got together for training on Thursday night, and began planning our Saturday night out. I'm not saying we weren't ambitious, but perhaps we weren't ambitious enough – we were perhaps just enjoying being one of the top clubs in the division, rather than the top one.

Jason Eaton, the striker who would achieve fame with a famous goal later on during the Robins' journey, echoes his former team-mate's recollections:

It had become very frustrating for everyone, and it was obvious that something was missing to get us promotion. The players were there, no question, but perhaps we just needed someone to get the best out of us. We always thought we were good enough, but after we kept just missing out I think some of the players lost a bit of their self belief. Chris Robinson used to quite like me as a player and I seemed to fit into his plans, but I had a lot of striking partners along the way, some for one or two games, which was difficult. The other thing was that we knew that the club was in debt and that every big gate or cup run was massive because it meant the directors could pay some of the debt off.

There were the usual comings and goings in terms of players over the summer, the most significant signing being that of Jamie Victory, who would be an important member of the team over the next six seasons. The defender made his debut in a pre-season friendly at Cinderford, and the story is that he was so impressive during the first half that a group of supporters saw Chris Robinson at half time, and virtually demanded that the manager sign Victory there and then – after just 45 minutes of football for the Robins. For the player himself it was a bit of a surprise:

I had left Bournemouth and was looking for a club when Chris Robinson phoned me up, and I decided to come down just to keep fit, and maybe to put myself in the shop

Cheltenham Town FC: 1996/97 team. From left to right, back row: John Atkinson (physiotherapist), Chris Robinson (manager), Bob Bloomer, Scott Starr, Kevin Maloy, Mark Freeman, Darren Wright, David Elsey, Chris Price (assistant manager). Middle row: Mark Bellingham, Paul Chenoweth, Jimmy Wring, Chris Banks, Andy Hughes, Jimmy Smith, Phil Sarjeant, Wally Attwood (kitman). Front row: Dean Clarke, Steve Benton, Martin Boyle, Jason Eaton.

window. I enjoyed it at the club and stayed, but I had not really intended to stay – it was just somewhere to go and train at first. I was nineteen, and had been at West Ham at first, so to suddenly find myself without a club was a big culture shock for me. I wanted to get back in the League and to be honest I didn't like part-time football because I was used to training all the time. In the end though I had to take what was available, and that's what I did – and I think I made the right decision.

The season opened on 17 August 1996. In 2002 this day would see the Robins at Tranmere, but six years previously, Sittingborne provided the opposition at Whaddon Road. Do you think you're a real Cheltenham fan? If so, then cover up the page quickly and try and recall the team that won that game 2-0.

The side that day was: Kevin Maloy, Dean Clarke, Jimmy Wring, Chris Banks, Mark Freeman, Jamie Victory, Darren Wright, Bob Bloomer, Jason Eaton, Mark Bellingham and Paul Chenoweth. The substitutes were Martin Boyle, Lee Howells and Andy Hughes. A crowd of 703 were in attendance. In fact the first three matches of the campaign were all won, Lee Howells getting two goals in the 3-1 victory at Dorchester in the second game, and Jamie Victory scoring in the 2-0 home win over Kings Lynn. Although the next match, at Salisbury, was lost 2-0, the side then won three matches in succession – a run that included the novelty of three goals in two games from Chris Banks (two in one game at home to Atherstone, where the gate was just 610).

Six wins out of seven was a pretty good start by anybody's standards, but it wasn't enough to lead the table at the start of September. Annoyingly for Robins fans, that honour went to their fierce local rivals, Gloucester City, who had an identical record, but with a certain Dale Watkins scoring plenty of goals, they enjoyed a better goal difference.

By late October, much of that early season optimism at Whaddon Road had started to wane and fans were already concerned that their chances of promotion were slipping away. A poor run of one win in five league games meant the team was down to sixth, as Gresley Rovers powered through to a top spot that they would only relinquish briefly during the season. Support was starting to drift away as well – only 536 saw a 1-1 home draw with Dorchester. This was the game in which Jamie Victory rescued a point with a late equaliser and a young defender called Michael Duff made his debut.

Mike Davis, who has worked under five different managers at the club since a brief spell as a player recalls how Duff came to join the club:

Derek Bragg and myself brought Duffo to the club. We saw him playing for Carterton and invited him to play in a trial game, and I remember this snotty-nosed, sixteen-year-old kid turning up. He was ill on the night and should not have played and didn't do very well, but Derek and I still strongly recommended to Chris Robinson that we should take him on and happily we managed to convince him. He had something about him.

The bad league run was ended with a 6-0 rout of Ashford at Whaddon Road – two more goals for Jamie Victory and two for Lee Howells as the biggest win of the season was achieved in fine style – and a 2-2 draw at local rivals Worcester City was another indication that things were perhaps picking up.

The League was then temporarily forgotten about as the Robins prepared for an FA Cup tie at Peterborough. This was the first time they had appeared in the first round proper since 1992, and only their fourth appearance since 1973. The cup run had, in truth, been just as unconvincing as the league form. A late goal by Chris Banks had given the Robins a 1-0 win at Gosport in round one, and this had been followed by a 4-3 home win over Salisbury in round two (Jason Eaton scoring a hat-trick). Weymouth, once proud members of the Conference but now a side fallen on hard times in the Dr Martens League Southern Division, were next up at Whaddon Road, and the visitors defended well before Jimmy Smith netted the winner 20 minutes from time. The fourth and final qualifying round saw one of the matches of the season, and indeed one of the matches of the last five years for drama.

The draw took them to Twerton Park, home of Conference side Bath City – a side with whom Cheltenham had a long history of epic matches, and a local derby of sorts as well. The first game was anything but memorable, a good number of travelling supporters coming back home happy after a 0-0 draw, but the replay will live long in the memory of the 1,018 (the first home four-figure gate of the season) who watched it. The visitors scored first on 36 minutes through Mike Davis, and it stayed that way until the last minute when Martin Boyle, a former Bath player, equalised to take the match into extra time. Within five minutes of the restart the game was effectively over as first Jason Eaton and then Jimmy Smith scored, and the icing on the proverbial cake was a fourth from Lee Howells. It was evidence of the potential of the side – if only they could be more consistent.

At Peterborough, then (as now) in the Second Division – and therefore three divisions above their visitors at the time – the Robins battled hard, and got a 0-0 draw. That meant a replay at Whaddon Road, and with the possibility of an upset, the cameras from *Sportsnight*, the classic BBC midweek sports programme (now, alas, no more), came to see if the *coup de grace* could be applied. Unfortunately, it wasn't to be. The home side gave another really good account of themselves, taking the game into extra time before the League side scored twice early in the added thirty minutes. A late Jimmy Smith penalty gave the Robins hope before a third Peterborough goal in the last minute finally ended their aspirations. Lee Howells remembers the games well:

To be honest we could have been easily beaten by 3 or 4-0 because they battered us up there. In the second half I don't really remember personally crossing the half-way line. It was men against boys really. Then in the replay, it was a cold night – very frosty – and we could have won it in normal time without the need for extra time. I guess though we were just chuffed to have reached the first round, and done ourselves justice.

Arthur Hayward was also pleased to have reached the first round – a gate of 4,160 for the home replay meant some useful extra cash for the club:

Cheltenham Town manager Chris Robinson celebrates Cheltenham's goal against Peterborough United.

I remember being very nervous up at Peterborough but I thought we did really well, and then brought them back to Whaddon Road on a high – the TV cameras were there, and again we did pretty well for 90 minutes.

Meanwhile, inconsistency was still a problem in the league. In between the Peterborough cup ties the side travelled back to the eastern side of the country to record a 1-0 win at Cambridge City, but the first league game after the replay was lost 1-0 at home to Gravesend on a cold December afternoon, and when they conceded a late goal to drop two points at Crawley a week later the side were down to seventh place, the lowest position of the season. Gresley Rovers, Halesowen Town and Gloucester City were starting to pull away, with a gap of eight points between the Robins and the top three.

A 5-1 midweek win at Newport, with two goals apiece for Martin Boyle and Paul Chenoweth, was a further indication of the inconsistency, and then the last game before Christmas was also won 2-0 at home against another Welsh side, Merthyr Tydfil.

We weren't to know it back then, but that game was highly significant, for on the bench that day was a new signing, Steve Cotterill, as he recalls:

I came back from Ireland and did a bit of scouting for Wimbledon, and actually saw a couple of Cheltenham games because I was asked to look at Lee Howells for them. Then I got a call from Ray Baverstock, who was manager at Cirencester, saying he was desperately short of players, so I had a game for them. That game obviously got covered in the local press, and I then got a call from Chris Robinson asking if I would have a couple of games for Cheltenham over the Christmas period.

To be honest I said I didn't think that would be fair, leaving Cirencester where I could have played for the rest of the season, and then just coming in for a couple for matches – I needed a longer term commitment than that. So, to cut a long story short I ended up signing a playing contract for a couple of months, and did some coaching with the YTS boys at the time who were Michael Duff, Michael Jackson, Ross Casey, Dave Parker and Christy Fenwick. I really enjoyed the coaching, and I think it was a bit of variety for them so it went down well with them, and after that I got asked to put on a couple of sessions for the first team, which they also enjoyed.

His arrival was generally greeted with enthusiasm in the dressing room as Jason Eaton recalls:

When Steve came to the club as a player, I remember he came up to me in the dressing room and said, 'I'm not here to take your place, don't worry'. When he came I didn't know a lot about him, just a bit about his background – he was a big name because he had been at Wimbledon and Bournemouth. To be honest, I was very surprised to see him in our dressing room.

Howells also remembers his future boss joining the club:

We knew that Steve had played for the club before, and of course Keith Knight was at the club who knew him from then as well. When Steve first came to the club he and I sat on the bench together for a couple of games and had a good laugh really, and he was really interested in what was happening at the club.

One of the great occasions in football generally is the local derby, you know the type, Everton *v.* Liverpool, Rangers *v.* Celtic, Manchester United *v.* Manchester City, Newcastle *v.* Sunderland, and er … Cheltenham *v.* Gloucester. No honest, if you lived in Gloucestershire and followed football down the years, the local derby, traditionally played at Christmas and Easter, was one of the big matches of the season. The match at Meadow Park, Gloucester was even bigger than usual – Gloucester were third at the start of play, Cheltenham were fourth.

It was to be another disappointment. The Robins lost 2-1, despite taking the lead midway through the second half through Jamie Victory, and despite Steve Cottterill making his debut at number 10. The Gloucester hero was a man who was to feature prominently in the Robins' rise, Dale Watkins, who scored twice, the second three minutes from time to seal what at the time felt a crucial win.

There was a strong sense around this time that another season was slipping away – not even successive home victories either side of New Year against Nuneaton and Baldock could change that. Steve Cotterill has particular cause to remember the second of these games, a 3-2 victory.

I think that was the game where I first showed my managerial ability at the club. In the time I was helping out with Chris it didn't bother me that much whether he played

Back at his home town club: Cheltenham Town's Steve Cotterill in action against Nuneaton.

me or not, although I knew I was good enough to play in the side even though I hadn't played for a couple of years. Anyway, for this particular game I wasn't even on the bench, which was fine, and Chris asked me to watch the game from the stand. Anyway, I think we went 1-0 up but then we seemed to lose it and by half time we were struggling, and for me the immediate problem was in the midfield area – it was blatantly obvious. So I came down about five minutes before half time to talk to Chris and told him what I'd seen, and he said 'fine, I understand'.

So we got in the dressing room, and I just stood there when he started talking and he said the problem is in the midfield, and he just turned to me and said, 'Steve you've been in the stand, just tell them.' I looked at him, because I was really surprised and said 'You're the manager, you should tell them,' but he said 'no problem, you go ahead'. So I explained what I thought we needed to do to sort things out, and we nearly ran out of time because the referee was buzzing and buzzing to get us out and I had to finish. Anyway we won the game 3-2, and I didn't say anything, but I knew I had won the respect of the players in that half time period.

The future boss was back on the bench for the following Saturday's game, a home FA Trophy tie with Dulwich Hamlet. It was to be Chris Robinson's last game in charge as, despite leading at half time thanks to an early Jamie Victory goal, the visitors scored two second-half goals to record a 2-1 win. For many fans it was an outrage, despite the fact that Dulwich, from what was then the ICIS Premier Division (now called the Ryman League) were at a similar level within the non-League pyramid, it was a match that few had expected Cheltenham to lose.

Not only had many supporters had enough, so too had the board. On the Tuesday after the Dulwich defeat, 21 January 1997, Chris Robinson was sacked, as Arthur Hayward recalls:

We were a bit concerned about Chris really at this stage because we really didn't feel that he was carrying the players, perhaps because he wasn't a top player himself. We had some rumblings from the dressing room, and decided we had to act quickly in order to make sure the club didn't suffer and that's what we did. It wasn't an easy decision to make – there were people for him staying in the boardroom as well as those who felt he should go, and if you look at the timing of the decision we replaced him when we were third in the league so that was a brave decision.

It was indeed a brave decision – few clubs replace a manager when their side are still in the running for promotion, despite the inconsistent form the league table still read as follows:

	P	W	D	L	F	A	Pts
Gresley Rovers	22	14	7	1	41	19	49
Halesowen	24	13	6	5	43	27	45
Cheltenham Town	22	13	3	6	45	24	42
Gloucester City	23	13	2	8	45	32	41

Paul Baker recalls the time as being a difficult one as well:

I think at the time we felt that we were flattered by where we were, and I'm not sure we felt that Chris Robinson would do it for us – he was a great bloke, and we didn't fall out with him, but we felt it was time for a change, we'd had a lot of near misses, and we were concerned about the manner of the performances.

Lee Howells has similar thoughts about his former manager:

Chris was a really nice person, and talked a good game, but to be honest I wasn't really convinced by him as a manager and I know a number of the lads thought the same. He brought in a number of new players, and I think some of them weren't any better than those we had… but he was a good guy.

The question was, who would take over. In the event the man who succeeded Robinson was already at the club, and, on 22 January 1997, the appointment of Steve Cotterill as manager, initially until the end of the season, was announced. The Cotterill era was under way.

Arthur Hayward recalls the momentous decision to appoint Steve Cotterill as manager:

Of course some of us, namely Colin Farmer, Rod Burge and myself, knew Steve from before when he was a young player with us – even in those days he was a very assured person, he knew what he wanted to do, and he spoke his mind, so we knew what we would be getting! We talked long and hard as a board as to whether he would be the right choice, and we just thought that given how successful John Murphy had been, having originally been a player with us, Steve might be able to do the same thing, so we decided to offer him the job until the end of the season to see what would happen. We felt we had to act quickly, and we just felt that Steve's experience of the professional game would help us, so we didn't consider anybody else.

At the time Hayward was quoted in the local press as saying that he believed that Cotterill 'could lead us to promotion'. Even more prophetically, he declared that his new manager was 'clearly a very ambitious young man who we believe has exactly the right credentials to succeed in management', citing not only his previous experience at Wimbledon, but also his spell with Sligo Rovers in Ireland, which included a campaign in the UEFA Cup. Nevertheless the chairman was still cautious – the new manager was only given a temporary contract until the end of the season.

Steve Cotterill remembers that time well:

They sacked Chris and I got a phone call out of the blue, asking me to take over until the end of the season. I said to them that I didn't think that to the end of the season was fair, because I knew they wanted to get promoted, and at that time, to be honest

Cheltenham Town's new manager, Steve Cotterill.

I think Gloucester City had a much bigger squad than we did, and it was going to be tough. But it was that thing about going back to your home town – looking back it was a big risk though, because I knew there were people thinking can he manage? The Cheltenham public didn't know I'd already managed in Europe with Sligo. Anyway I went back and signed up to the end of the season – to be fair, it wasn't a situation where it was, if you don't get us up you will lose your job, more that we'd have another look at it at the end of the season.

Lee Howells recalls that the new manager immediately made an impact:

From day one he had this presence to make you think hang on a minute, he's about, I'd better make sure I'm concentrating here or I'm going to get my collar felt. He was great though – he took all the players aside and talked to them and put little things into their heads about how to get better. Suddenly it was all much more professional, he was saying to us all, that if we wanted to be better players we had to sort our lives out and be more focused, things like not drinking during the week and diet. His ambition and enthusiasm just got everybody going.

Chris Banks, who was to skipper Cheltenham when they made the Football League, took it in his stride and remembers:

'I think we were a little surprised when he was appointed because he'd only been at the club for a short time. I was open-minded though because I try and take people as I find them, so I thought, let's give this guy a chance.'

The first game for the new manager was at Central Park, not in New York or even the one in Wigan, but in Sittingborne in Kent, a slightly different venue from Cotterill's final game in charge – the Millennium Stadium in Cardiff.

The match was lost 1-0, Gary Kemble scoring the winner for the home side 10 minutes from time against a side that lined up Gannaway as follows: Duff, Wring,

Banks, Freeman, Victory, Chenoweth, Clarke, Boyle, Smith, Bloomer. Subs: Wright, Symonds, Parker.

Worse was to follow a week later as the Robins lost again, this time at home to King's Lynn. As in the previous home game, under different management, Cheltenham let slip a half-time lead, and conceded a late goal to slump to a 2-1 defeat. This was despite the first appearance for a new signing, locally-born Keith Knight who, having started his career at the Robins and then moved into the League with Reading, came back to Whaddon Road on a month's loan from Halesowen.

Arthur Hayward remembers the inauspicious start:

We'd gone down to Sittingborne and lost, and then of course lost at home the following week, and I can remember looking across at the rest of the board and thinking 'what have we done here', but we knew that morale in the dressing room was pretty low when Steve was appointed and so it would take him a while to sort things out. I think that some of the players had got a bit cosy with Chris, and perhaps a bit complacent so Steve was like a breath of fresh air.

The manager was inclined to be less patient:

I said to the boys when I took over that I thought we could afford to lose four games out of the last twenty, and of course after two games it was two out of eighteen! We lost the first away at Sittingborne, which was a really dour game, and then we played King's Lynn at home and we were sensational that day. I'd signed Keith Knight, who was my first signing and he was outstanding but we still lost; however I think we were able to build from there.

One important factor when I came back was that Michael Duff wasn't there – he was on loan at Cirencester and I was being told from quite a few quarters that Michael Duff wasn't good enough. Well, well, well!

Duff himself is clear that the appointment of Cotterill as manager was a turning point in his career.

I was on loan at Cirencester when Steve came, but I was brought back straight away. He had been training with us during the day when he came back as a player, and he had seen me play in our first team. I'd done well in couple of the games, particularly one against Merthyr, and I think that even though he was only a player then, he still had his manager's head on.

I was then sent on loan, but I only played a couple of games for Cirencester, and then Steve brought me back and I played in his first game at Sittingborne. I'd only played in five or six first team matches before then after making my debut against Dorchester in the previous November.

I think he must have seen something that other people didn't because I'd been turned away by a number of people and clubs for being so small. I think one thing he liked was my desire to win. We would have games of head tennis and if my team lost I would lose my head a little bit, but I think he liked that as it was the same mentality as he had.

I have a huge amount of respect for Steve – when I was seventeen, people were not taking a chance on me, and were saying that I would not make it at Dr Martens League level. Now I am playing in Division Two, and I am a Northern Ireland international – I owe him my career.

With bad weather and cup ties causing postponements, it was in fact to be nearly a month before Cotterill recorded his first win as manager – a 2-1 home win against promotion rivals Halesowen; two further wins followed in succession to set up the important match at leaders Gresley Rovers on 22 February. Gresley Rovers are a good example of one of many non-League clubs that have had brief periods of glory which have not been able to be sustained. This was their greatest ever season, under the player-management of Paul Futcher, and with Garry Birtles playing a prominent role off the field. The Derbyshire side, based in Swadlincote, were playing at the highest level in their 115-year-old history, much of which had been spent in local leagues. They were setting a fearsome pace at the top of the league and had only lost two games all season.

It was an extremely tough test for the Robins, and in the event, despite dominating possession they were beaten 2-0, a win which put Gresley eight points clear of their visitors with a game in hand. That might have been the end of the promotion dreams, had it not been for one major fact – Gresley's ground was not of the appropriate standard for the Conference as, with a capacity of just 2,000 (and only 400 seats), it was too small. As they could not be promoted even if they won the league, the race was on for second place, which would now be enough to send the club that finished there into the Conference. Steve Cotterill acknowledged that the strength of their side was too great:

The result up there was about right – we weren't quite ready to play a side like them, and they deserved to beat us.

Despite this loss, the players were seeing a change in the way the club was being run, as Jason Eaton recalls:

When Steve took over from Chris Robinson, things changed straight away – he seemed to have this air about him. You knew from the off that he was the boss, and he made sure that you knew it as well! He had so much enthusiasm, and people looked up to him because he had played at a high level and it was obvious that he knew his stuff. His desire to win was huge, and he brought a bit of that Crazy Gang mentality into it – he must have learnt a lot from those days at Wimbledon.

Things were getting better and Arthur Hayward was soon starting to see the benefits of his new manager:

I think everyone knows that Steve is a stickler for doing things right, and some of the boys found that difficult to take early on, but as the weeks went by the smiles were returning round the club, and we were thinking that this appointment might be a good one. There was much more togetherness in the team – you could see that they were looking after each other.

One of the characteristics of the Robins in the Cotterill years has been their consistency, and as the new manager began to get to grips with his task, the side went on an eight-game unbeaten run, of which five were drawn. Of particular significance were the last three games in this run, which saw them pitted against three sides up with them at the top of the table: Gresley, Halesowen and Gloucester.

A season's best home league crowd saw an entertaining 2-2 draw against league leaders Gresley at Whaddon Road on 25 March. The Robins were unable to keep a 2-1 interval lead, in a match that saw a debut for midfielder Richard Dunwell, signed on loan from Barnet. Dunwell scored on his debut, but his spell at Cheltenham will be remembered for something completely different ...

Dunwell scored in his second match as well, twice in fact, in a remarkable 5-1 win at Halesowen; all this after the home side had led 1-0 at half time courtesy of a Mark Freeman own goal. It was a key win, and it set things up nicely for the Easter Monday clash at home to Gloucester City a crucial game as one glance of the league table at that stage confirms:

	P	W	D	L	F	A	Pts
Gresley Rovers	35	20	10	5	60	33	70
Cheltenham Town	35	19	7	9	69	40	64
Gloucester City	34	18	7	9	67	43	61
Halesowen Town	35	17	8	10	67	49	59
King's Lynn	36	17	8	11	56	53	56

The match, perhaps unsurprisingly, ended in a draw, in front of a season's best attendance of 3,005. Dave Webb gave the Tigers the lead, and although Darren Wright equalised shortly after half time, the Robins were unable to get the win that would have taken them six points clear of their local rivals. Steve Cotterill remembers the match, and also the state of the pitch, which by that stage of the season was raising doubts.

I remember the pitch was a real dust bowl – you could make a sandcastle in the middle of the pitch, it was an absolute disgrace. I remember thinking that if we ever got any money that would be the first thing that we would want to invest in. As for the game, I seem to remember Dale Watkins didn't get there for the start of the game for Gloucester, and I remember a real melee in the centre circle after Adie Mings got hold of Darren Wright by the hair. It was a tough game though, as you would expect.

Gloucester now turned their attention to a two-legged FA Trophy semi-final against Dagenham & Redbridge, and a ten-day break from league action. In fact it was to be longer, as with both legs drawn, the tie went to a third game at Slough, which caused a full two-week break from league action. To this day, many City supporters are convinced that it was the cup run that cost them promotion, as it was to leave them playing their last seven league games in a fortnight.

Meanwhile the Robins moved on to Manor Park, Nuneaton, with the chance to open up a six-point gap on their local rivals. Unfortunately, it wasn't to be as they failed to claw back an early goal and went down 1-0, only the fourth defeat under manager Cotterill. With Halesowen losing at home to Merthyr to find themselves five points behind the Robins with five to play, it was looking like a straight fight between the two Gloucestershire sides for the vital second position, although Nuneaton must have felt that they still had an outside chance as that win moved them to within six points of the Robins with one game in hand. Gresley's 2-0 win at King's Lynn meant that not only were Gresley now eight points clear and likely to finish as champions, but that King's Lynn looked to be out of the race.

The following Saturday, with Gloucester still otherwise engaged, the Robins took their chance to move six points clear of the men from Meadow Park. Darren Wright, who was scoring some crucial goals at this stage in the season, scored the winner six minutes into the second half against Hastings at Whaddon Road. Despite this win, the gap between Cheltenham and the third placed side was still only three points – with King's Lynn winning at Sittingborne to leave themselves just three points behind, albeit having played a game more.

We were now into mid-April, with just three Saturdays left of the league season. The Robins faced a long trip down to deepest Kent to play struggling Ashford Town – a reminder for those people currently advocating regional leagues that 'the south' of England can be a large geographical area. They weren't at their best, despite manager Cotterill including himself for the second week running in an unfamiliar number 4 shirt, and they were thankful to Darren Wright, once again. The midfielder scored with eight minutes left to rescue a point after Ashford had taken the lead in the first half. Gloucester meanwhile, having suffered the disappointment of defeat in their Trophy semi-final, bounced back with a 3-1 home win over Gravesend. They now held the upper hand, with their games in hand. Could they make the most of them? King's Lynn's challenge this time did seem over after a 1-0 home reverse to Crawley Town. The table on the evening of 19 April 1997 looked like this:

	P	W	D	L	F	A	Pts
Gresley Rovers	39	23	10	6	69	37	79
Cheltenham Town	39	20	9	10	72	43	69
Gloucester City	36	19	8	9	71	45	65
King's Lynn	40	19	8	13	60	56	65

Both sides played on Tuesday 22 April. Cheltenham won 4-1 at Sudbury, four first-half goals, including two for Jason Eaton, doing the trick, whilst Gloucester were held 2-2 at Dorchester, all four goals coming in the first 32 minutes. Even better news for the Robins came two days later as Gloucester faced another game in their hectic run in

Atherstone, coming away from Meadow Park with a draw. The gap was now five points, and Gloucester had just two games in hand.

On the penultimate Saturday of the season, Gloucester faced the daunting prospect of a trip to Gresley, with the Robins playing their last home game of the season at home to Newport AFC. Unsurprisingly, Gloucester lost, their tired side succumbing to a side who were crowned Southern League Champions. More surprisingly, Cheltenham failed to take full advantage, as on a frustrating afternoon at Whaddon Road they were held to a goal-less draw in front of 1,565, a hugely disappointing result against a side lying one off the bottom of the league. Manager Steve Cotterill, a subsitute on the day, was booked in unusual circumstances for allegedly coaching his players as he warmed up along the touchline. *The Pink 'Un* described Cotterill as being 'aggrieved' by the decision – which was surely something of an understatement!

So the gap was now six points, with Gloucester having two games to play, and with an inferior goal difference of eight goals. Halesowen still had a mathematical chance, but as they were lying three points behind Cheltenham with a much inferior goal difference, it was realistically not going to be them. It was all down to the last week of the season.

The run in was a tense one for chairman Arthur Hayward:

I can remember on several occasions Colin Farmer and I sitting in the bar, or in the manager's room waiting for the Gloucester City results to come through – we would phone up the club where they were playing to get the result. I remember one occasion, I can't remember who it was against, and they were losing 2-0 with about 15 minutes to go but had a tremendous last few minutes and won the game!

Looking back now to the events of five years ago, tribute should be paid to Gloucester for their efforts in that last week of the season. As we have already seen, they were facing a punishing schedule of matches, and were having to cope with the disappointment of missing out on a trip to Wembley in the FA Trophy. They knew that they had to win both their games on the Tuesday and the Thursday of the final week of the season to set up a grand finale.

In the event, they did just that. Firstly, Dorchester were beaten 3-1 at home, the Tigers coming back from a goal down, and then Baldock were beaten in sensational style away from home by 3-2 with two goals in the last six minutes keeping their promotion dream alive, after they had been 2-0 down.

So, it was all down to the final day. The table looked like this as the teams prepared for their final matches:

	P	W	D	L	F	A	Pts
Gresley Rovers	41	25	10	6	75	38	85
Cheltenham Town	41	21	10	10	76	44	73
Gloucester City	41	21	10	10	80	53	73

The situation was very simple. With their superior goal difference, a win would take Cheltenham up, unless Gloucester won by a cricket score. If they didn't win, then they would still get promotion, provided that their result was as good as, or better than their local rivals. With the Robins facing a tough away fixture at Burton Albion, and Gloucester at home to mid-table Salisbury, it was finely balanced.

Steve Cotterill had some history to deal with before the game at Burton:

We had a big fear factor in the club about the Burton game – there was a real sense of 'Oh, Cheltenham don't do very well at Burton Albion'. I think that my time at Burton enabled me to show the players that they had no need to have a fear factor. I'd had a good time at Burton, and that stood me in good stead, because when we walked through the gates usually at somewhere like Burton our lads would be stared at or frowned upon because they're the opposition. Instead, at Burton, everyone greeted me like the prodigal son, because of my time there as a player, and that really helped.

In the event, it was a dramatic afternoon. Promotion was achieved, but the Robins needed a helping hand to do so.

The game at Burton was an epic in its own way, and ended 0-0, a result that meant that Gloucester would be promoted if they could win their game. For much of the first half, it looked as if they would do just that, as an own goal, ironically from former

Burton Albion v. Cheltenham Town. Richard Dunwell misses Cheltenham's penalty.

Burton Albion 0 Cheltenham Town 0

Richard Dunwell saw his penalty brilliantly saved by Darren Acton as Cheltenham failed to win but still earned promotion to the Vauxhall Conference.

The goal-less drew against a battling Burton, who were reduced to ten men by injury, was enough to help the Robins go up.

Cheltenham were level on points with Gloucester City at the start of the last round of matches, but with a superior goal difference knew any win would guarantee them promotion. However, they had the hardest match against a Burton side who had been promotion contenders for much of the season, while City were at home to mid-table Salisbury.

But with City blowing their chance in style with a 3-1 home defeat, Cheltenham were promoted, although there were some jitters early on as Burton pressed and news came from Meadow Park that City had taken a 1-0 lead.

The Robins had to withstand some early pressure with Alan Davies having a free kick turned away for a corner before Mark Freeman managed to get his head in the way of a firm strike from Hornby.

Kevin Maloy in the Cheltenham goal took two attempts to hold a cross from Davies and Nuttell should have done better when he found space, but shot tamely.

However, after withstanding the initial onslaught Cheltenham came close to scoring. Keith Knight's corner was well volleyed by Jamie Victory from eight yards, but Acton pulled off a superb reflex save.

Cheltenham were beginning to pick up their game but Dunwell was off target after cutting in from the right and Burton came back midway through the first period.

Nuttell finished a good move by driving straight at Maloy, and when the Cheltenham goalkeeper failed to punch away Devaney's header, Chris Banks was on hand to make a crucial interception. Bob Bloomer had another chance for Cheltenham towards the end of the half, but his free kick just clipped the bar.

Cheltenham's defence looked more secure end less nervy after the break and it was the visitors who had the best of the chances. The wall did its job from a Lee Howells free kick after Benton had fouled Jason Eaton. Burton had the odd chance and Darren Wright did well to deny Spooner, but it was Cheltenham who were upping their work rate and beginning to get on top. However, they wasted their best chance when Burton almost gifted them a goal. Simon Redfern brought Howells down but Dunwell was unable to beat Acton with the spot kick.

With twenty minutes remaining, Spooner was forced to leave the pitch with an injury and, with Burton having already used their three substitutes, they were forced to finish the match with ten men. Cheltenham failed to capitalise on this and Burton had a couple of late chances. However, neither side could break the deadlock and the Robins were able to celebrate promotion.

Burton Albion v. Cheltenham Town. Promotion to the GM Vauxhall Conference. Steve Cotterill (manager) with the runners-up trophy.

Cheltenham player Matt Lovell, gave them an eighteenth minute lead. It stayed that way until the hour mark when Salisbury equalised – now Cheltenham, still goal-less at Burton, were going up. At this stage though, the Robins would have expected to have needed to have won – with half an hour left and Gloucester on top, surely City would score again.

In the event, there were further goals, but to Salisbury as two late goals gave them an unexpected 3-1 win. To make matters worse, Gloucester defender David Johnson was sent off three minutes from time, which led to a mini pitch invasion by frustrated home fans. As a result, the referee took the players off the field, which led to a late finish and a delay for the celebrations at Burton.

It was a great day for chairman Arthur Hayward:

I think it was the most nervous time that we had, because we were so close to getting back to where we thought we rightly belonged – the Conference. We knew we were okay off the field because we had settled the financial situation – two or three directors had written off a lot of money to make sure that our balance sheet was right for the Conference. So we went off to Burton – it was a warm day and we got there reasonably early, as we used to do, went into the bar and sank a few pints to try and relax. Then we heard that John Barton had left out a couple of their key players because of injury, so that was another pint, and by this time it was all too much for

Burton Albion v. Cheltenham Town. Promotion to the GM Vauxhall Conference. From left to right: Dave Midwinter, Steve Cotterill and Bob Bloomer celebrate their win.

Burton Albion v. Cheltenham Town. From left to right: Steve Cotterill, Paul Chenoweth and Bob Bloomer celebrate.

Paddy Wood, one of the other directors, and he had to go for a walk round the perimeter of the ground to try and calm down!

Then the game started; the support was unbelievable and I thought that we were on top. It was 0-0 at half time, and I think Gloucester were leading at that time, so we then realised that we had it all to do in the second half. Then we got the penalty and we all thought, well this is it, but of course he missed it, and then news came through that Salisbury had equalised and then taken the lead – one of our old players, Matt Lovell, was playing for Salisbury and we were in touch with his parents who were at the game. They told us that when we had got the penalty the whole ground at Gloucester had gone quiet because everyone was listening on their radio, and then when it was missed it got the biggest cheer of the day.

So our game finished but because of the crowd problems they had at Gloucester they were still playing, so we had to wait for them to finish. I can remember walking round the ground biting my nails waiting for that whistle, and coming across from the other side was Colin Farmer, and we gave each other a hug because we were both so emotionally drained. It was something the board had worked so hard for – we had been determined to get back into the Conference and when the news was confirmed that we were up it was just sheer delight. I can still remember all those smiling people after the game – people who I'd first met back in the early 1980s when the crowds were around 270-280; you knew all their names, their first names. After the match, we went into the car park to see all the supporters getting on their buses – it was the beginning of course of a fantastic five years, but it's still my favourite memory, mainly I think because of all the hard work by the board over so many years.

Paul Baker's memories are equally vivid:

I think obviously Gloucester City were favourites. It wasn't a great game, but I remember sitting up in the main stand with our goalkeeping coach at the time, Martin Thomas, watching the game. It was 0-0 and we got a penalty and we missed it and you think 'Oh no, it's not going to happen', but at the same time you've got the radio station [after slight prompt agreed on as BBC Radio Gloucestershire!] behind us with the live feed coming in from Gloucester and you realise it's going to be our day.

The manager was getting his score-flashes from Paul Godfrey, now club secretary:

Paul was up in the stand and he was shouting out the scores – you could hear him yelling, yes, it's 1-1, and then it's 2-1 to them. I really remember the final one though – he was standing with both hands punching the air, saying it's all over, Salisbury have won 3-1.

Paul Baker's memories of the celebration have become a little hazy:

At the end of the game it was unbelievable – we were on the pitch, and walking round in a daze really, we couldn't believe the way the unexpected had happened – it was just unreal. To be honest, I cannot remember too much about it – some of the moments just merge – I suppose because we've had so many of them over the years. If we'd had just one great match like Wembley or Yeovil it might be easier, but we've had so many great days, one after another that you can't just bring them all to mind immediately, and I guess you focus on the most recent memories.

Lee Howells will never forget his afternoon either:

It was a brilliant day, one of the best days I've had at the club – I think the first time you achieve something it's always special. I can remember being on the pitch and there was the great

Delighted Cheltenham Town chairman Arthur Hayward at the match against Burton Albion.

roar from our fans, and we realised that something must have happened at Gloucester – and it wasn't going to have been a goal for them.

The manager remembers his first success as a manager at his home-town club very well:

It was obviously the catalyst for all that we later achieved – it was a great, great day. I remember us getting the trophy up on the balcony and on the pitch there were supporters of both clubs on the pitch, and it was a great atmosphere. Looking further ahead, Burton even took a coach to the Trophy final, and there's a picture of me with the trophy wearing both a Cheltenham Town and a Burton Albion scarf, so I had a great affinity with them – they were as pleased as we were that we'd been promoted.

Talking with other players and directors who were at the club five years ago, one is struck by the real sense of achievement that still exists in relation to that promotion. Just as for Arthur Hayward, it remains a favourite memory for many, even after all the other successes that have happened – perhaps a reflection of the fact that it had been achieved after so many years of hard work and near misses; perhaps because it was the first success. What is clear is that, looking back, it was a slightly fortunate first step on

the road to the Second Division. Gresley were the best side in the league, and suffered because of off-field issues – a lesson that Cheltenham's directors noted carefully. As they rose up the league, they would make sure that the pace of change off the pitch would match the progress on it.

Equally, Cheltenham were perhaps fortunate that Gloucester City became victims of their own success, forced to play catch-up in terms of league fixtures as a result of their cup successes – this was a scenario that the Robins themselves would face five years later. Steve Cotterill acknowledges that it could have gone either way:

I think it's amazing what's happened to both Cheltenham Town and Glou-

Burton Albion v. Cheltenham Town.
Promotion to the GM Vauxhall Conference.
Keith Knight with the runners-up trophy.

Burton Albion v. Cheltenham Town. The Cheltenham Town players celebrate.

*cester City since that day – the difference is incredible. I'm sure though that given the
squad they had at that time they would have done well if they'd gone up.*

So, stage one was complete. The Robins advanced to the top flight of non-League
football, where in their previous spell lasting seven seasons they had finished no higher
than eleventh. It was time for lift-off.

2

The Conference Challenge
1997/98

Having negotiated part one of his long-term plan, albeit via a slightly unorthodox route, Steve Cotterill was all set to embark on the new Conference challenge ahead – once he had sorted out his own future.

He recalls:

I didn't know if I was going to take the club into the Conference. The first thing I had to do was to try and negotiate a contract and find out if they wanted me to have the job. They did want me to have the job and it should have been easy to sort it out. But then you go from being the hero to thinking 'Are they really bothered about keeping me?' as you don't get offered the money you are looking for – but that happens at every club. You have to draw a line under what you want and what they want, and try and come to an agreement. So I never signed initially for the money I would have liked, but I knew that if we were successful, I would start to earn a little bit more. I knew Cheltenham paid me what they could afford to pay me and I think in the last two or three years I didn't really have a rise because I knew where we were at. I was paid a good wage and there was little point in going in and asking for more as it was better that we had extra money for something else.

Cotterill's decision to stay on coincided with the arrival of the club's new chairman, Paul Baker, who succeeded the long-serving Arthur Hayward, who had been in the job for thirteen (often difficult) years. Baker, a former Cheltenham Borough councillor and head of a successful Cheltenham-based insurance company, had been on the board for a few seasons. He recalls:

I have always supported Cheltenham Town and I had been invited to join the board as I was a sponsor of the club. I remember when I was asked to join the board, I went to look at a set of financial accounts, and was told to steer clear of the club as it was insolvent. But, as ever, the heart rules the head so I joined the board when we were in the Dr Martens League. Following promotion to the Conference, a couple of directors asked me if I was willing to take over the chairmanship. Arthur had been in the chair for thirteen years and had seen the club through some very difficult times when the club had nearly gone out of business on more than one occasion. I was chuffed to be asked and pleased to accept, but first I made sure all the directors were happy about it and also that Arthur was happy, as I did not want to put his nose out of joint. It was not a case of me coming in and taking over now we were back in the big time. It was almost a natural succession as I had put a lot of my own money into the club, and some of the other directors were not always able to do that. It was felt that as I had put a lot of my money and a lot of my time into the club, that it was appropriate for me to take the chair. It was a difficult decision at the time but the support I have had from the rest of the board had made it a lot easier and I have been very proud to be chairman through some very successful years. As a board, we have turned it around from an insolvent club to a success story.

Baker was thrown straight in to helping Cotterill prepare for the new challenge ahead in the Conference. Baker remembers:

We had been second in the Dr Martens League I don't know how many times. Having taken so long to get into the Conference, it was important that we stayed there, and that was our first target. So we set about strengthening the squad, and the key thing was that we were able, with a bit of money, to bring in a few quality players, and that, along with Steve becoming the full-time manager, was the difference. All of the players we brought in that season cost money, and we started to pay out reasonable wages as well.'

Steve Cotterill signs as manager of Cheltenham Town, watched by directors Paul Baker and Brian Sandland.

Cheltenham Town FC: 1997/98 team. From left to right, back row: Mike Davis (reserve team manager), Steve Murphy, Chris Banks, Ross Casey, Mark Freeman, Steve Book, Steve Cotterill (manager), Ryan Gannaway, Michael Duff, Mark Crisp, Darren Wright, Jamie Victory, Bob Bloomer. Front row: Wally Attwood (kit man), Michael Jackson, Christy Fenwick, Jimmy Smith, Jason Eaton, Keith Knight, Lee Howells, Russell Milton, Dale Watkins, Steve Benton, John Atkinson (physiotherapist).

Cotterill says:

Paul was lucky that he came in when he did, and in a way he ended up reaping the benefits of Arthur and the others keeping the club alive for ten years or so. I worked with Arthur initially, and had no problems with him, and never had any problems with Paul. Both of them let me get on with the job, and I had more or less carte blanche with the football side, which helped me a lot.

Before he started on the team rebuilding, Cotterill also recruited a new assistant manager in Mike Davis, a local man who had been a regular fixture at the club over a number of years. Davis recalls:

I had known Steve for a number of years and he contacted me and asked if I would come back and work with him, and I was delighted to do so. I had played in the reserves as a left-back, but went to Australia to play semi-pro football. I had accepted that I would never be good enough, as I was a fringe player and played a couple of times for the first team, that was it. John Reid, an ex-Cheltenham player, invited me to go to Australia and I went out there for three years. When I came back, Lindsay Parsons was the manager and I took over the youth team. Lindsay was working on his own at the time, and Pete Higgins came in to help him, and I then took over the reserves. Lindsay then left and Pete Higgins took over, and I assisted him, then Chris Robinson took over. I was Chris's assistant to start with, then Chris Price came in. I then took over the youth development, where the likes of Michael Duff, Ross Casey, Michael Jackson, Christy Fenwick, Dave Parker and later on Gareth Hopkins came along. I was also helping Pat Casey run the reserves, but I was unemployed at the time and not being paid by the club, but got a job working for a company in Tewkesbury which imported Portuguese aluminium, so I left the club again. When Steve asked me back I was doing the job as well and it was very demanding for those two Conference seasons. I would finish work at 5 p.m., meet Steve at 5.30 p.m., go to a game somewhere and get to bed at 1 a.m. before getting up for work the following morning, so it was hard work. I was privileged to be given the opportunity and I like to think he chose me because we are like-minded people. He must have thought I had certain strengths that I could help him with, and there was mutual respect. I think we worked well together. Steve was much more in your face than me and I am happy to be the quiet man in the background. Graham Allner is now the fifth manager at the club that I have worked with as an assistant so I take that to mean I must be quite good at what I do, and I enjoy the challenge.

With his management team in place, Cotterill turned his attention to the playing side, and in came six new faces, while the exit door was beckoning for seven more. Cotterill knew major surgery was needed, and knew that several players could not stay if the club was to be successful.

I felt that when I first came to the club, the players were running the club. I thought there were a core of seven or eight players that were to a certain degree negative influences on some of the positive influences. I thought there were energizers and energy sappers, and there were more energy sappers than energizers, so with three days of getting promotion to the Conference, we needed to get rid of those energy sappers and take them away from the energizers. The first thing I went for was characters and not necessarily playing ability. You can fill a wheelbarrow full of apples, but if you leave a bad one in the bottom you will definitely turn the rest. From the start of the Conference, there has not been a bad apple at the club because I could shape and mould my own team, and by getting rid of six or seven players, it allowed me to do major surgery, so that's what I set about doing.

Both ends of the pitch were transformed, with Steve Book brought in to take over the number one shirt, as the Exeter postman Kevin Maloy departed for Dorchester Town. Book cost £8,000 from Forest Green Rovers and had a long tradition in the game, as his father Kim was once beaten six times by George Best in an FA Cup tie for Northampton against Manchester United, and his uncle, Tony, served Manchester City in various capacities. Bath-based Book, who worked as a carpenter fitting mini-bars in hotels all over Britain and Europe, had served his apprenticeship at places like Welton Rovers and Frome Town, after the likes of Brighton, Wycombe and Lincoln City told him he would not make a Football League goalkeeper.

Cotterill says:

I remember the same person who said Michael Duff wouldn't make it said Booky wouldn't do it for me either – now I don't judge his opinions much. If he tells me a player won't do it, I'll go and buy him for Stoke now.

In midfield, Cotterill beat off several clubs to land Russell Milton from Dover. Milton, a trained teacher, moved into the area as his wife, who originally came from the Ledbury area, got a teaching job, and Cotterill swooped immediately, beating off Kettering, Kidderminster – then managed by Graham Allner – Gloucester, Bath and Worcester for his signature.

The £4,000 he paid was to prove a bargain for a player whose left foot was to unpick many a defence and whose ability to put a set-piece on the proverbial sixpence would come in more than handy over the coming years, notably on a never-to-be-forgotten day in May 1998. Milton, a cheeky chappie with an engaging and ever-present smile, arrived at Whaddon Road with a good CV. Educated in the marble halls of Highbury, he was unable to make the breakthrough and headed east, where he turned out for South China in Hong Kong, and represented the colony, where his midfield partner was the legendary Brazilian Socrates, captain of their 1982 World Cup side. With a pedigree like that, Dover had not wanted to lose him, and they had wanted a fee in the region of £10,000.

Cotterill remembers:

Russell fell in my lap, but I had never seen Russell play, so I needed him to come in for a trial. We had a good chat, we took to each other at that meeting, and I said if you are good enough, I'll have you – the same situation as Dave Norton later on – and I told him I wouldn't mess around for five or six weeks. He was moving up here, but Dover were a bit awkward over the fee. We nailed them for £4,000 in the end, and he ended up being my sand kicker. I would call him that as I would bring him on for dead balls, and his accuracy was amazing. He ended up playing a key role with his ability to keep the ball.

Cotterill also shuffled around his strikers. Out, after only seven games and two goals, went John Symonds, a four-figure Chris Robinson signing from Bedworth United, and Martin Boyle, whose 84 appearances brought him a decent return of 35 goals. There was also no return for Richard Dunwell, whose loan spell yielded four goals in ten games – and a place in club folklore as the man who missed the Burton penalty. Stalwarts Jimmy Smith and Jason Eaton remained – Smith with over 100 goals for the club already, and Eaton approaching the landmark. Cotterill embellished them with Dale Watkins, a prolific striker with a reputation for scoring goals, goals and more goals.

'Super Dale' had done just that for Rushden & Diamonds and for Gloucester City, from where Cotterill procured him for £15,000. He was blessed with genuine pace –

something Cotterill did not have in Eaton and Smith, who were both penalty-box poachers. Says Cotterill:

Over a period of time we were like vultures a bit, as we stole from Gloucester City, and then Hereford later on. I would put that down to good business.

Young striker Simon Teague, released by Bristol Rovers, was also snapped up, but only managed a substitute's appearance against Boreham Wood in the FA Cup, while Cotterill also attracted the vastly experienced Mark Crisp to Whaddon Road. Crisp was a team-mate of the Robins' manager from his days at Alvechurch, and was a regular scorer for Bromsgrove on their rise to the Conference.

'Kipper' became a popular face at the club, and started with a last-minute winner against Wimbledon in a pre-season friendly, but a serious knee injury was to restrict his appearances, with one FA Cup goal in 23 games the sum total of his Robins career.

Cotterill says:

Booky, Russell and Dale were all very good lads, but good footballers as well. I knew Mark Crisp from years ago, and he was another good, solid, non-League player. He had been around, done the Conference, and was my old strike partner at Alvechurch. You talk about players like Lee Howells, Chris Banks and Neil Grayson, who played a major part in what happened, but the Mark Crisps and Keith Knights were not only good players but were fantastic characters as well. Get Mark Crisp and Keith Knight together, and I guarantee you would leave the room with your face and jaw aching with laughter. If you don't, you have no sense of humour whatsoever. You could hire those two as a double act. They are the funniest pair I have ever seen in my life. If I could get the chairman at Stoke to swallow a budget for team entertainment I would employ those two tomorrow, but it was all part of the spirit we were building.

The Robins had a good pre-season, beating the Wimbledon XI and Cardiff, but losing to Swansea and Bristol Rovers; however, no one quite knew what to expect from the season when it opened at Dover on 16 August.

The ninety minutes that followed left them in no doubt as the Robins came away from the Crabble on the wrong end of a 3-0 defeat, and survival was the word on everyone's lips as they wended wearily home from the Kent coast.

Lee Howells recalls:

I came off the pitch thinking 'we've been taught a lesson'. The coach back was very quiet. I think we were all thinking it was going to be a long season if we were going to have another forty-five games like that. I was thinking to myself, and I'm sure a lot of the other lads were too, that we just weren't going to be good enough for the Conference. But Steve was great. He just said 'Come on, don't be frightened, believe in yourself.' Then we played Hayes at home, and we won 2-1, but we were lucky to

Dover Athletic 3 Cheltenham Town 0

Cheltenham Town were celebrating at the end of last season when they just pipped arch-rivals Gloucester City to promotion on a thrilling final day. However, the Robins' return to the Conference was hardly a happy one as they went down 3-0 at Dover Athletic. Cheltenham began the match with four new players, including former Forest Green Rovers goalkeeper Steve Book. Russell Milton was also making his Conference debut for Cheltenham, after enjoying seven successful seasons with Dover. The match began tightly and Cheltenham made a confident start, although that confidence was dented when they went behind in the fourteenth minute. Gerry Dobbs received the ball on the right and sent over a fine cross, which Jimmy Strouts headed past Book into the top left-hand corner. This did not deter the Robins and they still worked hard and created a few chances.

However, they had little luck and when Dale Watkins found the net, his effort was ruled out for a foul on Daniels. They suffered another setback before the break when Phil Barber flicked the ball towards goal and Chris Banks deflected the ball into his own net. Dover were flattered by the half-time scoreline and Cheltenham probably had more of the play in the second period. Watkins was inches away from scoring his first and Lee Howells shot just wide as the Robins still could find no luck. Things became worse for Cheltenham when some good work from Munday, Wilson and Henry set up Neil Le Bihan and he fired home from fifteen yards. The Robins now must get ready to entertain Hayes tomorrow night.

win, and I remember thinking again, I don't really know that we're ready for this. Overall that season I think we really grew up quickly and that was down to Steve a lot with the new players he brought in.'

But as usual, there was no panic from the manager. Cotterill says:

We never did well anywhere on the first day of the season, which was a decent trait as it turned out. It was a real kick in the teeth, a real eye-opener, and it was welcome to the Conference. I think we learned more in that game than any other. It was a long way back on the coach and gave me a lot of thinking time. Then we played Hayes and got absolutely murdered in the first half, I think we came off giddy, but we got a 2-1 result, and that was the catalyst for Jason Eaton and Dale Watkins' partnership.

At half-time and with Hayes 1-0 up, Cotterill replaced Crisp with Eaton, and fired out some sharp words in the dressing room. Within five minutes of coming on, Eaton equalised and Jamie Victory netted the seventy-fifth minute winner. The same eleven who finished that game were sent out against Woking four days later and got a flyer when Victory headed them in front after 90 seconds, then after going 2-1 down, Watkins broke his duck with a penalty, and Eaton completed the 3-2 win. Eaton was clearly having no problems with the step up, and scored again at Hereford on Bank Holiday Monday, as did Watkins. But that was in a losing cause as a mistake from Book, dropping Ian Rodgerson's cross at Ian Foster's feet and two goals, one of them a stunning 25-yard strike, for Neil Grayson helped the Bulls to a 3-2 success.

Eaton recalls:

I came on in that Hayes game to play alongside Dale, and it felt that there was something between us straightaway. I was good at holding the ball up, and Dale was quick, and I think we could read each other's game well, too. It is great when it comes off like that – and I think that season we went on to score about fifty goals between us – not many strike partnerships do that.

That trip back from Edgar Street was to be the last time until New Year's Day that the Robins would sample the bitter taste of defeat. Smith secured the first away win of the campaign at Kettering with a 12th-minute winner, and then rejected a loan switch to Gloucester City before two home games in seventy-two hours. The clash with Rushden & Diamonds was put back after the death of Diana, Princess of Wales, but resulted in another goal each for Eaton and Watkins in a 2-0 success, then Eaton was on the mark again in the 1-1 draw with Leek. The Rushden game, however, was the last for Mark Freeman for a while, after a clash with Adrian Foster left the defender with twenty stitches in a leg wound.

Cotterill was forced into the transfer market, bringing in Bristol Rovers defender Billy Clark on loan, and he made his debut in a 1-1 draw at Hayes, where poacher supreme Eaton rescued a point with an 88th-minute goal. Two defeats in seven games was a better than expected start, and left the Robins lying in fifth place as they took the first steps on the FA Cup trail at Thatcham with a Watkins goal. Stalybridge were next to feel the force of Eaton and Watkins as the duo scored again in a 4-1 success, and then Victory clinched a 1-1 draw with Slough as Cheltenham climbed to third, when a victory would have put them level on points with early leaders Morecambe. The dynamic duo Eaton and Watkins saw off Merthyr in the Cup but the fine run continued in the Conference, as did the front two's scoring form. Watkins hit both goals as Kidderminster were beaten 2-1, then Eaton hit two as Northwich were edged out 3-2.

Away from the league, a comprehensive 5-0 Cup win over Paulton Rovers left the Robins a win away from the first round proper, Crisp grabbing what was to be his only goal for the club. Milton had been out for six weeks, then limped off again in a goal-less draw with Gateshead, as Cotterill continued his striker search, and netted Clark's services for a second month while chasing a permanent deal for the defender.

That FA Cup first round place was achieved with Keith Knight's goal seeing off those renowned Cup fighters Sutton United, but the draw was slightly disappointing, as it paired the Robins with Western League side Tiverton Town. Before that, however, came the small matter of Halifax Town, the Conference's unbeaten leaders. Eaton was the hero with a brilliant hat-trick, in a 4-0 Whaddon Road demolition.

Cheltenham Town 4 Halifax Town 0

By any standards this was an incredible result. A devastating second-half performance saw Cheltenham tear the previously unbeaten league leaders apart with four goals in a twelve minute spell. Jason Eaton claimed a hat-trick and Bob Bloomer added a spectacular goal to send most of the 2,505 crowd home happy. Unbeaten Halifax Town welcomed playmaker Jamie Patterson back from suspension, while Cheltenham, who were hoping to preserve their own unbeaten home record, fielded an unchanged side.

The first chance of note came in the seventh minute, when former Coventry City defender Brian Kilcline blasted a free kick straight at Steve Book. Five minutes later Bob Bloomer struck a shot from the edge of the box which was gathered well by goalkeeper Lee Martin despite an uneven bounce.

Halifax moved the giant Kilcline forward at every opportunity and from his flick-header Andy Thackery was given a chance that he put well wide. Lee Howells was then booked for a foul on Gary Brook as Halifax, strong, neat and well organised, applied pressure from the Cheltenham goal.

Ten minutes before half-time, Martin was called upon to make a good save when Jason Eaton produced a sharp turn and shot from twelve yards. Howells was given a stern talking to by the referee after a foul on Brown as the game entered a stop-start phase. There were too many fouls and too many stray passes, with neither side able to impose themselves on the game.

In the first half of injury time, Halifax midfielder Chris Hurst went into the referee's notebook for a nasty-looking jump tackle on Chris Banks. Cheltenham had their moments going forward in the first half, particularly when the ball was swept out to Keith Knight on the right, but the Halifax defence showed no signs of allowing a victory.

Three minutes into the second half, Cheltenham came close to scoring when Mark Bradshaw nodded a Jamie Victory header off the line. The game exploded into life in the 60th minute when a mistake by Kilcline let in Dale Watkins. He expertly rounded the goalkeeper, but his shot was cleared off the line by Kieran O'Regan. From the resulting corner Martin's weak punch hit Jason Eaton and went in off the post.

A minute later, Kilcline again lost his footing and Eaton nipped in to steal the ball beyond Martin and send the home fans into raptures. Even better was to follow when, five minutes later, Jimmy Smith found space on the left and his cross was expertly volleyed into the net by Bob Bloomer. Another swift cross, this time headed down by Howells, landed at the feet of Eaton who gleefully completed his hat-trick. Jimmy Smith turned from attacker to defender late in the game, bravely heading clear a Bradshaw cross under pressure from substitute Darren Lyons.

With the damage done, Cheltenham were content to keep possession in the closing stages and Jason Eaton, substituted late in the game, received a standing ovation.

Eaton recalls:

That was one for the archives. They had Brian Kilcline at the back, but that day everything I hit went in. However, I think it was all overshadowed by the other goal – a fantastic Bob Bloomer volley.

The euphoria of that win was still dying down when the club announced one of the biggest signings in its history. The rumours had started at a fans' forum where chairman Paul Baker announced that the club would be making a big signing, and, just days later, Clive Walker became a Cheltenham Town player.

Not since Jim Barron persuaded former Aston Villa, Everton and Scotland striker Andy Gray to pull on the red and white shirt in the early 1990s had Cheltenham had such a high-profile player on their books.

Said Baker:

I think Clive Walker's signing showed how far Cheltenham Town had come to bring in a someone of his pedigree. He had tremendous experience, had been there and done it all and had so much professionalism. He was also a lovely bloke – despite all he had achieved, he would speak to anyone, and to the fans, and he really had a good influence on the other players. He had a great attitude, and was a lovely person to have around the club both on and off the pitch – he was a very good signing by Steve.

The forty-year-old former Chelsea, QPR, Sunderland and Brighton winger was nothing short of a non-League legend. Cotterill had swooped quickly when Walker was sacked as Brentford's assistant manager.

Clive had probably made more of a name for himself playing for Woking than he did in his great League career at Chelsea and elsewhere. I remember

Cheltenham's new signing, Clive Walker.

asking him if he fancied it, and I don't think he did to start with. I had a headstart because we knew each other from Brighton, so I got him in, and as soon as he started training with us he knew he made the right choice.

Walker recalls:

I saw Steve at one of Brentford's reserve games and we got chatting. I hadn't seen him for a few years. At the time, I knew that my time at Brentford was drawing to a close, and when the time came that I left, Steve was one of about six managers who phoned me. There were a couple of Conference teams and four from the Ryman League, but I came down and had a look around. I knew the FA Cup was due so I needed to decide quickly if I was going to be eligible for it, but I wanted to check the journey out. I got to Cheltenham, and Steve, being his persuasive self, convinced me to give it a go. Neither of us made the other any promises, we would see how it went.

Walker made a brief debut in the 2-1 win at Slough, which made it eleven games unbeaten in the Conference, but he didn't wait too long to make a real impact against Tiverton in the first round of the FA Cup. Cotterill had sent Walker on, and with a midweek replay beckoning, he smashed in the winner two minutes from time.

Walker recalls:

I was nowhere near fit for the Slough game and Steve threw me on against Tiverton. I scored the winner – it was a great start and it's the perfect way to win people over. It wasn't a total surprise as the FA Cup was always good to me and in a way it was almost inevitable that I would do something as I was lucky where the Cup was concerned.

Cotterill remembers:

There was 86 or 87 minutes on the clock, and just before he went on I said to him 'Any chance of scoring the winner,' and he said 'Yeah, sure'. When he did, he came looking for me, and he turned out to be a fantastic signing for us. When he came to us he was unfit, and had probably put on a little bit of weight and it took him a while to get into it. Arguably, Cheltenham Town gave Clive his two best years in non-League football, winning the Trophy, league runners-up and then winning the league.

The draw paired the Robins with Boreham Wood, but first came clashes with Gateshead and Leek – and suspensions were starting to bite. Howells and Watkins missed the 2-0 win over Gateshead, and Watkins also missed the trip to Leek, where a goal-less draw kept the unbeaten run alive. Watkins was joined on the sidelines by Bob Bloomer as Boreham Wood came to town for the second round FA Cup tie.

A crowd of 3,525 – a figure which, three years later, would be a disappointing attendance – saw Shaun Marshall give Wood the lead, but Howells earned a replay with a

75th minute strike. Cheltenham's exploits were beginning to be noticed, and five players – Banks, Howells, Victory, Eaton, Book and Watkins – played in an England semi-professional trial match against the Dr Martens League at Gloucester City.

Banks, Victory, Howells and Watkins were given the full game, with Eaton and Book having a half each. Watkins grabbed the winner on his return from suspension against Morecambe, in a game where Darren Wright saw red on a rare first team start, but all eyes were on Boreham Wood. The prospective third round draw had handed Cheltenham a home tie with Division One side Reading, which would be special for Keith Knight, a former Royals' player. He was to get his reunion, and Cheltenham were to get their first FA Cup third round appearance for sixty-four years – but at a cost.

On a freezing cold night in Hertfordshire, it was perhaps fitting that two of the club's loyal stalwarts, Jimmy Smith and Bob Bloomer, should secure the 2-0 win.

However, Eaton limped off with an ankle injury after 14 minutes of the game, and was not seen again until the New Year. That gave Smith his chance, and he was determined to take it, scoring again with a deft chip at Stevenage in a 2-1 Friday night success. The other goal came from Watkins, who himself had passed a fitness test to play, but from a more unorthodox route. Bloomer, Smith and Watkins stood over a free-kick, and after a mock argument distracted the Stevenage defence – a routine Cotterill had seen Real Madrid try on satellite TV and had subsequently worked on in training for months – Bloomer tapped the ball for Watkins to drive home the winner. Those points cemented Cheltenham in second place as Yeovil came to Whaddon Road for a Boxing Day clash which saw Walker take centre stage with both goals in a 2-0 win.

1997 ended with a 1-1 draw with Welling, a last-gasp Watkins penalty saving the unbeaten run. The reprieve was only temporary as the four-month run ended on New Year's Day at Yeovil where Owen Pickard – the man who Cotterill nearly signed instead of Dale Watkins the previous summer – had a hand in ending the sequence at seventeen games. That almost went unnoticed as the club and the town waited for what was, at the time, the biggest game in 105 years – the FA Cup third round tiw with Reading. However, they had to wait a bit longer as Whaddon Road was waterlogged for the original date of 3 January, with the game put off for ten days by 48 hours of almost incessant rain.

The delay was good news for Jason Eaton, who had been sidelined with an ankle injury since the second round replay win over Boreham Wood, as it left him in with a chance of playing. Three days before, however, a different campaign got off to a low-key start at Enfield, as the Robins embarked on the FA Trophy with a 1-1 draw – only being pegged back by a last-minute penalty after Dale Watkins' early goal. That replay and a delay to the Reading tie was not ideal, and it was becoming obvious that a fixture backlog would rear its ugly head later in the season.

Baker recalled:

It was probably the first time we had a full house for a few years, and they were really crammed in. The fact that it was under floodlights as well made it a really special atmosphere and we played superbly to get a replay.

Cheltenham Town 1 Reading 1

Veteran striker Trevor Morley denied Cheltenham a famous FA Cup third round victory with a 71st-minute equaliser at a packed Whaddon Road last night. The 36-year-old Morley struck from the edge of the box, with the ball squirming under Steve Book's dive to give the Nationwide League Division One side a replay at Elm Park on Tuesday.

The Robins will have to do without midfielder Lee Howells, outstanding last night, as he starts a two-match ban on Saturday.

Cheltenham had gone in front after 22 minutes when Dale Watkins kept his cool to score his 17th goal of the season from the penalty spot after Clive Walker was challenged from behind by Gareth Davies. But they had to weather an early Reading storm which saw the Royals earn seven corners in the first 20 minutes as they threatened to win at a canter. Book produced a fantastic ninth minute tip-over from Phil Parkinson's 18-yard drive, then Morley and Stewart Lovell couldn't convert an almighty 12th-minute scramble.

Cheltenham were struggling to get out of their own half, but suddenly found themselves in front. Jamie Victory and Jimmy Smith linked up on the left flank and fed Walker just inside the box. Davies made a rash challenge from behind, and referee Ken Leach had no hesitation in pointing to the spot. Watkins followed his usual routine, and planted the ball to Nicky Hammond's left, the power taking the ball in, although the goalkeeper got a hand to it.

That was just the lift Cheltenham needed, and they dominated the rest of the half. A minute after the goal, Hammond had an escape when he punched Mike Duff's cross onto the head of Bob Bloomer, but the effort drifted just over as the goalkeeper back-pedalled furiously. Then, Victory glanced Walker's cross goalwards, with Hammond dropping on the ball just in time, and Keith Knight drilled a shot just over on the half-hour.

Watkins lifted a 35th-minute effort over the bar after Victory touched on a Walker free-kick. Watkins tried an audacious 25-yard chip after latching on to a Book clearance early in the second half, but Reading again had the better of the early exchanges. They won three early corners and forced Book to make a great low save by his post in the 57th minute to prevent Davies from making amends for his earlier misdemeanour.

Two minutes later, at the other end, Hammond spread himself well to block a Watkins effort as the striker turned well in the box. Reading were threatening down the flanks with Welsh international Jason Bowen and full-back Martyn Booty particularly impressive on the left, and Robins boss Steve Cotterill sent on the more defensively-minded Steve Benton for Smith. But a minute later, Reading were level when Morley played a clever one-two with Lovell, and shot, with the ball skidding through the sandy goalmouth and under the unlucky Book to bring the Royals level.

Cotterill then sent on 15-goal striker Jason Eaton for Walker as the Robins, far from being deflated by the goal, looked the stronger side in the closing stages with Reading happy to settle for a second chance. Former Reading player Keith Knight missed a golden chance to knock out his old club with nine minutes to go as he fired wide when well placed, then Eaton was marginally offside as he hit a post and Watkins put an effort wide.

Clive Walker won the penalty from which Dale Watkins scored:

That was a fantastic night. They were doing well and I remember the penalty as I dropped my shoulder to get into the box and he caught me.

The draw set up a massive cup week for the club, with the Trophy re-match with Enfield and the FA Cup trip to Reading falling within just two days of each other. The draws had been made for both, with a daunting trip to Cardiff the reward if Cheltenham could have seen off the Royals at Elm Park, while traditional foes Rushden & Diamonds were lying in wait for them in the Trophy. First, however, Smith's second-half winner returned the club to winning ways in the Vauxhall Conference against Hednesford Town, who were themselves in the top five of the division.

Action from the FA Cup third round tie between Cheltenham Town and Reading. Dale Watkins scores from the penalty spot.

Then it was off to Reading, and another great performance which ended in a gallant 2-1 defeat. Clive Walker's amazing FA Cup knack came up trumps with an equaliser, but Martyn Booty lashed a winner through a sea of legs.

Cotterill recalls:

I remember at Reading when it was 1-1, we had a big goalmouth scramble and Mark Crisp fired it over the bar, then Dale Watkins hit the post. We were a cat's whisker from knocking them out, and we got done in the end by a long shot from Martyn Booty, which went through about fifteen players and nestled in the corner. We had set standards and it put us on the map a bit as well.

Chairman Paul Baker remembers another great night:

When we went to Elm Park, that was the first example of the potential that the club had, as we must have taken 4,000 supporters with us. We were not a million miles away from getting a result and I remember being in the stand next to their chairman John Madejski, a multi, multi-millionaire, and thinking that we are moving in big circles now – and it has kept happening.

Left: Action from the FA Cup third round tie between Cheltenham Town and Reading. Dale Watkins celebrates scoring Cheltenham's goal. *Right:* Reading v. Cheltenham (FA Cup third round replay). Clive Walker celebrates scoring Cheltenham's goal.

Reading 2 Cheltenham Town 1

Cheltenham Town return to battling for their main goal of promotion to the Football League after bowing out of the FA Cup bathed in glory – with their First Division conquerors, Reading, backing them to succeed. The Vauxhall Conference side's narrow 2-1 defeat at Elm Park in their FA Cup third round replay last night leaves Stevenage Borough as the only non-League club left in the competition ahead of their own match against Newcastle on Sunday.

But the Robins, who have only ever beaten one League side – and that was almost sixty-five years ago – so nearly joined them in the fourth round for the first time in the club's history with a valiant performance against Reading, who now travel to Cardiff City on Saturday.

In the first encounter between the two sides a week ago Cheltenham were 19 minutes away from victory before Reading striker Trevor Morley equalised. In the replay Morley scored again to give Reading the first-half lead before a committed Cheltenham fightback led to an equaliser from Clive Walker, and was only dashed by a 72nd-minute winner from thirty yards by full-back Martyn Booty. Even then Cheltenham had chances to force extra time and a deflected effort from Jamie Victory hit the post, while Reading goalkeeper Nicky Hammond parried the follow-up from fit-again striker Jason Eaton and then substitute Jimmy Smith shot over the bar

Cheltenham, who are second in the Conference table after only being promoted to the division last season, were given a deserved standing ovation at the end of the game.

There was no hangover forty-eight hours later when Watkins' hat-trick, including a fortunate rebound off his thigh from a clearance by goalkeeper Andy Pape, secured a 5-1 win and a clash with Rushden. The punishing schedule – four games in eight days – did catch up with them at Northwich in a 2-1 defeat, with Mark Freeman on target, but when Rushden came in the Trophy, normal service was resumed.

That was after a seven-day break in the sun, the whole squad jetting out to Faro on the Algarve. On their return, Watkins hit two goals and missed a penalty against his old club as Cheltenham moved into the last sixteen, and a trip into the unknown at Unibond League Division One leaders Ashton United.

The unexpected success turned the spotlight off the field, as the board started to look at improving Whaddon Road, should League football ever become a reality. There was a £200,000 bill for safety work, floodlight improvements, new seats, better dressing rooms, work on the pitch and other minor work in the offing. Vice-chairman Colin Farmer has been the man in charge of the stadium improvements, and as he says:

I think that one thing that showed how we were progressing was in the first season in the Conference when we decided as a board to pay to be inspected for League status.

It was quite expensive for us at the time, but we decided that we wanted to be ready off the field for what was happening on the field.

As it was, of course, we came second, so the following season we knew we needed to get going and get things done ready for possible League football – we were determined to be ready off the field having seen other clubs fail on that score.

Chairman Paul Baker recalls:

We had to get the 'A' grading from the Football League. It was mainly the terraces and crash barriers which needed work doing, and that is another success story – the transformation of Whaddon Road, which is now unrecognisable from the ground we inherited.

February began with a bizarre finish to the 1-0 win at Hednesford, Eaton scoring in the final minute, but there was still time for Book to produce a stunning save from his opposite number Scott Cooksey, who came up for an injury-time corner.

The weirdness didn't end there as a bomb alert held up the home game with Stevenage for an hour, causing Whaddon Road to be evacuated. The players of Crescent United and Hardwicke weren't complaining as they suddenly had a massive crowd for their Northern Senior League encounter at nearby Whaddon Rec. The ground was searched, nothing was found and the game went on, finishing 1-1 after Dale Watkins put the Robins ahead.

Cotterill was also stepping up his bid for reinforcements with the Conference and Trophy campaigns moving into full swing. A striker and a centre half were still priority, as again injuries and suspensions were threatening to stretch the squad to breaking point. Russell Milton was struggling with a hamstring problem, Steve Benton was sidelined with an injury to his knee, which ruined his 1996/97 season and forced him to have another operation, Mark Crisp was stretchered off against Stevenage and Mark Freeman, Darren Wright and Bob Bloomer would all miss games through suspension.

As it turned out, Benton and Crisp would not play for the rest of the season – in fact, neither would wear the red and white stripes again. The centre half Cotterill found was Michael Thorp, recruited on loan from Reading to cover Mark Freeman's absence, but he too injured himself in the Stevenage game. The sight of Ross Casey, Paul Bloomfield and Simon Teague on the bench for the Trophy match at Ashton told its own story, and there was a start for young winger Dave Parker, so the 1-0 win, secured by Clive Walker, was very precious.

Says Lee Howells:

I think Ashton was the most important match in the Trophy run. We won 1-0, we had eight or nine players out, and I played centre-half. We won that one and then Jamie Victory scored against Hayes in the last minute and you think perhaps we're destined to get to the final.

Cotterill, however, was stressing that the Conference remained the priority, and it was to that end that he finally, after many months of searching, landed his striker. Neil Grayson, aged thirty-three, arrived from Hereford on a two-and-a-half year contract for £18,000 on 27 February, ending a six-month quest to land the former Northampton, York, Boston and Doncaster man. Hereford's financial state played a big part in the deal as the money Hereford wanted kept dropping lower and lower, but it was to turn out to be a brilliant bit of business.

Cotterill remembers:

It was a long quest to sign him, but in my career I have been quite a lucky person as most of the things I want I get. With Neil, it was case of striking at the right time when the club was right down, and we could negotiate a good deal. I first went for him and they said £50,000, maybe because it was Cheltenham Town. We said no chance. Then it got to £40,000, no chance, then £33,000, again no chance. Finally it came down to £18,000, which we could just about get to. So it was £18,000 for a thirty-three year old, and I had people asking 'Are you sure about that?' and I said 'Yes, we're sure about that'. And I was certainly proved right by Neil himself over a period of time.

Grayson remembers:

I got a telephone call from Graham Turner to say that Steve Cotterill had been in touch about the possibility of signing me. I met up with Steve and was impressed, talked it over with my wife and decided it seemed like it would be a good move, and of course it was tremendous. In one sense I was lucky in that Hereford needed the money and someone would have to be sold – lucky it was me as it turned out.

Grayson's arrival gave Cotterill the flexibility he wanted with his strikers, and added to the potency of Jason Eaton and Dale Watkins, whose partnership stood at 41 goals in 41 games, and was a blessing with Eaton's ankle and Achilles giving him problems.

New signing Neil Grayson (seated) with Paul Baker (left) and Steve Cotterill (right).

Says Baker:

I remember having a long chat with Steve about signing Neil Grayson. Again, it was a big signing for the club and showed we meant business as we were now taking players off clubs like Hereford. They were struggling at the time and as it turned out we would take two or three players off them in the end. As a board, we have always backed the manager, and I remember doing the bank transfer for the £18,000 we paid for Neil. What a fantastic signing he proved to be – a legend. He is probably up there as one of Steve's best signings for what he did for the club, and it is a shame he could not have been here forever.

Eaton remembers:

Steve had used me and Dale Watkins all season. I think he wanted another option for the league, and as Neil was cup-tied, it kept Dale and I fresh for the Trophy. It was a bit worrying for me when we signed a player of Neil's pedigree, but it was healthy for competition, and I was used to seeing them off.

As Cotterill points out:

It was a blessing in disguise that he was cup-tied for the Trophy if we wanted to finish as high as we could in the league. Eaton and Watkins were going well together and didn't deserve to be broken up, but it was worth breaking them up for the freshness, strength

Non-League internationals – England v. Holland. From left to right: Neil Grayson, Lee Howells, Dale Watkins, Jamie Victory, Chris Banks.

Non-League international – England v. Holland. Neil Grayson in action.

and power of Grayson. I am very team-orientated, as everyone knows, but Neil Grayson dragged us to second place in the Conference, without a shadow of a doubt.

Grayson's first game as a Cheltenham Town player was, however, not in the red and white stripes of the Robins, but proudly wearing the Three Lions of England, and, for good measure, the number nine shirt. Lee Howells, Chris Banks, Dale Watkins and Jamie Victory were already in the semi-professional party to face Holland at Crawley, and Grayson's arrival meant he was now a fifth Robin.

Grayson recalls:

I went for the trial at Gloucester City and did okay so I was selected to play against Holland. To be honest it was the first time I'd really met the Cheltenham lads. There were five of us playing that night and I played that game as a Cheltenham player, but

I hadn't actually made my debut for the club. Anyway, I played up front with Dale Watkins, we won 2-1, and to cap it all I scored as well.

Grayson's first Cheltenham game was an eventful one as well, a 4-1 defeat at Rushden & Diamonds, where Keith Knight was sent off for dissent, and things got progressively worse as Mark Freeman's memories of his earlier clash with Adrian Foster in September re-surfaced to such an extent that Freeman saw red as well. Lee Howells secured a 1-0 win over Farnborough in Grayson's home debut, and at the time there was an eerie atmosphere as the facelift to Whaddon Road had started with new terracing being put in to the Paddock and Family enclosure under the main stand, and at the Prestbury Road and Whaddon Road Ends.

Controversy reared its ugly head again in the Hayes Trophy clash, as the Robins made it third time lucky by reaching the last four, having twice previously gone out at the quarter-final stage. The game was heading for a replay in the 90th minute when Hayes goalkeeper Russell Meara was penalised for taking too many steps.

An ingenious free-kick routine ended with Dale Watkins having a shot blocked, but Jamie Victory followed up to score the winner. Hayes were incensed and fights broke out, with Nick Roddis of Hayes getting a red card and some Cheltenham fans and Hayes players later ending up in court after a melee in front of the main stand.

Having survived a replay at Barrow via a penalty shoot-out, Dover were to be the Robins' semi-final opponents, while Southport and Slough were the other semi-finalists. But the fixture pile-up was getting worse, and the Conference table showed Cheltenham in fourth place, fourteen points behind leaders Halifax, but with four games in hand on all the sides above them. That meant fourteen league games in six weeks, with eleven of those league games in April – plus the two-legged Trophy semi-final, the build-up for which was far from perfect, with two 1-0 defeats.

The first came at Morecambe and the second was at the hands of old foes Kidderminster at Whaddon Road. The man who scored Kidderminster's winner, and in the process ended a thirty-one-match unbeaten run at Whaddon Road (which stretched back to the 2-1 defeat by King's Lynn in Cotterill's first home game in charge back on 1 February 1997), was no stranger the the Robins. It was Paul 'Ocker' Davies, the nemesis of many a Cheltenham side in the past during Christmas meetings with Kidderminster. At thirty-seven he was all but retired – yet manager Graham Allner had to turn to him after an injury crisis and he responded with the 42nd-minute winner.

The Dover games were not without their drama, as Gerald Dobbs gave the Kent side an early lead at Whaddon Road before an inspired substitution with Jason Eaton coming on to score twice. Then at the Crabble, Dale Watkins and Eaton stretched the advantage to 4-1 on aggregate only for two long-range strikes from Neil Le Bihan and John Budden to make for a tense finish.

Eaton says:

I had a feeling that if I came on against Dover, I would do well. I borrowed a pair of shinpads from Keith Knight before every game, and they were my lucky omen. I scored

Cheltenham Town 2 Dover Athletic 1

Two second-half goals from substitute Jason Eaton gave Cheltenham Town a 2-1 lead to take them into the second leg of the FA Umbro trophy semi-final next Saturday. Cheltenham began with Trophy veteran Clive Walker partnering Dale Watkins in attack, but they were stunned just after two minutes when Dover opened the scoring. Goalkeeper Charlie Mitten launched a long clearance forward from just outside his area. The Cheltenham defence was caught half asleep and Gerald Dobbs raced through to fire past Book.

Cheltenham almost hit back immediately with a Jimmy Smith cross from the right. Jamie Victory met it firmly but his header was straight at Mitten. Smith received some rough treatment in the early stages and Dobbs was booked for hauling him to the ground. Cheltenham created a good opening after sixteen minutes when Smith and Lee Howells combined to set up Walker. He broke free but shot straight at the 'keeper from a tight angle. Cheltenham began to dictate the play and produced good football to pressure a heavily-manned Dover defence. On 27 minutes Watkins took a pass from Walker and headed for goal, only to lift his shot over the bar from the edge of the area. Walker was once again involved three minutes later when Howells found him in the penalty area but as he was about to shoot John Budden slid in to make an excellent saving tackle. Luck was not on Cheltenham's side ten minutes before half time when Howells set up Jamie Victory for a shot fifteen yards out. He struck it well enough but the ball hit Mike Duff on the back of the head and bounced away from goal.

After thirty minutes, trickery from Walker forged an opening for Watkins, but his shot lacked the power to trouble Mitten. Five minutes before half time Mike Duff won a free kick near the corner flag which Russell Milton floated to the far post. Duff played back to Mark Freeman but the defender blazed over the bar from eight yards. Mitten was called on to make a fine save a minute before the break, tipping over a Jimmy Smith shot after a good build-up involving Milton, Howells and Walker.

Ten minutes after the break, Dover broke upfield when Dobbs found Sam Ayorinde with a long ball and the former Nigerian Under 21 international forced Book to save. Jimmy Smith had to leave the field to have stitches after a clash of heads with Liburd Henry. Jason Eaton came on to replace him. Cheltenham had claims for a penalty turned down after 72 minutes.

Walker burst into the box and went over but the referee was well placed. Ayorinde charged into the box before firing in a shot that Book saved with his legs. A minute later it was Mitten's turn to save his team. Limping heavily, he turned a Howells shot over the bar. From the resulting corner Cheltenham finally got the goal their dominance deserved. Milton sent it over and substitute Eaton found the space to head into the corner of the net. Within a minute, Ayorinde hit the bar after Neil LeBihan had found him with a searching ball, Cheltenham took a dramatic lead nine minutes from time when Howells fed Victory, whose cross fell to Watkins. Watkins mis-hit his shot and, with the defence appealing for offside, Eaton deftly flicked a shot beyond Mitten.

Dover 2 Cheltenham Town 2 (agg 3-4)

Cheltenham Town will face Southport in the final of the FA Umbro Trophy at Wembley on 17 May. The Robins came through a nervy semi-final second leg at Dover, where the home side hit back from 2-0 down and nearly forced extra time. After goalkeeper Steve Book made an early save from Gerald Dobbs, Dale Watkins gave Cheltenham a flying start with a sixth-minute goal. Lee Howells crossed from the right end Watkins turned his marker before beating Charlie Mitten from twelve yards.

Sam Ayorinde missed a good chance to level for Dover, but Cheltenham looked to be cruising towards Wembley's twin towers when Russell Milton's corner caused panic and Jason Eaton scored his 100th Robins goal. After the break, Dover hit back when Neil Le Bihan smashed home a 69th-minute volley and John Budden made it a nervy last few minutes with a long-range equaliser.

Defender Lee Palmer nearly put one through his own net near the end, but was rescued by the bar, and Cheltenham were soon celebrating the first-ever Wembley trip in their 106-year history. In the final, the Robins will face Southport, who edged past Slough 2-1 on aggregate at Haig Avenue. Danny Bailey gave Slough the lead after half an hour, but Formby levelled after 66 minutes to book the Sandgrounders' final ticket.

Action from Dover Athletic v. Cheltenham Town. Dale Watkins celebrates the Robins' first goal.

FA Trophy semi-final – Action from Dover Athletic v. Cheltenham Town. Dale Watkins celebrates wth his team-mates after scoring the first goal.

twice when I came on and I had been itching to get on as I felt I would score. Down at Dover, I had the same feeling again – if I was playing I would score. I had my lucky shinpads on and the ball bounced in off them. The tension down there was unbeliev-able, and it was physically and mentally draining because of what was at stake. They came back with two great strikes but we hung on – it was amazing.

Lee Howells added:

The best game of the season was at Dover, even my wife came down for that one. It was a bit hairy towards the end, but the final whistle was fantastic – getting to Wembley was unbelievable.

For Cotterill, the latter stages of the second leg and the trip home are things he will never forget:

There were about twelve minutes to go and I was in the dug-out. I turned round to see what subs I had and Dover were chucking big balls in our box. Boka Freeman was

FA Trophy semi-final – Dover v. Cheltenham. Steve Cotterill and his team sing back to the crowd.

heading them all out as he did throughout his time – there was another who apparently couldn't play in the Conference, couldn't play in Division Three, but who did it. What a great character he was. Magnificent – another who lived the dream. Keith Knight was a sub, but I couldn't see him, then I turned round and he looked like a little hedgehog, curled up on the seat, so I asked what the hell he was doing. He said 'I can't watch any more of that.' There were twelve minutes to go.

Then when the whistle went I couldn't get him out of my face. He was like a rash, all over me. Being a local boy as well, we both knew what it meant to each other. I told the boys, as I always did, not to whoop it up in the tunnel, and be respectful to the opposition, and celebrate when our door was closed, not to be loud or arrogant. So we kept the volume down in the dressing room.

That certainly wasn't the case when the bus pulled out of the Crabble en route for Gloucestershire, as Steve Cotterill recalls:

We got on the bus and I told the driver to find the nearest off licence, and I told Paddy Wood to give me his credit card. We found an off-licence and all the lads were getting beer off the shelves, and filling trolleys up with bottles and cans. I saw this fridge and it was stacked, from top to bottom, full of champagne. There was a little tiny bottle in the front, so I took it out and put it on the floor. Then I got about six boxes and filled it with every bottle of champagne out of that fridge, then I picked the little bottle up and put it back in the middle of the fridge and shut the door. We were all back on the bus, and I had about three bottles left beside me. It was about a four hour trip back, but it could have been six or seven hours for all we cared. We were getting drunk, then more drunk, then legless and then clothesless. The singing got louder, and no one on that bus had a stitch of clothing on as we were dancing up and down. Eventually, everyone sat down and put clothes on, but people were wearing one blue sock, one black sock, someone else's pants, someone else's trousers. I don't think anyone had their own clothing on, and certainly nothing which matched anyway. That was the best bus ride I have ever had in my life. We had got to Wembley, and all the nerves were gone.

Southport came through the other semi-final, and with the Wembley place secured, the next target was to secure the Conference runners-up spot. Two days after the Dover draw, the Football League's grading committee gave Whaddon Road the green light after the completion of the £200,000 facelift was completed by the 1 April deadline. Dover were soon back at Whaddon Road for a league clash – and it marked Neil Grayson's first Cheltenham goals – he struck two in a 3-1 success, getting hectic April off to a winning start. Defeats at Woking and at home to Hereford ended any slight hopes of catching Halifax, who clinched the title on April 18 with a 2-0 win at Kidderminster, as Cheltenham beat Telford 3-1.

FA Trophy semi-final – Dover v. Cheltenham. Cheltenham 'keeper Steve Book meets the fans.

Steve Cotterill with the runners-up trophy.

For Cotterill, Wembley was then the priority, and he started to rest players to avoid injury and suspension, and shuffle the team around. He says:

We never ever gave the league up, but in the end Halifax wore us down because they must have had about five or six 1-0 wins. One game I remember we were disappointed when Geoff Horsfield scored with a deflected shot, which the goalkeeper fumbled in, and thought the title might be out of our reach. Our record between reaching the final and Wembley itself was still good, and I changed the team around. I know Paul Godfrey says I messed his programme up. I messed the numbers up for set-plays to confuse Southport, and gain any advantage I possibly could – and to annoy Paul, of course.

Lee Howells was one of those players to play a reduced role, as his eleven bookings saw him hauled in front of the FA, fined £75 and banned for a game.

He picked up two more in quick succession, and one more yellow could have seen him miss Wembley. Howells was on the bench for the Wembley rehearsal at Southport, where two Dale Watkins goals against a shadow Sandgrounders' side gave the Robins the psychological boost of a 2-1 win. He stayed there against Telford, and with Bob Bloomer also close to a ban, Chris Banks struggling with a thigh strain, and Russell Milton and Jimmy Smith also injured, Cotterill took the chance to blood some of his youngsters.

Ross Casey had come on as a substitute at Woking, and made his full debut in the 2-0 success over Stalybridge, while Michael Jackson came on in the 1-1 draw at Welling and against Stalybridge. Cotterill saved Jackson's full debut for the following weekend, Halifax's Championship party at The Shay in front of over 6,000 fans, where goal number 29 of Dale Watkins' season earned a 1-1 draw.

Lee Howells recalls:

That draw at Halifax was one of the really important games that season. They were presented with the Conference trophy, and Steve was saying to us 'Look at that trophy, you can do this'. I think we all thought he was out of his mind really, but we played really well and got a draw there.

A 2-0 win over Kettering and a 2-1 win at Farnborough, where Neil Grayson hit both goals, set up the final game of the campaign, a low-key meeting with Wembley opponents Southport. This finished 2-0 thanks to Neil Grayson and Jimmy Smith, as Steve Cotterill left out four regulars and opposite number Paul Futcher seven.

Cotterill's main headache in the run-up to Wembley was the fitness of Russell Milton, whose hamstring had been a problem all season. As it was, Cotterill left him on the bench, until choosing the perfect moment to introduce him and Jimmy Smith to the fray. With eleven minutes to go, Smith was fouled on the left touchline, Milton swung in the free-kick, Jamie Victory flicked it on and Jason Eaton stooped to nod in the winner.

Jason Eaton, who had to postpone his stag night, due to take place in Liverpool that weekend, remembers:

I had my lucky shinpads on again! Before the game I did not know if I would be fit as I picked up a hamstring injury and hadn't trained for a couple of weeks. The day

Cheltenham Town v. Southport, FA Trophy final, Wembley Stadium.

before the game, I went for a run with Steve and ended up in this field in the middle of nowhere. Lawrie Sanchez was there as well, and they put me through it. By the end, I was breathing through my backside. I thought I would struggle and did not know if I would last the game. I was nervous, but there was no way I was going to pull out.

Cotterill recalls:

I gave Jason a fitness test, but I was worried I had him out there too long, and thought I'd made a mistake, but I got away with it. Sanch came down and brought us twenty balls, they were Wycombe's match balls, to train with as they were the balls we would use the following day. Jason was really struggling, and we did some runs each, and he passed it. He was not 100 per cent, but wanted to play, and got his rewards.

Eaton adds:

The build-up was amazing. I took a video camera and filmed everything over the three days. It is a great memento to have and we went to Wembley the day before. I had been there for a concert once and remember thinking what it must be like to play there, and score there. The game itself was terrible – apart from that goal of course. I pulled off the back post when we got the free-kick, that was an instinctive thing to do. It came towards me and I had to think where I was going to put it. It was all a bit of a blur. I wanted to get a good connection on it and keep it down, to the 'keeper's left – and in

Cheltenham Town v. Southport, FA Trophy final. Jason Eaton *(far left)* scores.

Cheltenham Town 1 Southport 0

Jason Eaton's 79th-minute header sent the thousands who had embarked on the road to Wembley back to Gloucestershire in ecstasy. The Robins had struggled to make headway against nervous Southport who squandered several golden opportunities, most notably in the 63rd minute when Brian Ross got the better of Mark Freeman and ran through only to waste his chance with the goal at his mercy. But Town made the glorious breakthrough with ten minutes left after substitute Jimmy Smith was downed by Ged Kielty in a dangerous position on the right just two minutes after coming on for Keith Knight. His partner from the bench, Russell Milton (on for Clive Walker), floated in a dangerous free-kick which Jamie Victory flicked on for Eaton who nodded the ball past the despairing hand of Southport goalkeeper Billy Stewart. The goal sparked scenes of jubilation among the travelling army of Cheltenham supporters who had endured a slow and tortuous journey to the capital. From the outset, it looked as though their day might be ruined. The Robins were slow out of the starting blocks in the Wembley sunshine and gave Southport ample opportunity to press forward. They went close on 18 minutes when Dave Gamble set up Kevin Formby who blasted over and Town were let off the hook a minute before the interval when Dave Thompson dispossessed Chris Banks on the edge of the penalty area and pulled it back for Brian Butler – who was only denied by Bob Bloomer's lifesaving tackle. Veteran Clive Walker, now 40 years old, showed he could still mix it and almost added another fairytale to his collection on 36 minutes when he headed Knight's cross towards the danger zone only to see Stewart recover and make the save. Two minutes later, a sensational turn by Bob Bloomer and a deft flick by Eaton put Dale Watkins in the clear, and Stewart again had to be alert to dive at the striker's feet. Southport continued to create openings in the second period and after Ross's wasted effort, Mark Freeman was forced to clear Kevin Formby's header off the line with Cheltenham stretched. Formby again caused problems on 76 minutes but Freeman was again on hand to thwart him with a timely interception.

it went, and off I went. There were coachloads there from my dad's pub and from my work, but one of my mates, Dave, couldn't go, so I told him if I scored the celebration would be for him. Afterwards, the publicity was amazing. Everyone wanted to know me, and it felt weird to be singled out, as I had not experienced that before. I remember lifting the trophy with all our fans behind me – that picture is in pride of place at home.

Cotterill says:

It was fantastic to win it. We didn't win like we did at the Millennium Stadium, in style, but the one thing you realize is that you have to win. We had players who underachieved, but those you weren't so sure about played very well. Duffo, Jamie and

Cheltenham Town v. Southport, FA Trophy final, Wembley Stadium. Chris Banks lifts the FA Trophy.

Banksy didn't play as well as Mark Freeman did, Booky had a good game. Bob Bloomer overshadowed Lee Howells, and the wide men Keith Knight and Clive Walker came off for Russell and Jimmy Smith. Then you would have expected Dale to shine as he had scored 29 goals, but Jason got the winner.

Chairman Paul Baker remembers:

It was just unforgettable, and I remember Mark Freeman and I couldn't sleep and we were wandering about the hotel at 7.30 a.m. talking about the day ahead. Personally for me, it was amazing to be sitting in the Royal Box, and it was just as memorable for those 20,000 who came down from Cheltenham. It was coach after coach after coach all the way down the motorway and everyone was so enthusiastic about it. It wasn't the greatest game in the world but at that stage it was all about the result, but it gave the club a lot of national exposure, and we made well over £100,000 from it as well.

Assistant manager Mike Davis remembers:

Going to Wembley was a dream for me and the club. As a kid I had watched the FA Cup final and never imagined that me or Cheltenham Town would ever be involved in a game there. Going down Wembley Way I was in tears, and thought 'I can't believe this, someone pinch me'. I had seen the club in dire straits and had been around the club for a long time, and couldn't believe the club were involved in such a high profile game.

The following day, Cheltenham got a chance to hail its heroes as the team paraded the trophy through the town centre on a open-top bus. Hero Jason Eaton continues the tale:

We had a great night in Cheltenham and I could not believe the number of people who tuned out for the bus parade. I have got that on my video as well – we spent ages on

Cheltenham Town v. Southport, FA Trophy final, Wembley Stadium. Scorer Jason Eaton with the Trophy.

Steve Cotterill *(left)* and Jason Eaton *(right)* – the goalscorer – with the FA Trophy.

the roof of the town hall, and I was overwhelmed by it all – I couldn't believe what my goal had meant to the people of Cheltenham.

Little did anyone know it at the time, but this was to become a regular occurrence – but by popular consensus, none of the subsequent tours have topped this one.

Says Baker:

Cheltenham suddenly became aware it had a football team. Cheltenham is very conservative – with a small 'c' – and sometimes the people find it difficult to get excited about anything. But there were 12,000 people out that night and I will always remember Clive Walker on top of the town hall roof, and it showed everyone that the town had something to be proud of. It was great to be giving the fans something, and it was the start of more and more children wearing the Cheltenham shirts they had bought for Wembley instead of Manchester United or Arsenal shirts.

For Clive Walker it was a great day – his fourth Trophy final and his fourth winners' medal. He recalls:

People would keep telling me about breaking records, and at the time that was a record, although Matt Crossley has also done it now. Wembley was a fantastic place to play and I treated this as just one more time. People kept saying to me that I had never scored there, but although it would have been nice, winning there was the main thing. It was special with Cheltenham as it was a new club and the special thing was to see he looks on the faces of the other players, the youngsters like Michael Duff, and some of the others who I thought would probably not play there again. I would like to think I helped a bit, and Steve would say 'If you have any questions about Wembley, ask the guy in the corner', and nod towards me. The open-top bus tour sticks in my mind as well. We did that at Woking, but there was nothing at the end like the Town Hall thing we did in Cheltenham. I don't know what hit me but I lifted the Trophy once and everyone cheered, so I did it again, and they cheered again and in the end I couldn't put the thing down. It was really special, and that night is the most abiding memory I have of my time at the club.

The final word is Cotterill's as he reveals the psychology which took his team to Trophy glory:

I had told them at the start, that at the moment the tunnel is long, and there's a corner in it, and it's very long, and it's all dark in there. But the sooner we get to the corner, you might see a little glimpse of daylight. We needed to get to that fourth or fifth round, and then everyone starts to see those Twin Towers. It was a continuous drip feed thing, and you embed things in their heads bit by bit about going to Wembley. It was a continual dream or vision that I built up in them about walking out there, scoring there, and winning there and they lived that dream in the end.

Cheltenham Town v. Southport, FA Trophy final, Wembley Stadium. The Robins celebrate winning the FA Trophy.

Cheltenham Town bring the Trophy home – Clive Walker shows it to the fans.

The glorious homecoming – manager and players at the Town Hall.

3

Onwards and Upwards
1998/99

The summer of 1998 was dominated by one question among Cheltenham Town's directors, management, players and supporters – how could the club follow the most successful season in their history? After winning the FA Trophy and finishing second in the Conference, the only way to do it would be to win the Conference, and retain the Trophy – which is exactly what Steve Cotterill set out to do when the players reported back in early July.

Cotterill remembers:

It was 7 July, and it was 6.30 p.m., the first day back in pre-season training. I sat the boys down on a lush pitch at Whaddon Road, and said 'Right then, how do we top that? Here we go – we are going to win the Trophy again and win the league – that's the only way we can top it. Let's not be afraid of it. Let's take the challenge on and everyone will tell you that the second year is harder than the first. If you believe them it will be, but if you don't then we'll have another right crack at it.' Everyone did know us then, but what we had done was coped with the fear factor, the side was getting stronger and the players were getting better. If we could tweak a few things, I knew we could do well.

Howells recalls that speech:

I think we'd taken the league a bit cold last the previous year, and there were a lot of people saying that we couldn't do that again. But Steve was going around saying why not, and I think we were starting to have more self belief.

As chairman Paul Baker adds:

We couldn't believe the success of the previous season. Everyone was talking about consolidation and to come second in that league, with so many full-time clubs in it when we were still very much a part-time outfit was incredible.

Cotterill, having finally ended his long striker hunt with the signing of Neil Grayson the previous February, went for the 'if it ain't broke, don't fix it' approach, as only two players were added to the squad. Both came down the road from Hereford, first John

Cheltenham Town v. Hayes. Jason Eaton chases after Hayes' no. 2 Nathan Bunce.

Brough, a strong, versatile player who had spent most of his life as a central defender but was just as useful at the other end of the field. He had proved that at Whaddon Road the previous Easter with a goal in Hereford's 2-1 win. Another player who had suffered the ultimate agony – relegation from the Football League – with the Bulls joined him.

David Norton, with vast experience behind him at Aston Villa, Northampton and Hull City, was all set to retire at thirty-three having left Edgar Street. He had been released after a bad injury, cured by an operation, but was surplus to requirements. Thus it was a surprise for the Robins fans who turned up at Harrow Hill for a pre-season friendly to see him lining up for Cheltenham.

Norton remembers:

I had left Hereford after their first season in the Conference, and I had effectively retired. The PFA paid for an operation as at the time it was difficult for me to be very active, and I got the Football League's insurance pay-out. John Brough and Neil Grayson had gone to Cheltenham from Hereford, and Steve called and asked me to go down for pre-season. He gave me a chance, and there was no pressure on either side – but it turned out to be the most fantastic year of my life. Other clubs wanted me, but as soon as Steve called, I was not going anywhere else. Everyone knew there was only one way to better what had gone on the previous season, and it seemed that everyone at the club, from the bottom to the top, knew we would win the Conference. That excited me a lot as I said that if I was going to play again, it would be with a club who would help me get my pride back after the relegation with Hereford. That was the worst moment of my career and as soon as I went to Cheltenham there was only one club I wanted to play for. I could have made better money elsewhere but as soon as I met Steve that was that.

Chairman Baker says:

Over the close season we had a sneaky feeling that we were not a million miles away. The previous season we had not been hammered by anyone, had more than held our own and were a difficult side to beat, so we didn't bring in many players. David

Norton was a gamble but he proved to be a massive influence as he had done it at the highest level. He was another great character like Clive Walker, as was John Brough, a very strong, versatile player, and I suppose those two were the difference for us.

Says Cotterill:

Broughy came on a free and Norts had had a couple of bad injuries, but he was one of those characters – another good one – and a good, solid, honest pro. who would do what you told him, live off it and drive others on. He had a burning desire to put right his relegation with Hereford, and they bulked the squad up a bit, meaning we had competition. I think we could have won the league the year before with a stronger squad as we had no room for any injuries, and we set about starting to have a crack at it. We got off to a good start when Chris Banks scored at Welling after seven minutes, then got our mandatory bad start by losing 2-1.

Norton took his place in the side and John Brough was there too, standing in for the suspended Mark Freeman alongside Chris Banks. At Welling Neil Grayson was Jason Eaton's partner as Dale Watkins suffered a pre-season pelvic injury. The new Whaddon Road pitch was christened by a goal-less draw against Hednesford, before a six-goal thriller against Hayes really got the season off and running. David Norton made his first real impact on the Whaddon Road faithful with a spectacular diving header – unfortunately it was past Steve Book, into his own net. After being 2-0 and 3-1 down, a point was secured in the final minute with that penalty king of many years' standing, Jimmy Smith, coming off the bench to become the hero.

Three games, two points – this was not the script that Steve Cotterill was hoping for, but the shortest trip of the season provided just the impetus needed to get things moving. Nailsworth's Forest Green Rovers had made it to the non-League elite via successive Championship triumphs twenty years after meeting Cheltenham in a Dr Martens Mid-land Division game, and their meet-ing at The Lawn was very eagerly anticipated. What was not anticipated was Steve Cotterill's change of formation – a switch which was to prove an inspired one. Cotterill changed from his trademark 4-4-2 to employ three centre-halves, Chris Banks, John Brough and Mark Freeman, who was back from suspension. That allowed

Cheltenham Town v. Hayes. New arrival David Norton on the ball.

Clive Walker to have more freedom, and he turned in a dazzling display at The Lawn, where Jason Eaton and David Norton hit the target.

Remembers Cotterill:

We started playing 5-2-1-2 and we took off from there. We were good that night, and I remember Clive Walker was sensational, and we went on as the players' mental strength and character enabled us to go on a good run of results.

For Norton, it was a huge relief after the own goal days earlier, and goals from Neil Grayson and Jamie Victory at Leek built on the win.

Norton remembers:

That diving header was spectacular. What a way to start in front of the fans at Whaddon Road – I wanted the ground to open up. But I scored at Forest Green and the fans practically mobbed me – it was great the way they took me to their hearts straightaway. I had expected some questions from them but they were brilliant and that goal was special – it was my way of saying thanks to them for believing in me.

Norton's stay could have been a brief one, as seven games in to the season, business partner Gary Mills tried to entice him to King's Lynn.

Norton recalls:

He offered me the chance to go there and coach with him. It was tempting – he was my best mate and my business partner but by then Steve had sold himself to me, along with the directors, players and fans and I realized it would be a big mistake if I left.

With Norton now bedded into a central midfield role, Cheltenham Town were on the move. Before they knew it, they were in the top three thanks to two successive 4-1 wins, over Barrow and Morecambe. The first, against Barrow, was Clive Walker's match as the forty-one year old reached the landmark of 100 non-League goals, becoming the first player to reach the mark after scoring more than 100 Football League goals. The 2,005 Whaddon Road crowd rose to a man as he put away Lee Howells' pass, and for good measure he added number 101. Walker had stayed at the club for another season after a pre-season chat with Steve Cotterill.

Walker remembers:

I didn't have a contract, Steve and I had a verbal agreement and both parties stuck to it. My legs were coming to the end of their time and I said I would do the best I could, and as it turned out I couldn't play as much as I would have liked to. At the start of the season though, I was on a roll – it was the same roll that I had been on for about five years, with only the time at Brentford in between. My age didn't bother me, but in the end my Achilles injury would stop me. That 100th non-League goal was a very special moment as I had been stuck on 99 for a while, and I was determined to carry on until I got it.

Neil Grayson and Lee Howells shared the goals against Morecambe as Grayson and Jason Eaton made the most of their chance with Dale Watkins out.

Watkins scored in a reserve game at Gloucester, but was still some way from full fitness, so the 'Jason-Grayson' duo was born. They hit a goal apiece at Kettering in a 2-0 success, then Eaton and Mark Freeman saw off Kingstonian as the winning run reached six. A 3-0 win over Southport made it seven, courtesy of Eaton again, David Norton and Clive Walker, and already observers were predicting a two-horse title race between Cheltenham and their old foes Rushden & Diamonds.

The winning run ended thanks to Steve West's long-range effort for Woking at Whaddon Road on 22 September, cancelled out by Neil Grayson, but bizarre happenings 120 miles to the north meant history was made. Many of the 2,406 at Whaddon Road that night left the ground disappointed, but a look at Teletext cheered them up quickly. Rushden were in action at Leek, and were leading 1-0 thanks to Paul Underwood's goal, and were set to stay top until fate intervened. Some chemical tanks at the Courtalds factory adjoining Leek's Harrison Park ground caught fire, and eventually the game was abandoned – Cheltenham were on top of the Conference.

Cotterill recalls:

It was good to be top of the table. We had an iffy start but once we had got back on an even keel, we carried on winning, and the players had that belief that the run would carry on, and so it did.

A Clive Walker inspired 4-2 win at Farnborough extended the advantage to three points and the lead was cut to two when Dover left Whaddon Road with a point from a 1-1 draw.

But Cotterill was not resting on his laurels, and was scouring the transfer market, a move for Hednesford's former Aston Villa defender Andy Comyn hitting the buffers, but soon it was Cotterill himself in demand. Swindon Town were the suitors, and Cotterill was interviewed for the post, but he missed out in favour of Jimmy Quinn, so it was back to the job in hand.

His main problem surrounded Dale Watkins, who after four substitute appearances, was still struggling with his mystery pelvic injury, despite a County Cup goal at Cinderford. The mystery was eventually solved as Watkins underwent a double hernia operation, which ruled him out for two months. But Neil Grayson was still in the goals, scoring at Yeovil alongside David Norton's screamer, but the Glovers hit back for a draw before an eventful home win over Doncaster.

After Whaddon Road passed a lunchtime inspection, John Brough and Michael Duff's first Cheltenham goal earned the 2-1 win, with Jason Eaton missing a penalty. The game marked the debut of Cotterill's latest signing, Richard Walker, the result of his fourth raid on Hereford in a matter of months, a £15,000 fee seeing the defender follow Neil Grayson, John Brough and David Norton on the well-worn track down from Edgar Street.

Cotterill was less successful in his bid to obtain cover for Dale Watkins, with John Norman, the Morecambe striker, saying no to a move due to the travelling distance to Cheltenham from his home on the Wirral.

Says Cotterill:

I had to keep trying to make the squad stronger. I like to bring players in November and the end of January or beginning of February. Every year I would try and leave space in my budget for a player or two, as I would normally need something after Christmas to bolster us a bit.

So thoughts turned to the FA Cup, and two wins over Western League opposition in Barnstaple and Taunton set up a home tie with Division Two strugglers Lincoln City. Preparations for the big day were not ideal – the fourteen-match unbeaten run ended with a 1-0 defeat at Woking, as Clive Walker missed a penalty at the club where he had enjoyed so much success, leaving Cheltenham top only on goal difference from Stevenage, who had pushed themselves into the picture.

Any hopes of upsetting Lincoln in front of the *Match of the Day* cameras were dashed by Lee Thorpe's goal eleven minutes from time, so with the FA Cup over, crunch time was coming on two fronts.

Says Cotterill:

The Lincoln game was disappointing, as it was probably the only time we did not do ourselves justice in the FA Cup.

Attention then switched to the Trophy, where Bashley were the first hurdle in the quest for a return to Wembley, and Neil Grayson scored twice in an unconvincing 2-1 win before the Trophy was locked away until January. But the main focus was the visit of title rivals Rushden & Diamonds, in a game which saw 4,051 flock to Whaddon Road.

There was an early shock as Steve Book saved a penalty from Colin West, and a tense game was settled by Keith Knight's 32nd minute goal – however, seven days later, Cheltenham were off the top for the first time in over two months. A 0-0 draw at Dover was the cause, letting Kettering take over, and they were soon four points clear after Cheltenham's second successive goal-less draw, at home to Leek.

By now, Cheltenham were an established force, and the annual round of England non-League trials saw nine of the side play against the Dr Martens League at Bath. Steve Book, Richard Walker, Chris Banks, Michael Duff, Jamie Victory, Russell Milton, Lee Howells, the newly-fit Dale Watkins and Jason Eaton lined up in a 0-0 draw – with future Robin Shane Higgs keeping them at bay – while Neil Grayson played in another trial game.

The league was developing into a four-horse race with Kettering and Stevenage joining Rushden in the chase for the title, and Stevenage were next to come to Whaddon Road. The game was played against a backdrop of injuries, with Neil Grayson and Richard Walker spending time in an oxygen chamber to speed up their recoveries, Bob Bloomer and long-term victim Mark Crisp still sidelined and Clive Walker nursing his Achilles problem. That meant Dale Watkins' recovery from his hernia operation was a blessing, and he came in for his first start of the campaign to revive his successful partnership with Jason Eaton – and to good effect as they shared the goals in a comfortable 3-0 win. The pair were at it again on Boxing Day in a 3-0 win at Telford, and the Christmas cheer was complete when Watkins scored at Kidderminster as 1998 finished strongly.

The momentum continued into the start of 1999 as well, with Clive Walker and Lee Howells seeing off Telford, with another clean sheet for the defenders, amazingly their eighth in a row in the Conference. That record ended at Doncaster, who hit back from 2-0 down to grab a 2-2 draw after Watkins again proved he was back to form and fitness with two first-half goals in a game which saw John Brough sent off. Kettering thumped Morecambe 6-0 and held a four-point lead, but Cheltenham had three games in hand, while Rushden were 12 points adrift of their Northamptonshire rivals having played six games less. The bookmakers were backing the Robins, installing them as 11-10 favourites for the title as the squad jetted off to Marbella for their now-customary mid-season break.

They returned to face the challenge of the next stage of the FA Trophy defence, with Canvey Island – later to lift the Trophy themselves – showing some of that potential in a 2-1 defeat, progress only secured by Mark Freeman's late winner.

The draw was not kind – an away trip to Stevenage – but that was forgotten as the unbeaten Conference home record disappeared in the unlucky 13th game thanks to Paul Tait's winner for Northwich. As it turned out, the damage wasn't too great – Kettering's game at Woking was abandoned and Rushden lost at home to Doncaster, a result which allowed Yeovil to just about stay in touch after they edged out Barrow. Again, Steve Cotterill responded with a foray into the transfer market, and this

A familiar sight: Neil Grayson celebrates scoring a goal.

signing would turn out to be another resounding success. He landed Mark Yates from Kidderminster Harriers, paying out £25,000 for a player who would go on to the be the cornerstone of future glory, and who started the 2002/03 season as the club's skipper. He had played for Birmingham, Doncaster and Burnley before joining Harriers during Graham Allner's reign, where he was a key cog in their midfield machine.

Chairman Paul Baker recalls:

Mark Yates was a crucial signing. I remember I was on a train talking to Steve as he was doing the deal and the reception kept coming and going. Mark is another nice bloke – we have always had nice lads at the club, who cause no trouble for us. They all seem to blend in, and we have had no prima donnas, and we always meant to strengthen the squad if there was a push for us to go up. We have always been able to do that, and seemed to bring in the right players at the right time.

Cotterill's view:

I could fill a book on my own on Mark Yates, even though he doesn't go right back to the beginning like some others. He was one of my best signings.

He didn't take long to make his mark either, featuring in a run of three tricky looking away games which could make or break the title challenge. The first stop was Southport, on what was to prove a significant afternoon, as Lee Howells and Neil Grayson sealed a 2-0 win while Rushden fell at Northwich and Doncaster grabbed a win at Kettering. The deficit was now one point on Kettering with two games in hand – and Rushden's three games in hand meant little as they had slipped 11 points behind the Robins.

Rushden used one of those games in hand, drawing 1-1 with Kidderminster, before the Trophy interrupted things again, with what was to be an eventful tie with Stevenage. A 0-0 scoreline at Whaddon Road was only half the story. Jason Eaton saw red after a fracas with former Robins goalkeeper Chris Taylor, but elsewhere Kettering's home Conference defeat by Dover lifted the mood.

After the game, Cotterill revealed he had rejected the chance to join his friend Lawrie Sanchez at Wycombe Wanderers, then the Stevenage replay the following Monday turned into complete farce. Mark Freeman never scored a better goal than the 20-yard volley he fizzed in at Broadhall Way, but a snowstorm and a convenient lack of brooms to sweep the snow off the lines led to an abandonment at half time.

There was no snow at Whaddon Road the following day as youth was given its head against Hayes in the Endsleigh Trophy, Gareth Hopkins scoring both in a 2-1 win. The news that six Robins (Steve Book, Chris Banks, Mark Yates, Lee Howells, Dale Watkins and Neil Grayson) were in line for England semi-professional caps was a huge boost as the Conference away days tour headed for Morecambe.

The result was another 2-0 win, this time courtesy of Dale Watkins and Neil Grayson, before it was back to Stevenage again to try and settle the Trophy saga. Again, the fates didn't conspire to make things easy – a 0-0 draw after 120 minutes meant penalties, and it was David Norton who kept his cool to earn a 5-4 shoot-out success.

Norton was the centre of attention again at Hereford days later, when he was abused by the home fans at Edgar Street, but had the last laugh as Mark Freeman and Jamie Victory made it nine points out of nine from the three away trips, with no goals conceded – surely championship form. Norton remembers that day:

There was a section of small-minded people who didn't understand why I had left Hereford – but there were 1,500 Cheltenham fans chanting my name, who drowned them out. The abuse hurt at the time, but I would have gone through twenty-five games like that if I knew there was a Championship medal at the end of it.

That win left Cheltenham three points behind Kettering, but with five games in hand. Rushden had now played the same number of games (28) and were six points behind. Kettering used up another game – drawing 1-1 with Welling – while Cheltenham were reaching the last eight of the Trophy again as two Jamie Victory goals and a Dale Watkins effort saw off Hendon. Before that game, there was another new arrival – Neil Howarth coming in from Macclesfield for another rock-bottom price, £7,500. Howarth had skippered Macclesfield to Conference title glory, but it was concerns over Chris Banks' fitness which prompted Steve Cotterill to take the plunge.

The six in line for England semi-professional caps had been reduced to four as Chris Banks and Lee Howells pulled out injured, but Steve Book, Neil Grayson, Dale Watkins and Mark Yates featured against Italy at Hayes in a 4-1 win, Grayson scoring twice. Book and Grayson were to play again later in the season in a 1-1 draw with Holland.

Keith Knight, back from an injury lay-off, secured a 1-1 draw at Barrow, and then Hereford came for the return at Whaddon Road, with John Brough netting against his old club in a 2-2 draw that was followed by another at Stevenage. Lee Howells, after seven games out injured, came off the bench to grab a point for the Robins with Brough also on target, while Bob Bloomer was sent off.

Banks made a surprise return in the 0-0 draw with Farnborough, who had just lost their leading scorer Dennis Bailey to Cheltenham as Cotterill swooped for a £15,000 signing. Bailey has his name etched in football folklore as the last visiting player to score a hat-trick against Manchester United at Old Trafford, in a 4-1 success for QPR, and he had hit 21 goals for the struggling Hampshire side.

Recalls Cotterill:

Dennis Bailey was a short-term quick fix. I was only getting him for the run-in, to put a spanner in the works of others as I knew they would fear Dennis as he could nick a goal.

That's how it turned out, as Bailey moved to Forest Green the following May as Cheltenham recouped the £15,000 – but not before the experienced striker had played his part. He was booked thirty-six seconds into his debut against Kettering in a real top-

Action from Whaddon Road, Cheltenham Town v. Kettering Town. Dennis Bailey salutes the crowd after Kettering score their first own goal with their 'keeper flat on the ground.

of-the-table clash at Whaddon Road, which saw the gate break the 5,000 barrier for the first time, as 5,202 crammed themselves in.

A Martin Matthews own goal and a cracker from Neil Grayson made it 2-0 at the interval, and Cheltenham were back on top when Grayson added his second and the Robins' third after the break.

They had four games in hand on Kettering as both sides were locked on 66 points, with Rushden just three points behind. Bailey grabbed his first goal at Hednesford two days after the Kettering victory, but it was a late consolation in a 3-2 defeat, and with Rushden winning by the same score at Leek, Cheltenham, Rushden and Kettering were locked together on 66 points.

'A game too far' was how Cotterill described that Hednesford defeat at the time as he battled with an injury list which numbered Chris Banks, John Brough, Richard Walker, Mark Yates and Dale Watkins.

The Trophy interrupted things again as Cheltenham reached the semi-finals thanks to Neil Howarth's goal at Emley, while down south at Rockingham Road, 5,017 people saw Kettering and Rushden slug out a 0-0 draw which put Rushden top by a point as their Easter Saturday clash with Cheltenham loomed large.

All roads literally led to Nene Park that day, and anyone driving into their impressive complex knew straightaway that it was no ordinary match.

Chairman Paul Baker:

My overriding memory of that day at Nene Park is of the queues stretching away from the turnstiles. I could not believe how many people there were. They seemed to go on and on, and I remember thinking that there was no way everyone was going to get in. I stayed outside the ground for about half an hour trying to find ways to get people in. I bought a ticket from a supporter who had a spare one, and got some in as directors' partners.

As it turned out, conservative estimates say that some 700 Robins fans were locked out, and they missed a classic. The Nene Park scoreboard read 'Rushden 1 Cheltenham 0' after 90 minutes, and, still reading 90 minutes, it said 'Rushden 1, Cheltenham 2' after Mark Freeman and Neil Grayson turned around Miguel De Souza's first-half goal.

Paul Baker:

I remember looking at the scoreboard which said 1-0 to Rushden after 90 minutes, and thinking to myself that it wasn't going to change. Then Mark Freeman scored – another Cheltenham legend and a guy who would go through walls for you – and then we had Neil Grayson's amazing winner.

Rushden and Diamonds v. Cheltenham Town, Nene Park. Cheltenham fans queueing up outside the ground before the match.

Rushden and Diamonds 1 Cheltenham Town 2

Cheltenham Town snatched an incredible victory over their deadly Nationwide Conference title rivals with two goals in the last two minutes. In front of 6,312 fans – and with 400 Robins fans locked out – the Robins' promotion hopes looked set for a big jolt as they trailed to Miguel De Souza's 21st-minute goal. But in the 89th minute substitute Mark Freeman crashed in Mike Duff's cross and looked to have sealed a deserved point, but a minute later it got better when Neil Grayson squeezed home a winner after John Brough touched on Freeman's long downfield ball.

Freeman was the odd man out in the Robins defence. Chris Banks, Neil Howarth and John Brough formed the back three, while in midfield Bob Bloomer got the nod ahead of Russell Milton alongside David Norton and Lee Howells, who made a positive start from the kick-off which led to Dennis Bailey having a shot blocked. Michael McElhatton fizzed a fourth minute effort wide, then Steve Book had to make a confident catch as Guy Branston looked to get on the end of an Underwood cross. Jim Rodwell went in the book for a foul on Bailey, and Rushden went close after 12 minutes after Carl Heggs beat Bloomer and crossed for Collins, who headed wide.

Cheltenham had been under the cosh but won the first corner after 16 minutes, only for Rushden's pressure to pay off after 21 minutes. Michael Duff was harshly booked for a high challenge on Underwood, who swung in the free-kick, which Branston knocked down for Miguel De Souza, who was left with the easy task of beating Book. Cheltenham reacted well to going a goal behind, and started to cause Rushden some problems.

On the half-hour, Duff was sent away up the right and tried a cheeky effort which hit the outside of the post, nearly catching Smith unawares. Then good battling by Bailey and Howells in midfield saw the ball break for Norton, whose low effort was touched round by Smith. From the resulting corner, Grayson had a volley blocked and Howarth a shot charged down, and after 35 minutes Smith did well to clutch Norton's stinging 25-yarder into his midriff. Cheltenham, who won six corners to Rushden's none in the first half, then saw Brough glance a header over the angle as they finished the half strongly. Howells was booked after 36 minutes for a foul on Heggs, and Collins took the booking tally to four after scything down Bloomer.

Cheltenham started the second half attacking towards their own fans but had an early scare when Collins outpaced Howarth and cut back to Heggs, but fortunately for Book his shot lacked power. A minute later, Rushden won their first corner, and the Robins had another scare when Howarth had to clear a Heggs cross with De Souza lurking. Cheltenham hit back and Branston's toe denied Howells as he went through and Darren Bradshaw hacked away when Smith missed a deep Norton cross. Grayson put a volley over from Victory's cross from the left by-line, while the outstanding Banks did well at the other end, keeping cool after Collins headed a deep Underwood cross back across the face of goal.

Book was a relieved man after 63 minutes when a Mark Cooper corner flashed straight across the face of goal without a touch, and a minute later Steve Cotterill made a double change in an effort to break what looked like an impenetrable Diamonds defence. Milton replaced Bloomer and Freeman came on for Howarth, with Milton's first contribution being a yellow card. Ten minutes later, Bailey was forced to limp off after receiving treatment to a leg injury, with Keith Knight coming on and Brough joining Grayson up front.

Brough had an instant impact, being fouled by Bradshaw and nearly getting on the end of Milton's free kick. With 10 minutes left, Heggs was booked for a foul on Knight, and Rushden sub Colin West, warming up on the touchline, also got cautioned for delaying a Robins throw-in. As the minutes ticked by, it looked as if all the Robins' efforts would be in vain, as the game drew to its incredible finish. A short corner was played to Duff and Freeman barged through the congested box to crash the ball home and send the 1,500 Robins fans behind the goal delirious. Seconds later, they were positively euphoric as the Robins pinched an incredible winner. Freeman whacked the ball forward and Brough touched it on and played it towards goal with Grayson nipping in ahead of Rodwell to guide it into the roof of the net for what could be a vital goal in a month's time.

Rushden and Diamonds v. Cheltenham Town, Nene Park. Neil Grayson and team-mates celebrate his winning goal, watched by Rushden goalie Mark Smith.

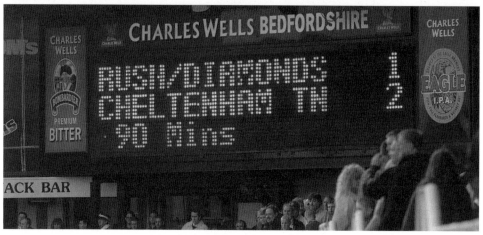

Rushden and Diamonds v. Cheltenham Town. *From top to bottom:* The score at 90 minutes wasn't the final score *(1)*. With the scoreboard still showing 90 minutes, the scores are level *(2)*. The final result is a last-gasp 2-1 victory to Cheltenham *(3)*.

Did Steve Cotterill think it was all over? His reply:

Until the whistle is gone there's always a chance. We had the corner before the equaliser and I thought there was small chance. I remember cursing Michael Duff for getting the ball. He is six foot three, and there he was going short for a corner when he should have been in there to head it in, but he crossed it for Boka. Then to go and get the winner was sensational, and very disappointing for them, but they were always magnanimous in defeat, as they were at Cardiff in the play-off final as well.

Grayson's winner cemented him into Robins history. He says:

That goal was probably the worst goal I've ever scored to be honest. It was just a toe poke. John Brough hit the first shot and he still swears it was going in before I got to it, but I don't think anyone believes him. We would obviously have settled for 1-1 so to score again so late on was just incredible really.

For Steve Cotterill, that game and the subsequent 1-0 home win over Kidderminster convinced him that Cheltenham would win the Conference. He says:

That's the weekend we won it. Had we beaten Rushden and lost to Kidderminster on Monday, and they had gone and won at Woking again, it was game on. We beat them, which was a real kick in the teeth, and we beat Kidderminster 1-0, on the same day as Woking beat Rushden 1-0. That weekend we nailed them down.

After the Kidderminster win, the FA Trophy semi-final clashes with Kingstonian took priority. Steve Cotterill still wanted the double:

I was proud of what we had done the year before but anyone can win a cup. Not everyone can win a league, and I thought we could do both so my feeling was let's push it as far as we can.

Neil Grayson and his makeshift strike partner John Brough earned a 2-2 draw at Kingsmeadow in the first leg, and it appeared then that the return to Wembley was on. Amazingly, the sides met again in the midweek encounter between the two legs, with Cheltenham getting the Conference points thanks to a Neil Grayson penalty, but that was to count for nothing. The Trophy dream died at Whaddon Road as Matt Crossley, David Leworthy and Gary Patterson sent Geoff Chapple's side to the final, where they would lift the silverware as Tarkan Mustafa's goal sunk Forest Green Rovers 1-0 – everything rested on the title.

Cheltenham had five games left, and led the table by two points from Kettering, who only had one game to play. Hayes had sneaked into third, five points behind with two matches left, but Rushden were still the main threat. They had four games to play and were seven points behind Cheltenham, while Yeovil, with five games left were ten points behind in fifth place.

The permutations were simple – Cheltenham needed six points from five games to make sure of the title – wins in home games against county rivals Forest Green as well as Yeovil – who were still title outsiders themselves – would be enough. Dennis Bailey gave the Robins a half-time lead against Rovers, but a late equaliser from substitute Matthew Coupe pegged Cheltenham back.

Recalls Steve Cotterill:

It was all very tense and we had to play on Saturday, Tuesday and Thursday. I knew that four points from Forest Green and Yeovil would probably do it, and we had looked at beating Forest Green and getting a draw against Yeovil. I got them all to the ground early, and it was clear there was going to be a big atmosphere.

That was something of an understatement – the official crowd figure is 6,150, but the general consensus is that the actual number on the terraces was nearer 7,000.

Steve Cotterill remembers:

Yeovil could still have won the league themselves if they had beaten us. They went 1-0 up in the first minute, then 2-1 up, when Warren Patmore got a penalty, but we came back each time.

So 2-2 was how it stayed until the seventh minute of injury time, when the winning goal came – but the riddle over who scored that goal has never really been solved. Keith Knight swung the free kick over, and Michael Duff and Jamie Victory both went for it, and the ball flew past Tony Pennock to send Whaddon Road into delirium.

Cotterill's take on the dispute is:

I always say that Jamie Duff and Michael Victory headed it in. I actually think both of them headed it, and they are very close to each other. They both swear they headed it, and it is possible. To be honest, I don't really care now who headed it, and I know is that it was scored by a Cheltenham Town player, and we won the game.

To this day, Duff and Victory both claim the goal. Duff, whose name is in the club's official records as the scorer, says:

It is my goal. At the time, I wasn't so sure, but now I am 100 per cent certain. If Jamie had scored it, why did he not celebrate madly like I did? It is in the records as being mine, and that's enough for me, so I'm keeping it. I don't score too many, so it is nice to have scored 'the goal'.

The celebrations are the reason that most people have given the goal to Duff – he headed off for the fans while Victory simply turned away.

Cheltenham Town 3 Yeovil 2

A dramatic winner deep into injury time from Michael Duff sent Cheltenham Town into the Nationwide League at Whaddon Road last night. After a breathless match which sent the 6,150 crammed into the ground through a rollercoaster of emotions, Duff headed home Keith Knight's inswinging free kick to spark the promotion party.

As the game ended in high drama, it had started in the same way as Yeovil went in front within a minute. Kevan Brown's free kick was flicked on by Warren Patmore and Owen Pickard stole in to loop a header past Steve Book. Whaddon Road was silenced, but two minutes later came to life again as the Robins equalised. Mike Duff's cross was headed against the post by Dennis Bailey, and the rebound fell to Victory, who needed two bites before putting the ball in the net.

That breathless opening set the tone for the rest of the game and the tempo barely let up. There were half chances at both ends before Cheltenham inched in front after 20 minutes when Duff's right wing cross was met by Grayson's head at the near post. That inspired the Robins, who had a good spell until half-time. After 28 minutes Dean Chandler was forced to clear at the far post as Victory headed a ball down to Grayson, Duff put a header inches wide from a David Norton cross and Tony Pennock saved from Bob Bloomer.

However, 60 seconds after the break the champagne was back on ice as Victory handled a far post corner and Patmore despatched the penalty to make it 2-2. Worse looked to have followed after 51 minutes when Pickard touched in Rob Cousins' through ball, but the Robins were rescued by an offside flag. The tension rose and Brown, Grayson, Paul Steele and Mark Freeman were all booked, then Bloomer had a shot saved and Lee Howells hit the inside of the post with Pennock beaten.

As the minutes ticked by, it seemed that Saturday's game at Hayes would be the one where the title was decided. Then Steele was sent off after 78 minutes for a late tackle on Grayson and the Robins went for the jugular. Victory headed wide after 78 minutes, then Pennock pulled off four brilliant saves. He somehow denied Grayson after 85 minutes, and got up to block the rebound, then after Victory headed wide again Pennock turned a Knight curler around the post as the game moved into injury time. Norton was next to be denied as Pennock turned his 20-yarder away, and it seemed that the promotion party would be delayed until Duff popped up to spark euphoric scenes.

Victory says:

I am a bit disappointed about it as I know why people think he scored – because he celebrated and I didn't, but I know I scored it. People ask why I didn't celebrate if I

Cheltenham Town v. Yeovil Town. Cheltenham Town become Conference Champions.

did score it, but my overwhelming feeling was one of relief as I had missed three or four headers in the game before that. So when I scored, I was so relieved as I could not have lived with myself if those misses meant that we missed out on going up. Duffo said at the time that he did not touch it, which he now denies, and we still have arguments about it now whenever it is mentioned. But we got into the League, so it does not really matter but it would be nice if it could be cleared up once and for all.

At around 9.52 p.m. on 22 April 1999 the final whistle went, and the seemingly impossible had happened – Cheltenham Town were a Football League club.

Skipper Chris Banks:

Yeovil will always stick in the memory as the day that we clinched promotion. There were a lot of memorable games that season, but Yeovil was the best and the one people will always remember. It was a very open game and enjoyable to play in – a real roller-coaster. I haven't got a clue who scored the winner, and I don't care.

The celebrations went on for most of the night, and into the early morning, and everyone who was there has their own special memories. There are many stories, including the unnamed player who spent the night under a supporters' Union Jack flag on the steps of the old club shop, and managed to lose one of his shoes. Lee Howells recalls:

Yeovil was one of the best games the club has ever had – we all knew that we'd be up if we won it. I hit the post at 2-2, but to do it in the last minute was fantastic. I got in at 3 o'clock the following morning and rang my boss and told him I wouldn't be in for a while. It meant a lot to go straight up and to do it with such a small squad and an inexperienced manager.

Neil Grayson, scorer of the second goal, says:

What a night! I remember us going 1-0 down and even then so early on you think perhaps it isn't going to happen tonight. Then Jamie equalised and I scored from a corner so we were ahead at half time, but we then gave away a penalty at the start of the second half and although we really bombarded them, especially after Paul Steele was sent off, it didn't look as if we would win it. To score so late on was superb really and then the celebrations were something else – I don't think I've ever seen so many people on a pitch before. Then in the bar afterwards, everyone was coming up and hugging you – just unbelievable.

Steve Cotterill:

I remember being in tears at the final whistle as that was the culmination of everything. It was all the pressures if being a local lad, and I had the whole family at that game. Emotions are a measure of what you have put in, and that night was a measure of what we all put into that season. I remember going into the ground and it was daylight, and going back to my car it was daylight. I left the ground at 6.45 a.m., got a lift home as there was no way I could drive, got showered and changed

Cheltenham Town v. Yeovil Town. The Champions celebrate.

and was back at my desk two hours later reading all the faxes. The fax machine was like an Andrex toilet roll, and it took me ages to plough through them all.

Says David Norton:

You can't buy moments like that winner against Yeovil. I had to wait nineteen years for that night and over the season we were by far the best side in that league. Until about November we were the best footballing side, then we ground the results out and we had match winners throughout the team – there was not a team who could live with us.

After all the euphoria of that night, there were still three games left to play, but the Robins failed to win any of them. They went down 3-2 to an injury-time winner at Hayes in a game which saw Steve Cotterill ordered from the dug-out; they then suffered a 1-0 reverse at Northwich. The Conference trophy was presented after the final game a 0-0 home draw with Welling, which took Cheltenham to the 80-point mark and meant they won the title with a four-point cushion over Kettering, whose final-day win at Rushden clinched them the runners-up spot.

Cotterill says:

For the Welling game I changed the team, as players like Bob Bloomer hadn't been in the team, and played a lop-sided midfield to give some of the longer-serving players a game. We had won the League and I wanted them to have a chance for some of the others to say goodbye.

It was indeed goodbye to Cheltenham Town for some players after yet another open-top bus celebration, as David Norton, Keith Knight, Clive Walker and Jason Eaton did not make the transition to full-time football.

Cotterill adds:

I remember asking David Norton if he wanted a coaching job, but he wanted to carry on playing, so that was him out of the equation. I offered Jason Eaton a one-year contract, but he had a good job and was getting promotion after promotion. I remember doing his contract at Yeovil, and with that and his job we could not have matched that anyway. Keith Knight looked at it, would only have been a contract for a year or two, and he decided he was happy with his job, and Clive Walker I decided not to take, because of his age really. Also, he was struggling with his Achilles injury, and I felt he would have been better off in non-League.

For Norton, it marked the end of his golden season at Cheltenham as the insurance pay-out he had received barred him from making the step into the League.

He says:

Champions: Captain Chris Banks lifts the Conference Trophy.

Steve offered me a job on the management side with himself and Mike Davis, and that was very tempting. I couldn't play in the League and although Cheltenham have since gone on to wonderful things, I made the right decision. I wanted to keep playing, and I went to Yeovil, but within a few months Colin Lippiatt left. Steve Thompson took over, but I felt there was a lot of competition between him and me for a place in the team, and I wasn't going to drive from Nottingham to sit on the bench.

Forest Green came in for me and I really enjoyed myself there. There were a lot of lads I knew and a year later I became the joint manager with Nigel Spink. We kept the club in the Conference and got to the Trophy final, but I left and joined Gary Mills at Tamworth. Three months later, a job came up at Gainsborough Trinity and I went there, but I had to keep reducing the wage bill and ended the season with ten players despite reaching a Cup final, which we lost to Barrow.

Norton, who contributed 3 goals in his 46 starts, is now player-assistant manager back at Tamworth, and says of his time at Cheltenham:

You can't replace memories like I have of that season. Cheltenham and Steve Cotterill helped me get my pride back and now everyone knows about Cheltenham Town and everyone knows about Steve Cotterill.

That was also the end of the Cheltenham line for Walker, who signed off with the final goal of the season, the third in the 3-0 Gloucestershire Senior Cup final win at old rivals Gloucester City – a game which saw Michael Duff sustain the knee injury which delayed his arrival as a Football League player. Walker, whose two-season stay brought him 12 goals in 70 appearances, says:

It was brilliant to finally get a championship medal after being second twice, third and fifth with Woking, then second with Cheltenham. That was it for me at Cheltenham, and it would have been the end even if we had not won the league because of my

Mission accomplished: manager Steve Cotterill kisses the trophy.

Achilles – it was in bits. At my age I didn't want an operation, so it made sense to stop then. I did nothing for nine months out of choice, and the rest cured the problem, although I was sleeping in plaster casts – that was the price for twenty odd years of wear and tear.

Everything about my time at Cheltenham was good, but I am happy I don't have to do that drive any more, although at the time it was a joy to go down there. The people were brilliant, the fans, directors, and a great bunch of players, and Steve – he was always very determined to succeed and improve himself, which he has done, and it was a lovely place.

After his nine-month sabbatical from the game, Walker went into corporate hospitality, but the lure was too strong, and Ryman League side Molesey tempted him back. He continues:

I started playing there and then the manager left, so I took it on, along with my old Woking colleague Lawrence Batty. I wanted to see what I could do and I enjoyed the job, and did it for a year, then in February I called it a day there and now I do some television work for Sky which I really enjoy, but I would go back to management again.

Jason Eaton, after 115 goals in 247 starts plus 55 substitute appearances, and with his name forever down in history after the FA Trophy final winning goal, chose his career in the fitness business ahead of the full-time game which lay ahead for his colleagues.

Says Eaton:

I didn't want it to end, as I felt a lot for the club, and still do. For me, it was not tempting at any time to go into the Football League. I had made my mind up all along but it hit me when the start of the following season came along, as Cheltenham were in the Football League, I had helped to get them there, but now I was not part of it. It was hard to leave, and very hard to tell Steve my final decision, and it is only after I left that I realised just what a great club it is – one of the best in the non-League game. To find that again is difficult, and I have not found a 'home' in the game since I left. I have been to Yeovil, Newport, Forest Green, Merthyr and Basingstoke. Yeovil was good until the new manager came in, I did okay at Forest Green, then was loaned out to Merthyr and Basingstoke, who I eventually signed for full time.

Eaton left Basingstoke and started the 2002/03 season with Bath City. He admits:

I still see Steve Book, Lee Howells and Bob Bloomer, and it is hard at times. When they played Bristol City in the Worthington Cup, they came to Redwood Lodge for the pre-match meal. It would have been my dream to play at Ashton Gate for Cheltenham.

Jimmy Smith also left after becoming the club's second highest goalscorer with 131 goals in 307 games, while the unfortunate Mark Crisp also said farewell, as did reserve goalkeeper Ryan Gannaway, and youngsters Steve Murphy and Ross Casey. It was the start of a whole new era – and Cheltenham Town FC would never be the same again.

4

Life in the League
1999/2000

Of all the challenges that Cheltenham Town had faced in the previous 107 years of their history, the one they faced in the 1999/2000 season was arguably the largest. They had made it to the big time – the Football League, that elite band of ninety-two clubs which represents the top tier of English football. It was a dream that many who had been involved with the club for many years never thought would happen, but it was now a reality.

That challenge would not only be faced on the pitch by Steve Cotterill and his amazing squad of players, who seemingly had the gift of taking every step up in their stride. It would also ask questions off the pitch: of the board, who had run such a tight ship as the club had moved up and up; of the manager and his players, could they perform more miracles; and also of the town of Cheltenham and county of Gloucestershire. How would the football fans around the area, who had previously travelled to Birmingham and Bristol, react to finally having a Football League club on their doorstep?

Chairman Paul Baker describes his initial feelings about the step up as 'a massive fear of the unknown'.

It was all so different, and we would not know how different until we got into it. There was an awful lot of work to be done off the field in terms of the ground. That meant a massive investment in money and time, and Colin Farmer deserves a massive amount of credit for the work he did to get that ground right.

It was a busy summer for Farmer, and it all started the night of that unforgettable Yeovil game. He remembers:

What a lot of people don't realise is that once your ground has been approved as being of League standard you can get into the League, but you cannot play your first match without making further improvements identified by the inspectors. So, the night of the Yeovil game, although I was celebrating with the rest of them, I knew I faced a busy summer to get things ready for League football, like building the new control tower.

The biggest difference of all was that Cheltenham was now a full-time club. There would be no more training two nights a week after players had spent a hard day in the office, on the building site, fitting windows or at the scrap-yard – now it was training every day.

Cheltenham Town FC: 1999/2000 team. From left to right, back row: Brian Tarren (kit man), Andrew Mitchell (physiotherapist), Martin Devaney, Russell Milton, Hugh McAuley, Antony Griffin, Dale Watkins, Stuart Mitchinson, Mike Heather (groundsman), John Atkinson (reserve team physiotherapist). Middle row: Mike Davis (assistant manager), Jamie Victory, Mark Freeman, Gareth Hopkins, Steve Book, Steve Benbow, Shane Higgs, Michael Duff, John Brough, Neil Grayson, Bob Bloomer. Front row: Mike Jackson, Lee Howells, Chris Banks, Steve Cotterill (manager) Mark Yates, Neil Howarth, Richard Walker.

Chairman Paul Baker's simplistic description of what the change meant at board level is:

Going from part time to full time, added a '0' on to everything. The hobby suddenly became a business. Before we went up, you could buy someone for £10,000 and he could make a difference – £10,000 in the Football League wouldn't get you a lot. A lot of the players who became full time had been part time with us, and they relished the chance to go full time. I think they did well as they were benefiting from full-time training, a full-time physio, and all the things which go with that.

Cotterill also reaped the benefits from day-to-day contact with his players:

One of the best things was offering players like Lee Howells, Chris Banks, Jamie Victory and Michael Duff the chance to be a pro footballer. But my proudest moment was when I told Mike Davis he could go and hand his notice in and come and work with me full time. That was the great buzz I got from it, and having them all in every morning as opposed to 6.30 p.m. on a Tuesday and a Thursday was a breath of fresh air for me, and them.

Left: Mike Davis, assistant manager. *Right:* Dale Watkins.

Cotterill wanted to strengthen his squad, but he was able to resist the temptation to go down the 'boom and bust' road. He could so easily have cleared out all the players who had done the hard work and got the club promoted in favour of players who know their way round Division Three, but instead he put his faith in the players who had not let him down in the past.

Says chairman Paul Baker:

We had to look at budgets, and the squad, and talk to Steve, but one of the big things to consider was the additional money that the club got as a Football League club. It would have been easy to say 'let's go and spend it all', get rid of half the players, bring new ones in, but that would have been a fatal mistake. We didn't do it, we stuck with those same players and they haven't let us down. Clubs that go and make wholesale changes when they go up have found it is not the thing to do. Continuity at Cheltenham Town has always been so important and that is part of the reason why we appointed Graham Allner as manager when Steve left, to keep the team spirit and organisation.

Cotterill brought in three players for transfer fees – the last time the club paid money for a new signing. Cotterill went back to his former club Bournemouth for Antony Griffin, a twenty-year-old right-sided player with searing pace. The Robins' manager had first noticed the quiet Griffin, who would eventually make the right-back berth his own, during his long lay-off with the knee injury which ended his playing career. Cotterill was taking the Bournemouth youth team to the Isle of Wight and the teenaged Griffin was one of his charges, and he knew then that the player had potential. A tribunal eventually decreed that Cheltenham had to pay £25,000 for Griffin – £5,000 more than Leek Town received for Hugh McAuley.

McAuley had scored 18 goals in a Leek side which went down from the Conference – form which attracted plenty of suitors. There is a story that Rushden signed McAuley from Leek, but they failed to get the registration through to the Conference office before the March transfer deadline. McAuley had trials at Portsmouth and Sheffield United, Crystal Palace also showed interest and Stevenage made a bid, but Cheltenham won the day. McAuley's father had been a winger for Liverpool, Tranmere, Plymouth, Charlton and Carlisle, and is a youth coach at Liverpool, where McAuley junior spent some time.

The third arrival was to put pressure on Steve Book, as goalkeeper Shane Higgs was bought for £10,000. Higgs had been on Bristol Rovers' books, but found his way to Worcester, where he played for future Robins manager Graham Allner. Steve Cotterill had seen him play superbly for a Dr Martens League side against an FA XI which included nine Cheltenham players at Bath. Cotterill also snapped up local lad Martin Devaney, a teenage striker who had been on Coventry City's books under Ron Atkinson and Gordon Strachan without making the breakthrough into the first team.

Off the field, the Robins attracted a shirt sponsorship deal with Towergate Insurance, which helped to fund a development in the main stand, giving the club much-needed hospitality facilities.

Paul Baker says:

The sponsorship deal with Towergate Insurance was very significant. It was a six-figure deal, and it funded the hospitality development and executive boxes. Without it, we would have been coming into the Football League with no hospitality facilities at all, so that was a major investment, and we opened the boxes in October.

On the field, pre-season matches brought three wins, over Worcester, Telford and on tour in Cheltenham's twin town of Göttingen, as well as defeats by Wolves, in a richly-deserved testimonial for Lee Howells, and Birmingham City.

Recalls Lee Howells:

The hardest thing about going full time was the pre-season training. Steve really put us through it, and I remember it was a hot summer too, but that really helped as the season went on.

It was a proud day when the club ran out on 7 August 1999 for their first-ever League game, with Rochdale at Whaddon Road. Three players, Steve Book, Mark Freeman and Lee Howells, made their Football League debuts as a new world of squad numbers and names

Cheltenham Town 0 Rochdale 2

There was to be no dream start for the Robins in the Nationwide League as two first-half goals gave a slick Rochdale side victory at Whaddon Road. However, the defeat may yet turn out to be a good omen for Steve Cotterill's side as they lost their opening game in each of the past two seasons, and ended them with a trip to Wembley and the Nationwide Conference title triumph respectively.

In the first half, Cheltenham looked overawed and were out-passed and out-manoeuvred by Rochdale, who scored twice and could have gone in with a bigger lead had Dave Bayliss not hit the post in between Graeme Atkinson's 26th-minute goal and Tony Ford's second 16 minutes later. It could have been different had Neil Grayson's half-chance on the stroke of the interval gone in, but that seemed to lift the Robins and they competed better after the break, but could not find a way back into the contest. The Robins were without the injured Mike Duff, Richard Walker and Russell Milton, with summer signing Anthony Griffin filling Duff's right wing-back role.

Chris Banks, John Brough and Mark Freeman formed the back three, Freeman enjoying a good battle with Andy Morris, a veteran of Chesterfield's run to the FA Cup semi-finals three seasons ago. Freeman was one of three players in the starting eleven, along with Lee Howells and goalkeeper Steve Book, making their League debuts, Howells partnering Bob Bloomer and Mark Yates in midfield, with Grayson and Dale Watkins in attack. Rochdale always looked the more settled side in the first half, and their 39-year-old assistant manger Ford, who is closing in on 1,000 League games, fired a warning shot across Book's goal after 16 minutes. Brough hacked away another chance after 21 minutes after Morris beat the outcoming Book to a long through ball, and a goal seemed inevitable five minutes later it came. Morris was involved as he nodded a Wayne Evans cross down to Lancashire, who pulled the ball back for Atkinson to drill home from eight yards.

That gave Rochdale more confidence, and after Bayliss' 20-yarder hit the woodwork, Ford headed number two after 42 minutes from Atkinson's left wing cross. In injury time, Grayson had his first real sniff of goal and it nearly pulled the Robins back. But after Jamie Victory surged forward and rolled him into range 16 yards out, his shot went agonisingly wide – a goal then and it could have been so different.

As it was, the Robins came out fighting in the second half and Watkins burst through, fighting off Bayliss and Keith Hill, but his toe-ended effort sailed over. Watkins was replaced by Hugh McAuley after 67 minutes, and the £20,000 signing from Leek looked bright, as did 19-year-old Cheltenham-born Martin Devaney, who replaced Bloomer.

Cheltenham did their best to mount a grandstand finish, but there was to be no fairytale comeback. The best of the late chances saw a 71st-minute Howells cross drop just too far ahead of Brough, charging in at the far post, then four minutes later another good Robins move, which started with McAuley's cross-field pass to Griffin, ended with the youngster's cross being headed straight at Neil Edwards by Grayson.

Cheltenham Town v. Rochdale, Andy Morris and Mark Freeman.

on the backs of shirts came to Cheltenham. However, Graeme Atkinson and Tony Ford made sure there was no fairytale start as Rochdale claimed a 2-0 win.

Says Steve Cotterill:

As usual, we started with a kick in the teeth on the first day. It was another rude awakening, but it took them a dozen games, a bit longer than usual, to get used to it.

Lee Howells:

Rochdale was an anti-climax. I mean we now know what a good side they are, but I think we thought at the time 'well they'll be a good test to start with'. We came in on Sunday to look at the video, and you thought 'this is going to be a long season'. It was a bit like after the first game in the Conference – you worry whether you're going to be good enough.

Another upshot of Football League membership was a place in the Worthington Cup – and the draw handed Cheltenham a two-legged encounter with Norwich City. Five years previously, Norwich had been battling it out in the UEFA Cup with the likes of Bayern Munich and Inter Milan, while the Robins were facing the Bashleys and Baldocks, a fact not lost on chairman Paul Baker, who had a novel way of travelling to Carrow Road for the first leg:

Norwich was probably the biggest club we could have drawn and they were so friendly. It was the first time I chartered a plane, and four of us got together to fly to Norwich.

Norwich 2 Cheltenham 0

Iwan Roberts grabbed a first-half double to give Norwich City the first leg advantage in their Worthington Cup first round tie with Cheltenham Town. However, the Robins left Carrow Road last night with their heads held high after a spirited performance which sets up what could be a dramatic second leg at Whaddon Road in a fortnight.

Manager Steve Cotterill fielded the side which finished Saturday's 2-0 defeat by Rochdale, and the Robins were never overawed by their First Division opponents with the youthful exuberance of wide men Antony Griffin and Martin Devaney leading the way. Griffin and Devaney showed a healthy willingness to run at defenders and full-backs Daryl Sutch and Erik Fuglestad were given a tough time. The young pair were backed up by midfield duo Mark Yates – who had his best game in a Cheltenham shirt – and Lee Howells, who more than held their own as Norwich looked time and again to pass their way through Cheltenham's defence.

Norwich had the ball in the net after five minutes when Cedric Anselin fired home from fifteen yards but the goal was wiped out for a foul by Roberts on Jamie Victory as he knocked the ball down to the Frenchman. The respite was short-lived as Norwich took a fourteenth minute lead when Cheltenham were caught napping from a short corner and Phil Mulryne whipped in a cross and Roberts nipped in front of Mark Freeman and powered a header which Steve Book got a hand to, but could only divert into the roof of the net. That was the signal for Cheltenham to take the game to Norwich and their best chance to equalise came on 25 minutes when the impressive Yates fired just wide from 25 yards. But Norwich increased their lead after 37 minutes when Paul Dalglish, who was the main thorn in the Robins' side in the first half, played an exquisite pass into the path of Roberts, who broke into the box and drilled his shot across Book into the corner. Cheltenham had a good penalty call turned down after 43 minutes when Fuglestad upended Griffin, but they kept up the tempo after the break.

The Robins had a great chance after 62 minutes when a Yates cross was flicked on by Neil Grayson and Neil Howarth to Victory, who volleyed wide. Cheltenham managed to restrict Norwich to long-range efforts, the best one coming after 78 minutes when Mulryne blasted a shot just wide, but Cheltenham's performance deserved to give them a fighting chance of a second leg upset.

Norwich City v. Cheltenham Town in the first round, first leg of the Worthington Cup. Lee Howells tries to get the boot in.

There was no other way I would have got there, and it was an unbelievable experience. What a fantastic stadium it was, and there we were playing a side just out of the Premiership, who had recently played in Europe. But we have never been taken apart by any of these teams. We have always competed very well and acquitted ourselves well.

That was the case at Carrow Road, where two Iwan Roberts goals gave the Canaries the advantage for the Whaddon Road return, where the Robins gave Bruce Rioch's side the fright of their lives. A Neil Grayson penalty and Jamie Victory's header forced the tie into extra time, before a goal from Lee Marshall decided it in Norwich's favour. Says Steve Cotterill:

I would still say that their goal in extra time was offside. But we won over a few friends in those games, and also got together a lot of belief in our ability from those games.

Cheltenham Town v. Norwich, Whaddon Road. Neil Grayson takes the penalty and the goalkeeper dives, but the ball is in the net.

Cheltenham 2 Norwich 1 (agg 2-3)

A controversial extra-time goal ended Cheltenham Town's dreams of a Worthington Cup upset against two-time winners Norwich City at Whaddon Road last night. The Robins had clawed back the first leg deficit and forced the extra half-hour with a Neil Grayson penalty and a header from Jamie Victory. However, ten minutes into extra time, Jean-Yves De Blasiis sent Iwan Roberts away down the right, and with Cheltenham's defence asking for an offside flag which never came, Roberts squared for Lee Marshall to score at the far post.

It was rough justice on the Robins, who gave their Division One opponents an almighty fright right from the off. Norwich came with an adventurous 4-3-3 formation, but the back four snuffed out Chris Llewellyn and Paul Dalglish, while it took Roberts sixty minutes to carve out a worthwhile chance. Mark Yates, Cheltenham's best player at Norwich, lasted ten minutes before a tight hamstring forced him off, but teenager Michael Jackson rose to the occasion superbly alongside Lee Howells, who had a storming game.

As was the case at Carrow Road, Cheltenham got a lot of joy when the ball went wide, and Antony Griffin and Martin Devaney again caused Norwich problems, while Neil Grayson and Hugh McAuley were always a threat. An early goal was Cheltenham's aim, and it nearly came after nine minutes when McAuley's head met Devaney's free-kick, but the ball skimmed wide. The goal they deserved finally came two minutes after the break as Howells put Griffin through and he went down under Craig Fleming's rash challenge. Referee Phil Dowd had no hesitation in giving a penalty, and Neil Grayson smashed the ball home. Not surprisingly, the noise level rose and Cheltenham came close to a second after 56 minutes. McAuley sent Griffin away, then hared into the box for the return ball but screwed the effort wide.

Norwich just seemed to have taken the sting out of Cheltenham and silenced the crowd when the Robins hauled themselves level on aggregate after 69 minutes. Devaney swung over a corner and Jamie Victory rose highest to plant his header wide of Andy Marshall. The Robins could not force a fairytale third, and after Lee Marshall's goal, which meant Cheltenham needed to score twice to go through, the relieved Canaries were happy to hang on.

Sandwiched in between the Norwich double-header came two pieces of history. First, the club's first Nationwide League goal, a 64th minute bullet header from Neil Grayson at Mansfield which secured the club's first victory in the League.

Grayson recalls:

We didn't play particularly well to be honest and the goal actually came after Mansfield had a corner. I was running up to the other end, and Antony Griffin put in a great cross. I didn't have to change stride at all and headed it running at full speed. At the time you

Mansfield 0 Cheltenham 1

Neil Grayson, whose goals fired Cheltenham Town into the Nationwide League, headed the 64th minute winner which gave the Robins their first win in the professional ranks. It was a battling performance from the Robins, who had to use all their resilience to withstand some Mansfield pressure, as well as the awful weather, and the celebrations at the final whistle showed just how much the win meant.

Manager Steve Cotterill went into the game with the same side which performed so admirably at Norwich in the Worthington Cup and sprung a surprise by naming Mike Duff among the substitutes after his injury lay-off, but twenty minutes before kick-off Duff limped off after the pre-match warm-up clutching his troublesome knee. Cotterill was able to change his team sheet, Michael Jackson taking over from Duff on the bench.

The win at Field Mill was founded on a fine performance from the back four: Neil Howarth, Chris Banks, Mark Freeman and Jamie Victory, who dealt with all Mansfield could throw at them. Andy Roscoe and Lee Williams were dangerous on the flanks, sending over some testing crosses, but the defence stood up well to keep Tony Lormor and Lee Peacock at a safe distance. In front of them, Mark Yates and Lee Howells kept up their good start to the season, and they look like forming a useful team in the centre of midfield. Wingers Antony Griffin and Martin Devaney, so effective at Norwich, again tried to attack their defenders at every opportunity, but found the going tough as Mansfield managed, for the most part, to cut off the supply to strikers Hugh McAuley and Grayson.

Cheltenham had a couple of early scares as hesitation between Steve Book, and first Freeman and then Howarth, nearly let Mansfield in, but Grayson saw his 20th-minute effort deflected wide by David Linighan after a nice move down the left. Lormor scooped an excellent 27th-minute chance over and a header on the half-hour from the burly striker was inches over after a Williams free-kick tested the Robins defence.

With the rain lashing down, referee Roy Pearson had been lenient in allowing for the conditions, but abandoned that idea to book Howarth and Banks within seven minutes as Cheltenham found themselves under early second-half pressure. But they broke the shackles in the best way possible to grab the lead. From a Mansfield corner, McAuley broke away and linked up with Griffin, who popped up on the left. He reached the by-line and sent over a cross and Grayson powered in and sent a bullet header into the corner, giving Barry Richardson no chance.

After the goal, Cheltenham still had some defending to do, and the back four did their job. Victory blocked a Neil Richardson shot on the six-yard line and substitute Michael Boulding tested Book with an angled drive, which he parried away. Cheltenham nearly gave themselves some breathing space in the dying seconds as Freeman headed over a Howells corner. Freeman, the pick of the defence, nearly became a villain at the death when a long ball skidded off his head and forced Book into a full-length save.

Mansfield v. Cheltenham Town. McAuley and Devaney jump on top of Grayson to celebrate his goal.

don't think 'I've just scored the first ever goal for Cheltenham in the League', you're just focused on having put them in the lead. It's only afterwards that you think you'll be remembered for that first goal, which is nice really.

A week later, Hugh McAuley scored Whaddon Road's first League goal from the penalty spot as Hull were beaten 1-0. That win was also down to a magnificent goalkeeping display from Steve Book, who repeated the dose at Hartlepool in a 1-0 win, secured by a Neil Howarth goal. So, 9 points from a possible 12 – and things were looking rosy.

Steve Cotterill recalls:

We got 9 points out of 12, but had sombreros and masks on, as we were bandits. They were all ram raids, and it came back to haunt us as we lost five on the spin. The points we had were justifiable, as in those defeats we didn't deserve to lose some of them, and might have nicked a draw, but we soon had 9 points out of 9 games.

Lee Howells says:

We then won three on the run, but we were lucky against Mansfield and then just nicked it against Hull and Hartlepool. I think deep down I thought that we had a lot of work to do and that we were a long way off the pace. You do wonder if you're good enough, and you've got to remind yourselves about just how good you are and what you've done.

The losing run began when Barnet left Whaddon Road with a 2-1 victory, despite a John Brough goal, before the club celebrated yet another first. The Sky TV cameras came to Cheltenham for the game with the Shrews, but Lee Steele's early goal took the points for Shrewsbury. Single-goal defeats at Peterborough and Brighton followed, and John Brough, Michael Duff and Richard Walker were joined on the injured list by Antony Griffin, who suffered a nasty facial injury at Brighton.

For Duff especially, it was a bitter pill to have to miss out on the early weeks of the new adventure:

It went from highs to lows, having scored the goal which got us there. It was a recurrence of an injury I got from a bad tackle in a game at Gloucester. The scan said I had roughed the bone up, then against Birmingham in pre-season Dele Adebola fell on me. I had an MRI scan, but it did not feel right and I missed the Rochdale game, then Steve put me on the bench against Mansfield. It lashed it down, and I had studs on, and was running down the line when someone passed me the ball. I didn't want it, so flicked it away with the outside of my boot, my studs got caught and I twisted the knee. After five minutes I could not walk, but in the end that was the best thing that could have happened as I tore my cartilage and within five weeks I was back. When I did come back, I had to play out of position in midfield as Neil Howarth had come in at right back and done well. I was only twenty, so I couldn't walk in to the manager and say I wanted to play at right back, and Neil had something like three or four man of the match awards. Steve thought I could do a job wide on the right and I wanted to play, but that found me out a bit, and it took about ten games for me to adjust.

Cheltenham Town v. Brighton. Paul Watson *(left)* and Jamie Victory *(right)*.

The worrying aspect of the run of defeats was the lack of goals, and the drought had extended to 369 minutes when Rotherham left Whaddon Road with a 2-0 win on 2 October. A glance at the Division Three table that night saw Cheltenham lying fourth from bottom, and their tally of four goals was the worst in Division Three.

Even the Conference Championship Shield game with Kingstonian could not end the drought – the K's won that 1-0 – so action was needed. It came in the form of loan signing Mark Jones, a twenty-year-old striker borrowed from Wolves, and he came into the side against Southend, which had suddenly become a must-win game.

Jamie Victory recalls:

We had a dodgy start when we lost 8 out of 11. The problem was that we tended to read the papers and look at the table. But we knew we had to keep playing because we were doing okay – if we had been playing badly then that would have been the time to worry
.

Despite not getting on the scoresheet himself, Jones made an impact. Cotterill recalls:

He could have scored three in that game.

Jones helped to end the losing run, and the goal drought, which extended to 375 minutes before Neil Grayson's sixth-minute opener. Russell Milton added a second, and

despite Martin Carruthers' consolation strike, the losing run was over, and the relief was palpable. It didn't last long though – another single goal defeat, this time at Darlington despite winning eight corners to the Quakers' none, meant the Robins were back in the bottom four. Four days later came the low point – a 2-1 defeat at eventually-relegated Chester, where the fantastically-named Manuel Junior Agogo scored twice, but they recovered from that as a battling performance earned a 0-0 draw with Brighton, despite a red card for Neil Grayson.

Off the field, Cotterill was, as ever, looking for ways to increase team spirit, and took his squad on a paintballing trip, and was also trying to strengthen

Cheltenham Town v. Southend. Lee Howells in action.

Cheltenham Town v. Southend. Russell Milton celebrates scoring the Robins' second goal.

the squad. On FA Cup first round weekend, he arranged a deal to sign thirty-four-year-old midfielder Nicky Marker, a player with over 600 games behind him at Exeter, Plymouth, Blackburn – where he was involved in the Premiership championship success – and Sheffield United. That was just the sort of experience Cotterill was looking for, and Ally Pickering and Ray Wallace were two other targets, both of whom played in reserve games.

Marker did not play in the Cup game, which saw John Brough's equaliser cancel out a mistake by Steve Book, who dropped a cross at the feet of Gillingham's Nicky Southall. In fact, Marker did not get further than the bench, failing to make an appearance on the pitch in his short stay with the club. Of more pressing concern still was the lack of goals, and Cotterill was making concerted efforts to bolster the strikepower at his disposal. But he was about to lose one of his mainstays, and had Martin Devaney in plaster with a fractured ankle. Dale Watkins had struggled to make an impact at Football League level, and several Conference sides, notably Stevenage, Telford and Kettering, were interested in prising him away.

Kettering won in the end, taking him on loan at first and eventually signing him permanently for £25,000 to end a spell which yielded 38 goals in 99 starts. Cotterill tried to sign Manuel Junior Agogo, who had sunk the Robins less than a month before, and tried to set up loan deals for Jason Brissett from Walsall, Adrian Coote from Norwich and Isaiah Rankin from Bradford City, all without success. So at Halifax, it was down again to the player rapidly becoming prolific in front of goal, Russell Milton, to secure a point from a 1-1 draw. Mark Freeman's first League goal set up a 3-1 home win over Carlisle, achieved without the suspended Neil Grayson. Jamie Victory and Hugh McAuley – partnering John Brough in a somewhat makeshift forward line – were also on target.

The FA Cup run ended in typically brave fashion at Gillingham, Brian McGlinchey's deflected winner knocking the Robins out after cracking strikes from Neil Howarth and Russell Milton cancelled out Gillingham's 2-0 lead. The search for a new striker finally succeeded as Cotterill brought Jason Brissett to the club on loan from Walsall, ironically just when it seemed as though the problems in front of goal were over.

Brissett, a former team-mate of the manager's at Bournemouth, would give Cotterill something he did not have at his disposal – sheer pace. He came on for his debut in another thrilling 3-2 defeat, this time at Northampton, which meant the Robins had hit seven goals in a week. The game, switched to Friday to avoid England's Euro 2000 play-off with Scotland, saw Neil Grayson back in the side and back on the scoresheet against his former club, whose fans had given him a superb reception, while Hugh McAuley kept up his good form.

But a fatal late slip by Steve Book, who was beaten by a low shot from a future Robins loan player, Daryl Clare, gave the Cobblers the points and left Cheltenham still dangerously close to the bottom of the pile. A 0-0 draw at high-flying Swansea was a large confidence booster, and was followed by a pair of 2-0 home wins, and all of a sudden things were looking much brighter. The first win, over Plymouth, featured one of the best goals ever seen at Whaddon Road, a dipping, 30-yard volley by Neil Grayson after Hugh McAuley flicked on a Steve Book clearance. Book was also heavily involved in the other win, over Leyton Orient, saving a penalty as Neil Howarth and Lee Howells scored, and a glance at the table made for healthier reading all of a sudden, with Cheltenham now eighth from bottom – and climbing. A trip to Rochdale yielded a 0-0 draw, which sounds fairly unremarkable, but featured one of the most bizarre incidents Cheltenham Town can ever have been involved in.

After nineteen minutes, there was little danger as Damon Searle put a cross into the Cheltenham box, but Jason Brissett, thinking he heard a whistle from the crowd, picked the ball up and gave away a penalty. For the second game running however, Steve Book guessed right and saved Tony Ellis's kick – only marginally sparing Brissett's blushes, and it didn't stop his loan being extended for a second month. Not even the Auto Windscreens Shield could disrupt what had become an amazing turnaround in form, Russell Milton scoring the only goal at Southend to make it five clean sheets in a row.

Before that game, Steve Cotterill made what was to prove to be a very significant appointment. Feeling that himself and assistant Mike Davis needed a hand, he recruited his eventual successor Graham Allner to help on the coaching side and to manage the reserves. Allner, who had been Cheltenham's assistant manager in the early 1980s, was highly successful at Kidderminster Harriers, taking them to the Conference title in 1994, when the club were denied promotion as the ground at Aggborough was then not up to standard. There was also an FA Trophy win in 1987 and two losing finals, and two Welsh Cup finals – and lots of wins over the Robins in Conference clashes, notably a 6-2 win at Whaddon Road which Allner has often described as the best performance ever by one of his sides:

I've known Steve for years, and I remember him coming up to Kidderminster with Mark Buckland when he was just a young lad. Bucko said he wanted to sign for us, but I couldn't offer him anything at that time. Steve and I have always kept in touch though, and he got in touch with me when he came back from Ireland to see if I could offer him anything. When he called, I'd left Worcester and was just a bit drained really, which was the reason I'd left. I'd had a fair few years in the front-lines and didn't feel I wanted to manage a club, but I did want to stay involved in football. Steve just called and said come and help out on the coaching side, and as my big love has always been the coaching I was happy to come. My first impressions were of a well organised club, and a good set of lads who responded well to the manager. There was such a determination to succeed that you could feel it. Steve said he wanted me to help him develop a mix of what he already had and the type of team I'd had at Kiddy. The first game I did was the Auto Windscreens Shield match at Southend. We won 1-0 and Russell Milton scored. I think in the early days I was there you could see that the club was new to the Football League, just like I was, and I think most people would have settled for consolidation.

But consolidation was not Steve Cotterill's sole aim – he had his eyes on the play-offs. A 1-1 draw with Macclesfield was followed by three first half strikes, from Russell Milton, Michael Duff and Mark Freeman, which saw off Exeter City on Boxing Day, and a goal from Neil Grayson against his home town York sealed a 2-1 win.

The year 2000 started badly, with a 2-0 home defeat by Lincoln, but that was merely a blip, a bad-tempered 2-1 win at Macclesfield with Neil Grayson and a Russell Milton penalty resuming what was becoming normal service. It was interrupted slightly by the Auto Windscreens Shield, as more than 1,400 fans made their way down the M5 to Ashton Gate for a 3-1 defeat which marked the end of Jason Brissett's eventful loan spell as he missed a penalty. In the League, however, there seemed to be no stopping the Robins.

Neil Grayson sealed a double against Mansfield with the only goal at Whaddon Road, then Martin Devaney made a staggering entrance at Hull to score with his first touch, earning a 1-1 draw after Cheltenham had gone a goal down in 35 seconds. Hartlepool were next to fall victim to the resurgent Robins – Neil Grayson and Hugh McAuley secured a 2-1 win, and also a place in Division Three's top ten. As February dawned, it was 2 defeats in 12 games for the Robins – a far cry from those dark days of September and clear evidence that the players had found their feet in the professional ranks.

Steve Cotterill could ponder that improvement on the plane to Spain as he took the players on their now-customary week-long break in the sun, but the return from Fuengirola to Barnet's Underhill proved too much. A 3-2 defeat was not the ideal start to the play-off push, and injuries to Neil Grayson and Hugh McAuley only served to compound matters, so it was back on the loan trail for the manager before the Sunday showdown with Swansea City.

He turned to Chris Freestone, a twenty-eight-year-old striker borrowed from Hartlepool, who made his debut against the Swans in the second goal-less draw between the clubs. He was unable to hit the target at Leyton Orient, where a Steve Book slip gave the Londoners a 1-0 win, but helped end the run of three winless games with a goal as Peterborough were vanquished 2-1 at Whaddon Road.

That prompted Barry Fry to dub Cheltenham the 'Land Of The Giants' – and proved just how much the Robins were getting under the skin of the more established clubs as they maintained their push towards the play-offs. Lee Howells and Russell Milton claimed the goals in a 2-0 win at Shrewsbury, and Halifax were beaten 3-0 – the biggest win of the campaign so far – with Neil Grayson, Russell Milton and Chris Freestone on the mark.

Chris Freestone *(left)*, Cheltenham's new loan signing, is pictured with Steve Cotterill *(right)*.

That took the Robins past Steve Cotterill's seasonal target of fifty points and into ninth place – the highest position of the season so far in the week that plans were unveiled for the new Wymans Road stand, which would give Whaddon Road 2,000 more seats. That goal against Halifax was Freestone's last contribution – Cotterill wanted to keep him, but he opted to return to Hartlepool's reserves, and that coincided with Neil Grayson limping off at Torquay. He suffered a stomach injury in the 1-1 draw at Plainmoor, where Martin Devaney scored, and missed the game at Plymouth as John Brough and Devaney made a makeshift strike partnership.

Steve Cotterill was never a fan of loan signings, but he put that to one side by capturing Ian Stevens from Wrexham in time for what was a crucial midweek clash with Northampton at Whaddon Road. The vastly experienced Stevens had an excellent game for 73 minutes against the Cobblers as Cheltenham won 2-1 with goals from Michael Duff and Jamie Victory. But that was all the Robins fans got to see of Stevens, who decided two days later that the travelling from his home in Lancaster was too much.

Cotterill recalls:

That was a strange one. He played his part, but the good thing was that we didn't have to pay his wages for that night. In hindsight, it would have been a good idea for Ian to look at a map before he said yes. If he saw a map he might have said no. He played very well in that game and it was annoying at the time as I had put a lot of work and time into getting him.

It was doubly annoying because Stevens delivered his snub on transfer deadline day – so Cotterill was left high and dry, and had to soldier on despite a late bid to bring Jason Eaton back on a part-time basis from Yeovil Town.

As it turned out, Neil Grayson was fit again, and played in the 2-1 win at Exeter, secured by Jamie Victory and Martin Devaney, which sent the Robins into the play-off positions with eight matches to go. More Devon delight followed as Russell Milton and Martin Devaney, who was developing a penchant for playing against sides from that county, saw off Torquay 2-0.

A late equaliser from Steve Soley in far-off Carlisle denied the Robins the chance to climb to fourth in the table after Mark Yates' screamer looked to have sealed a victory. Four days later, however, fourth place was a reality – Martin Devaney again on target at Lincoln, along with Jamie Victory, celebrating his 150th consecutive game for the club. But the play-off momentum crashed when Mark Sertori – who was wearing the red and white for a brief spell twelve months later – hit York's winner at Whaddon Road, and the Robins were out of the top seven after a goal-less draw with Darlington, in which Russell Milton missed a penalty.

High-flyers Rotherham gained a 2-0 win at Millmoor on Easter Monday – Jason White scoring the second a matter of weeks before joining the club – and a straight fight was developing with Hartlepool for the last play-off place. It was advantage Cheltenham after their penultimate game, when John Brough struck late on to beat stubborn Chester while Hartlepool went down 2-1 at home to Rotherham. So it was all or nothing on the final day of the season at Southend, and more than 1,500 made the trip to Roots Hall. Victory, and there was nothing Hartlepool could do, but a draw or a defeat would let Chris Turner's side in through the back door. It started well enough, with Lee Howells scoring inside seven minutes, but an equaliser from Steve Jones and a last-gasp wonder-strike from Nathan Jones meant desperate disappointment for Cotterill, the players and the travelling army.

Skipper Chris Banks says:

We thought we'd hold our own as other clubs had done. Macclesfield had done well in Division Three and got promoted, and Halifax and done well since coming back into the League. I always felt that there was real ability in the team to do well and I wasn't surprised we finished where we did. We'd always aimed for the play-offs and to fail at the last hurdle was very frustrating, but we'd proved that we were a good side, and we just had to roll our sleeves up and do it the next year.

For Cotterill, it was just a few games too far, but it was still desperately hard to take:

We had been used to playing forty-two games, and the last few were too many for us. We were running on a few hernias – Neil Grayson, Mark Yates, Steve Book, and a couple of others had them by the end of the season. I remember at Southend that we were pushing for the winner right at the end, and their goalkeeper Mel Capleton was like a man possessed. By this time, we were playing something like 3-2-5 with Michael Jackson as one

Southend 2 Cheltenham Town 1

A goal deep into injury time robbed brave Cheltenham of a play-off spot when news filtered through that rivals Hartlepool had won at Hull. But in truth the Gloucestershire outfit only had themselves to blame for missing a series of great chances. Cheltenham started brightly and a long free-kick caused the home defence problems after only a minute, but they were saved when Martin Devaney strayed off-side. Three minutes later a strong run down the right by Lee Howells ended with Antony Griffin setting up Devaney, who saw his shot blocked by desperate Southend defender Nathan Jones. But Cheltenham were not to be denied and when Chris Banks had a shot blocked for a corner, Russell Milton's flag kick got through to Howells, whose shot from the edge of the area was deflected over the helpless Mel Capleton and into the roof of the net. Cheltenham came close to a second goal after 14 minutes when Capleton's clearance was straight at Howells but, luckily for the home side, Mark Beard was on hand to kick clear the loose ball. Southend's response first saw a Scott Houghton effort balloon way over the bar after 16 minutes, and two minutes later Steve Jones went past Jamie Victory and Banks but drove his shot across the face of the goal. Cheltenham were left owing a huge debt to goalkeeper Steve Book when he somehow clawed out a close range header from Leo Roget. At the other end a 25th-minute volley from Mark Yates was tipped over the bar by Capleton. Book did well to save Simon Coleman's 35th-minute header at the second attempt. But Southend were not to be denied and equalised two minutes before the break. Dave Morley's free-kick was knocked on by Martin Carruthers for Steve Jones to squeeze a header just inside a post. Cheltenham had a great chance to regain the lead on the stroke of half-time when Devaney caught Morley in possession and took the ball wide of Capleton, but lost control and allowed it to run out of play. The 1,464 Cheltenham fans in the crowd were on their toes when Milton hit a free-kick straight from the restart which Coleman just cleared as Devaney closed in. Devaney then looked certain to score after 49 minutes when he raced clear of Coleman on the halfway line but Roget recovered to make a great saving tackle at the expense of a corner. From Milton's flag kick the ball fell perfectly for Mark Freeman but he somehow scooped his shot over the bar from just six yards out. Cheltenham again went close when a long free-kick from Book was knocked down by Devaney for John Brough, but his fierce 20-yard effort flashed wide of the target. Capleton did well to hold a superb 59th-minute left wing cross from Devaney as Brough lurked at the far post ready to apply the finishing touch. Cheltenham made their intentions obvious when they pulled off defender Freeman and brought on striker Neil Grayson in the 64th minute. Grayson looked sure to score within six minutes of coming on when Howells set him away but Coleman stretched out to nick the ball off his toe. Cheltenham were on top but almost paid for a silly 75th-minute mistake. Book and Walker got in a tangle trying to clear the ball and let Carruthers in but Walker got back to slide the ball behind for a corner. Cheltenham were starting to get desperate and threw players forward, leaving themselves exposed at the back. Deep into injury time Southend broke those Cheltenham hearts. Wing back Nathan Jones jinked his way through from the halfway line, beating four men before coolly slotting the ball wide of Book and into the net.

of the three defenders. We were battering them, and the ball just would not go in, then they broke away and Nathan Jones scored in something like the 93rd minute. It was just such an empty feeling as I was not ready for the season to be over that day – I was preparing for it to continue for another month. Mentally I was not ready to let it go – I wasn't accepting that we were not in the play-offs. I remember going on the pitch and I was absolutely devastated, and after the highs of the end of the two previous seasons, this was the other side of what we had put into it. There were tears of sadness this time, and I had to try and pick the boys up. They didn't know what they were going to get from me afterwards, and I remember walking in and the dressing room was absolutely dead. I told them to remember this feeling, and remember it again when we played them the following season, and carry on remembering it every time we played Southend – and we always had a good record against them. But Southend just proved to be one too many for us and was too much of a strain in the end.

Lee Howells agrees:

We had a great season and it was sad that we just missed out, but I think we'd just shot our bolt. There were a lot of players struggling with injuries at the end. I think what made it more special was the fact that we'd done it with the same players. Look at Rushden and Kidderminster – Rushden especially. Since they came into the League they've brought in a lot of new players. I don't think that doing what we've done with the same players will ever be done again and I think that is great testimony to everybody.

Despite that devastation, Cotterill and his squad had again exceeded many expectations. Says Paul Baker:

It was our first season in the Football League, and after all the changes, notably going from part time to full time, to be in with a shout of the play-offs with the potential of going to Wembley again was fantastic. Southend was one of the longest trips, and we took a lot of supporters, and yet in the end it was very disappointing to have come so far, only to face that long journey home again. We just had to realize what we had achieved and it was a really successful season.

5

So Frustrating
2000/01

After the disappointment of coming so close to the play-offs in their first season in the League, Cheltenham regrouped over the summer. Manager Steve Cotterill's first priority was to strengthen his strike force in readiness for the new season. To do so, he raided the playing staffs of two of his main rivals from the previous season, both of whom were ultimately successful in gaining promotion – Rotherham and Swansea

Rotherham provided Jason White, a strong and pacy striker who had once partnered Neil Grayson up front at Northampton and had also played for Scunthorpe and Scarborough. Swansea, the side who narrowly beat Rotherham to the Championship, were the providers of Julian Alsop. Alsop was in some ways the more controversial signing – standing at 6ft 5in, and with a physique to match, he was hardly likely to go unnoticed, and he had attracted his fair share of abuse from the home fans for his physical approach when the Welsh side had played at Whaddon Road in February. The manager was hoping that the addition of the two new strikers would aid a side whose League total of 50 goals in the previous season was one of the lowest ones in the division. Steve Cotterill recalls his two signings:

They obviously had contrasting fortunes in the end and it's amazing how their careers ended up. Jason would probably argue that he didn't perhaps get a long enough run, and it took Julian a year before he got going, and then he struck gold.

Ultimately it was to be a frustrating season for both players, who, for a variety of reasons, ended up contributing just 5 League goals between them. Whilst Alsop would blossom in quite spectacular fashion in the following season, White would struggle to make an impact throughout his time in Gloucestershire.

There weren't just new players at the club, there was also a new stand, as director Colin Farmer recalls:

We were really keen to develop the 'home end' during the summer, and build some proper terracing at the Prestbury Road end of the ground. C&G were really generous and gave us some money and we built it all using sub-contractors – each one doing part of the stand. I acted as overall supervisor and we did it for just under £50,000, which was really good value – if we had used an outside agency to do it then we would have been looking at £200,000 upwards.

The team were optimistic at the start of the season, as Lee Howells explains:

I think we were very determined at the start of the season because of some of the comments going round about us being just a 'big and strong' side which really got up our noses. Okay, so we were big and strong, but we also played good football and we got fed up with people just jumping on the bandwagon about us being a physical side.

Some fans were concerned about just how well the team might do second time round as teams adjusted to the Cheltenham way of playing. Chairman Paul Baker shared some of these concerns:

Don't forget that the directors of Cheltenham Town are fans too – that's very much the case here, although not always at other football clubs. I think, yes we had been

New signing Jason White *(left)* is pictured with manager Steve Cotterill *(right)*.

Cheltenham Town FC: 2000/01 team. From left to right, back row: Brian Tarren, Andy Mitchell, Martin Devaney, Russell Milton, Hugh McAuley, Antony Griffin, Bob Bloomer, Stuart Mitchinson, Mike Heather, John Atkinson. Middle row: Mike Davis, Jamie Victory, Mark

surprise packages – people didn't know what to expect from Cheltenham Town, they hadn't been to Whaddon Road before, so inevitably the second season was going to be more difficult. We do play in a certain way, but, to be fair, I think Steve did try and change things a little in the second season, not massively so, because he wasn't able to go into the transfer market and make radical changes, so we went in with much the same squad.

Freeman, Gareth Hopkins, Steve Book, Steve Benbow, Shane Higgs, Mike Duff, John Brough, Neil Grayson, Graham Allner. Front row: Julian Alsop, Mike Jackson, Lee Howells, Chris Banks, Steve Cotterill, Mark Yates, Neil Howarth, Richard Walker, Jason White.

So, yes, I think we all thought it would be a difficult season, and didn't think we'd do as well as we eventually did. The other concern was what would happen to the crowds, because it's always a honeymoon period in your first season, but what would the crowds be like second time around, how is that going to affect your budget, are you going to be able to hang on to your players, are you going to be able to strengthen your squad …?

119

Graham Allner, Cheltenham's coach.

The management team were also cautiously optimistic, as Graham Allner recalls:

I think we all hoped that on the back of just missing out the previous season we might go one stage further, but we knew it would be really tough.

The season kicked off at home to Mansfield. An early Mansfield own goal gave the Robins the lead, but this was cancelled out by one of the most memorable goals scored at Whaddon Road all season when Chris Greenacre swung his foot at a loose ball and half-volleyed over Steve Book from all of forty-five yards. When Mansfield skipper Mark Blake put his side ahead with time running out, another opening day home defeat loomed, but a scrambled Neil Howarth goal two minutes from time saved a point. The equaliser came after Julian Alsop challenged the visitors' goalkeeper, Ian Bowling, who obligingly dropped the ball at Howarth's feet, but in truth neither White or Alsop, who both came on as second half-substitutes, made much impact.

It had been a mixed opening day, and it would be fair to say that most fans were surprised by what happened next – a run of four unbeaten games without conceding a goal which took the side to the top of the Third Division – then the highest placing in their history. The run started at York, where in one of the most complete away performances seen under Cotterill, the Robins won 2-0, Grayson scoring both, and then continued with a home win against Torquay, despite having both Alsop and Bloomer (from the bench) sent off, a draw at Hartlepool and another 2-0 away success, this time at Hull. After five League games, Cheltenham sat proudly at the top of the table. Graham Allner remembers it well:

One of the reasons I remember that run so well was that Steve was banned from the bench, and Mike Davis and I were on the touchline for that run with Steve up in the stand. I think to be honest we were amazed to find ourselves top, and whether we were strong enough to stay there was always open to question. The other thing was that the good start created real expectations at the club and amongst the fans, which really put the pressure on and made it very hard.

Sadly, despite the positive feelings associated with this good start, there was already a cloud on the horizon. The major theme of the campaign had already developed – injuries. By the end of the Torquay game, the third League game of the season, there were already two players out with long-term injuries. Neil Grayson had broken his ankle in scoring the second goal at York, and Jamie Victory suffered a severe knee injury in the game against Torquay. Victory would not play again that season; for Grayson, it was to be a stop-start season – he would start under half of the club's League matches. Despite that massive setback, however, to his enormous credit he still finished top scorer. Steve Cotterill's most frustrating season yet as a manager had started how it was to continue:

The injuries we had were incredible really – for both Jamie Victory and John Brough they were really serious ones, career threatening. Thankfully we had a cracking physio in Andy Mitchell but we really suffered badly.

121

For Jamie Victory, missing virtually the whole of the season was a huge blow:

I was the type of player who never got injured so it was a real shock. As I had never had a bad injury, I had never really thought about the possibility. When I went down I was in excruciating pain for about two minutes, then it went. I tried to run and my leg felt a bit loose, so I kept jogging and played on for about four or five minutes before I went down again. The leg was swollen but it was not until I had the scan a couple of days later that I knew the full extent of it, and to be honest I didn't want to hear the news. The surgeon did a great job and I couldn't have asked for any better, then it was up to me with the help of Andy Mitchell and Steve Cotterill to get it right again. You can only do so much to help it, and I was in the gym, on the weights, on the bike, in the pool whenever I could be, and thankfully it's all right now and I've had no problems since.

In the middle of the League run, the Robins faced Watford in the Worthington Cup, with the first leg away from home. Supporters recalled the exploits against Norwich in the previous season's competition and were full of hope, but were well aware that their opponents had only just been relegated from the Premiership, and under the management of former England boss Graham Taylor they were one of the favourites for promotion. At Vicarage Road, on 22 August, the Robins gave a wonderful performance, and were unlucky to only come away with a 0-0 draw.

Suddenly Cheltenham were potential giant-killers. By the time of the second leg, they had reached the top of the table, and, with the hint of an upset it was the match chosen by *Sky Sports* for live coverage, something that pleased Paul Baker:

I think Sky are always looking for an upset, aren't they? I mean, this was Watford, a big club, against Cheltenham Town, just out of the Conference, and we had played very well at Watford. It was good money for us – around £40,000, which we could put away as a nest egg in case things didn't turn out as we'd hoped.

In the end, Watford were too strong, two early goals putting them into the driving seat, a position they never looked like relinquishing. However, it had been a good experience for the players.

After the first defeat of the season, the first League defeat came on the Saturday, Chesterfield taking over from the Robins at the top of the table in a match that saw the full League debut of Cheltenham-born Gareth Hopkins, in for the injured Alsop. The successive defeats seemed to have had limited impact at first, as the side lost only one of the next five matches – 3-0 at Cotterill's old side Brighton during the middle of the fuel crisis. Incidentally, this was one of only two matches not covered by BBC Radio Gloucestershire during the three League seasons (the other being the match at Lincoln in the third season). Sadly, despite the protestations of the commentary team, station management decided that road travel was to be for 'priority events only' – and this one didn't count. As an aside, the seventy-seven Darlington fans who beat fuel shortages and protestor 'go-slows' to make the Tuesday evening game in Gloucestershire on 12 September surely deserved a medal.

Watford 0 Cheltenham Town 0

Of all Cheltenham Town's achievements during the three-year reign of Steve Cotterill, this must rank alongside the very best. Not only did they visit a side playing Premiership football last season and return with a draw, they could and should have taken at least a one-goal lead into the second leg of this Worthington Cup first round tie.

The Robins hit the woodwork twice and had countless other chances to punish a Watford side that manager Graham Taylor described as 'woeful'. Taylor was so disgusted with the display that he suggested every Watford supporter at the game be given their money back, yet that could take nothing away from a jubilant Cheltenham side who were graciously applauded off the field by the home fans.

Cheltenham could have gone ahead as early as the fifth minute when Welsh international defender Robert Page made a mess of a back header from a Mark Yates lobbed pass. Hugh McAuley crossed for Julian Alsop, who reached the ball before Espen Baardsen but his header came back off the crossbar. Cheltenham produced by far the more careful and considered build-up play but two of the game's better chances fell to Michael Duff, a man not accustomed to finding himself in front of goal.

Jamie Victory sent Hugh McAuley scuttling down the left and his cross found Duff wide open in space at the far post. He could have brought the ball under control but elected to shoot first time and the effort flew into the side-netting.

Then, five minutes from time Duff collected a poor clearance from goalkeeper Baardsen but sent his shot straight at the grateful custodian. Watford barely flickered as an attacking force until late in the game although Chris Banks, who produced one of the many heroic Cheltenham performances on the night, kicked away a shot from David Perpetuini that appeared to have beaten Book. Tommy Mooney spooned a shot inches over in the dying seconds and Neil Cox had an on-target shot deflected wide. Hugh McAuley, enjoying another profitable night, this time in a five-man midfield with just Julian Alsop up front, saw a 20-yarder pushed round the post and drifted another shot agonisingly close, although the closest thing to a goal arrived in the 57th minute.

McAuley's corner was met with a firm header from Richard Walker, unmarked eight yards out, and was going in until substitute Johann Gudmundsson headed it off the line and onto a post. Watford will not relish a visit to Whaddon Road on 6 September and a no doubt sell-out crowd will gather in hope of a cup upset, the like of which Cheltenham has never seen before.

With Neil Grayson injured, Jason White struggling for form, and Hugh McAuley now being deployed in midfield, Martin Devaney was brought into the team for the home game with Plymouth to partner Alsop up front. He responded with a hat-trick the first ever by a Cheltenham player in the Football League, and he then scored two

Cheltenham Town v. Watford, Worthington Cup first round, televised by Sky.

more away at Exeter City following week. Graham Allner was one of those impressed by his form:

Martin was really on fire and was being talked about a lot in the press – he really had exploded onto the scene and was doing really well. Perhaps it was all a little too early for him because he lost consistency for a while after this, but it gave us a real glimpse of what you know he can do.

By the time the Robins travelled to Macclesfield on 14 October, they were in second place, lying behind Chesterfield who were already showing signs of running away with the division. It was to be another significant day in the season, not so much because of a 2-1 defeat after Julian Alsop had given them the lead, but because of a serious injury to John Brough, deputising for Mark Freeman in the centre of defence. Like Victory, Brough would not play again that season.

It was to herald a run of four defeats in five matches, the one bright spot being a win at Halifax through goals by Yates and McAuley. Injuries were now beginning to cause real problems – not just the long-term casualties, but a run of other less serious injuries, which meant that fielding a settled side was impossible. The last of three successive defeats was at home to Blackpool, in a match that saw a new face in the starting line-up: Grant McCann, a young Irish full-back, signed on loan for the rest of the season from West Ham to replace both Jamie Victory and Richard Walker, who had himself been injured after taking over at left-back. Steve Cotterill recalled the deal:

I remember the dialogue I had with Harry Redknapp, who was of course at West Ham at the time. I think Harry phrased it that 'it would be good for Grant to spend six months with you because you might put a rocket up his arse'. I think we did as well. I knew what Harry meant and Grant did need a rocket but what I will say is once he accepted it and got on with things, that was the year that Grant grew up, and when it came to naming the young player of the year I felt he had no real competition.

Despite all the disruptions, the side showed great character in going on a run of five League and cup games during November and the early part of December. One of those unbeaten games was at old local rivals Kidderminster Harriers, who had been promoted from the Conference the previous season. It was a game which produced a real collectors' item – a goal from Chris Banks:

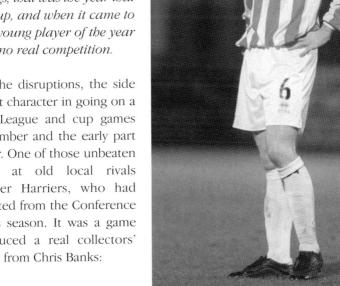

Loan signing Grant McCann.

125

I never usually go up for set-pieces – I'm normally left manning the fort. To be honest I'm not sure why I went up in the first place – I suspect it was because we had personnel changes due to injuries. Anyway, I went forward for this one and when it came to me I slotted it away. I'm not allowed up now – so I just say I have a 100 per cent record in terms of converting chances!

The last of the unbeaten games was at home to Barnet. The Hertfordshire side were now under the management of Tony Cottee, and were challenging for the play-off positions – a far cry from their subsequent decline and ultimate relegation back to the Conference. It was a topsy-turvy game, with a last-minute Julian Alsop winner bringing three points to the Robins. We weren't to know it, but that was to be the last home win until February.

Confidence was improving as the Robins faced the first of two successive trips to Ninian Park, Cardiff – never an easy place to visit. The first match was in the FA Cup second round, which had been reached after a comfortable 4-1 home victory against Shrewsbury, and players and supporters travelled to South Wales hopeful of another third round appearance, and the chance of playing a Premiership side.

Sadly, it wasn't to be. A bad-tempered game saw Cardiff win 3-1 with Julian Alsop sent off, and the following week in the League there was an identical scoreline, and another Robins sending-off: this time Michael Duff. Graham Allner didn't enjoy the games:

Both games were really disappointing, but there was a horrible atmosphere – really hostile, and maybe that got to the players. We didn't really perform and I don't think we could complain about the results – the reality was that there was a difference between us and Cardiff at that stage.

The following week, at Scunthorpe, Cheltenham achieved an unwanted hat-trick-of sendings-off in three successive games. On this occasion, Lee Howells was the player dismissed, but the side battled well to gain a 1-1 draw. A further 1-1 draw followed on Boxing Day at home to Shrewsbury, and by the end of the year the Robins were hovering around a play-off place. Optimists talked about the run as being only one defeat in the last seven League games; those of a more pessimistic nature pointed to a record of two wins in the last ten.

The first match of the New Year was away at Torquay on 8 January. In years to come the side that played will surely be the subject of one of the most difficult Cheltenham Town related quiz questions. Unavailable because of injury or suspension were the following: Neil Howarth, John Brough, Michael Duff, Richard Walker, Jamie Victory, Antony Griffin, Mark Yates, Lee Howells, Julian Alsop, and Neil Grayson. You could say that there was a full team of absentees. The Robins were down to their last eleven senior players, and only got to eleven because Cotterill signed Daryl Clare, a striker, on loan from Grimsby. In midfield, Marcus Jones, signed from Scarborough in November also made his debut. On the bench, reserve goalkeeper Shane Higgs was joined by Gareth Hopkins, and Michael Jackson, who had made just two first-team appearances. To complete the required five substitutes, squad numbers had to be given to Lee Burby and

Shane Duff, who had never been involved in the first team at League level before. For the record the side (playing a 4-5-1 formation) was as follows: Book; Bloomer, Freeman, Banks, McCann; White, McAuley, Jones, Milton, Devaney; Clare. Subsitutes: S. Duff, Burby, Higgs, Jackson and Hopkins. Steve Cotterill had never seen anything like it:

We had something like ten first-team players out – I remember looking at the players sat in the stand and thinking that the team up there was stronger than the team out on the park, with all due respect to the players who did play that day. I think that you could argue that win was one of the best Cheltenham Town have had in the Football League. It was a tribute to the team spirit and work ethic of every player who took part.

Even the captain was concerned:

We were literally down to the bare bones that day – I think it was one of the most amazing results in my time at the club.

Remarkably, the Robins won 2-1, with two goals from Martin Devaney, who continued to enjoy playing against Devon clubs. However such a patched up team could not expect to defy the odds each week, and as the injuries continued to bite, the side lost five games on the trot, a run that – despite a brave late-season rally – was to cost them a play-off place.

The first of these was at home to Hartlepool, where two second-half goals over-turned a Robins half-time lead, and then this was followed by 1-0 defeats away at Shrewsbury and at home to Hull City. The press conference after the first of these defeats could best be described as tense, as an obviously frustrated manager was crowded by reporters in the old press box at Gay Meadow. Long pauses were the order of the day, as Steve Cotterill tried to come to terms with the way the dice were being stacked against his side.

In the fourth match the Robins were once again on *Sky*. This time the match was away from home at leaders Chesterfield. One of your authors was unable to make this trip and watched a somewhat surreal evening's entertainment on television, wincing as the Sky reporter asked Cotterill why his side were 'failing' (to his credit, this inane question was greeted by nothing more than a wry smile and a bland denial by the manager), and then wincing again as the side made two basic defensive errors to find themselves 2-0 down within the first twenty minutes. These goals become even more difficult viewing when, loyally trying to watch the game with the sound turned down, listening to BBC Radio Gloucestershire's commentary, as the satellite delay meant that the ball was still some way from goal on the television pictures as the radio described the home side scoring.

The fifth and final defeat was at Mansfield, in a match which saw the debut of another loan striker. Daryl Clare, having played four games without scoring, returned to Grimsby, and Cotterill turned to Chris Iwelumo, signed from Stoke. The powerfully built centre forward scored on his debut as the Robins, 2-0 down at half time, mounted a spirited second-half comeback, but in the end it was to no avail as the home side ran out 2-1 winners. Lee Howells remembers the run only too well:

Cheltenham 3 Brighton 1

Cheltenham Town produced a stunning show of grit and determination to beat second-in-the-table Brighton, despite being down to ten men for seventy minutes. Lee Howells was sent off for two bookings in quick succession, but Cheltenham already had a 2-1 advantage by then.

Amid a cup tie atmosphere at Whaddon Road, Bob Bloomer sealed victory with a well-taken goal as Brighton conceded three goals for the first time this season. Cheltenham were forced into two changes to the side that lost 2-1 at Mansfield Town in midweek. Michael Duff (groin) and on-loan striker Chris Iwelumo (knee) were both missing through injury, their replacements being Grant McCann and Martin Devaney.

Brighton had the first chance of the game in the fourth minute when Darren Freeman crossed from the right finding Paul Watson, but he could not keep his shot down. Neil Howarth then found Julian Alsop with a ball over the top of the Brighton defence, but the giant target man screwed his shot wide from a tight angle. Eight minutes had elapsed when Cheltenham took a surprise but very welcome lead.

Hugh McAuley played a quickly-taken free-kick across field to McCann in space, his low drive from thirty-five yards seemed to catch goalkeeper Mark Cartwright unaware and crept inside the far post as he scrambled across. Three minutes later, Cheltenham blasted themselves two goals in front when McAuley's corner was flicked on by Richard Walker and Alsop directed a header in off the underside of the crossbar. The two-goal cushion lasted only three minutes until Brighton centre-back Danny Cullip got up to send a flick-header beyond Steve Book from a Paul Watson free kick.

The game had an aggressive undercurrent right from the first minute and matters came to a head after eighteen minutes when Richard Carpenter and Kerry Mayo of Brighton and Cheltenham's Lee Howells were booked following a brawl in the centre circle.

Howells lasted only two more minutes before being shown the red card for a second booking after a high tackle on Watson. But there was some confusion as to whether it was he or Devaney that committed the offence. Despite their man disadvantage, Cheltenham went close to a third goal when Neil Howarth produced a sharp turn onto a Mark Freeman free kick and stabbed his shot inches wide.

Book touched a free kick from Watson and a volley from Matthew Wicks over the bar, and parried a drive from Watson round the posts as Brighton heaped the pressure on. Brighton manager Micky Adams made a change for the second half, sending forward Paul Brooker on for defender Mayo, and the visitors created a good chance moments after the re-start when Darren Freeman found himself in space 10 yards from goal, but he snatched at his shot and it sailed over the bar.

Cheltenham were indebted to goalkeeper Steve Book shortly afterwards when Cullip met a cross from Charlie Oatway with a glancing header, but the Cheltenham stopper flew to make a remarkable save.

Ten-man Cheltenham were having to chase and tackle like terriers to contain a confident Brighton outfit, and they managed to frustrate the south coast side into throwing on two more attacking players in Nathan Jones and Gary Hart. Brighton were now playing with four up front, but it was Cheltenham who created the next good chance, Mark Yates warming the gloves of goalkeeper Cartwright with a fierce shot following a clever flick from Antony Griffin.

Book held a dangerous-looking header from leading scorer Bobby Zamora and Brighton went close to an equaliser when Andy Crosby nodded a ball across the six-yard box and Hart headed inches over the bar. But the game turned on its head again when Cheltenham regained their two-goal lead twenty minutes from time with a spectacular goal from substitute Bob Bloomer.

Receiving the ball thirty-five yards from goal, he held it up before cutting inside a defender and unleashing a left-foot shot which nestled inside the far post. A delighted Bloomer then proceeded to sprint all round the pitch in celebration of the goal. Brighton's decision to go all out for attack had backfired on them and the sheer number of blue and white shirts pushing forward meant that players were often getting in each other's way. Book dived to block a powerful close-range drive from Zamora in the last meaningful action of a memorable game.

I think it was the worst five weeks or so of my footballing life. Steve was going off his nut every day, particularly with the injuries. The truth is though that we were really unlucky in some of the games – we played some good football, but no-one remembers that.

Paul Baker was, for once, very worried:

I remember us going to Mansfield and thinking I just cannot see us getting another win – Steve looked down, he looked like he didn't know what to do about it, the body language of the players I think told a story – we were very concerned. To be fair it doesn't help when you've got a lot of injuries and such a small squad, and you're bringing in loan players – they take three games to settle in.

You're trying to think what you can do, but you know what you cannot do – you can't just go and spend money in the transfer market so you got to try and knuckle down and turn things round and thankfully that's what we did. That was the worst run in my time at the club, and all we could do was try and support Steve – and all credit to him and the players, they turned it round.

For Chris Banks, things were going from bad to worse:

The injuries were awful, and we were struggling badly; then at Chesterfield I gave away a goal and then got an injury so I came off after thirty minutes – and it was all live on Sky. I missed the game at Mansfield. To be fair I thought the spirit was really good, and I don't think we played that badly – we just didn't get the breaks.

Steve Cotterill remembers how he sought to help end the run:

We went paintballing after the fifth defeat. There was nothing we could do on the training ground – we'd exhausted all areas there, so we had to do something else and get away from football.

The run was to end in spectacular fashion. Brighton, with their large fan base were now challenging for promotion and arrived at Whaddon Road, in confident fashion. Ninety minutes later they had been well beaten, as ten-man Cheltenham won 3-1.

After a Mark Freeman own goal resulted in a 1-0 defeat at Darlington, in a match where they should have at least gained a draw, from somewhere the team regrouped, and went on an unbeaten run of 12 games. Long unbeaten runs were a feature of Steve Cotterill's reign at Cheltenham, so what was the big secret? The manager explains:

Mental strength was key, and that was down to the players really. They were able to keep a degree of consistency that was just great and the team spirit kept us going when we weren't playing so well.

The first match of the twelve was at Plymouth, where another loan player was unveiled by the manager – Greg Goodridge, signed from Bristol City. For many, his signing was a surprise – a man of enormous individual talent, who could beat a man with ease going down the wing, but perhaps not as hard-working as some of Cotterill's signings.

Graham Allner recalls:

We felt we needed some width and Greg was available, he obviously had a top pedigree and perhaps was able to give a little more to the team, particularly down the flanks. He could produce some quality stuff, but perhaps the consistency wasn't quite there.

There was some good news for the following game after the 0-0 draw in Devon – Neil Grayson was back. It had been a frustrating season for the popular striker, who, after battling back from his broken ankle had had another spell on the sidelines after an injury picked up on Boxing Day. Again he came back, but on his return, as subsitute against Hull, he limped off and had to be substituted himself. He left the field in tears, and the fans wondered if this was the end for one of their most favoured sons.

Grayson remembers:

I was gutted because it was different pain from when I'd injured the ankle and when I was back in the dressing room you do think, 'I wonder what's going to happen now'. Everyone picked me up when they got back in though, and Andy Mitchell, who was always brilliant for me, helped me get going again, and thankfully I was soon playing again.

As the season moved from February to March, both the next two games with Scunthorpe and Exeter were won 1-0, the latter with a goal by Mark Yates, who now embarked on a run of four goals in five games. Only one of these goals was in a win though, as the Robins dropped costly home points to Macclesfield, after a rare Steve Book mistake, and then York, where Yates rescued a point in the last minute. Graham Allner of course knew all about Yates' goalscoring abilities.

One of my things about Mark was that I didn't think he scored enough goals for us. I'd had him at Kidderminster and he must have scored around 40 goals in 200 games for me so I knew he was capable of scoring. It's a big bonus if people in his position can score goals because it takes pressure off the strikers and it can make a huge difference to the team. I think he should score more goals for us and I've told him that.

Sandwiched in between the Macclesfield and the York games was the home game with Halifax. The Robins won 4-2 and no-one there will forget the quality of the goals, particularly a superb volley from by Gregory Goodridge. There were though two more players making their debuts that day. Mark Sertori had scored for York City in their win at Whaddon Road the previous season; now after his release he joined Cheltenham as defensive cover – there was no sign of let-up in the injuries. Up front there was a third loan striker – Charlie MacDonald from Premiership side Charlton Athletic, Iwelumo having returned to Stoke. Cotterill was using the loan system to the full.

Loan signings aren't really something I favour, because they don't know how you play or what you expect from them. They're not really your players so are they going to give everything. Sometimes you get lucky I guess. It was different with Grant McCann because Grant was going to be there all year. I'd rather have my own players though, especially defenders.

The side were now playing catch-up, desperately trying to make up lost ground to try and make the play-off positions. By the time Cardiff City came to Whaddon Road for a Sunday game on the last day of March, the side were in eighth position, level on points with the two sides above them, and the side below them, with just seven games to go. After four draws in five games, the side needed to win, and they did so in convincing fashion, thanks to a hat-trick from Neil Grayson.

Grayson recalls:

I always seem to do well against Cardiff and remember beating them in the play-offs when I was at Northampton. I was getting some stick from their fans that day – perhaps they remembered me from the Northampton days so it was good to score, and to get a hat-trick was even better.

Now it was getting close. With just six games to go, the table now looked like this:

	P	W	D	L	F	A	PTS
Chesterfield	39	23	13	3	70	31	82
Brighton	38	23	6	9	62	31	75
Cardiff	39	21	11	7	82	43	74
Hartlepool	40	18	14	8	64	47	68
Orient	39	16	13	10	49	46	61
Blackpool	39	18	5	16	61	49	59
Scunthorpe	40	16	11	13	56	46	59
Cheltenham	40	16	11	13	50	43	59
Hull City	39	15	14	10	38	36	59

The next game saw the Robins at Barnet. The London side had parted company with manager Tony Cottee after a terrible run of form and were in danger of dropping out of the League. Both sides needed to win. In the event, neither side did. Cheltenham took an early lead through Michael Duff, but were then hit by yet another injury, this time to goalkeeper Steve Book. On came Shane Higgs for his Robins League debut, but he could do nothing about a turnaround that left Barnet leading 2-1 until Grant McCann scored from a free-kick in the last minute to secure a draw.

The next game, at home to Lincoln on Easter Saturday, was won with two goals from Michael Duff, and the side then faced a crucial away game at Blackpool on Easter Monday. Over 700 Robins fans made the journey north, many of them no doubt making a mini-holiday of the trip, to see a spirited performance bring a 2-2 draw – both goals coming from Charlie MacDonald, the only goals of his loan spell. Afterwards, Blackpool manager Steve McMahon commented that the result felt 'like a defeat' to his side, and there was no doubt who was happier with the point.

There were now three games left. The promotion and play-offs situation at this stage was made even more confusing by what would happen to Chesterfield. The long-time League leaders had been convicted of irregular payments and business practices by the Football League, and there was widespread speculation that their punishment might be severe – either a substantial docking of points to put them out of the promotion play-off positions, or even relegation to the Conference. Whilst seventh place would definitely guarantee a play-off place, even eighth might therefore be enough…

Paul Baker remembers it well:

Cheltenham Town 3 Cardiff City 1

Cheltenham Town's swashbuckling end to the season continued with a remarkable win over big-spending Cardiff City at Whaddon Road yesterday. The Cheltenham squad, assembled at a fraction of the cost of Cardiff owner Sam Hammam's Bluebirds, out-fought their Welsh counterparts in a victory of heart and spirit over expensively assembled performers. Nowhere was this contrast more keenly witnessed than in the battle between the opposing strikers. Cheltenham's Neil Grayson, thirty-six years old but with the vibrance of a man half his age, produced a typically all-action performance to plunder his first hat-trick for the club, while Cardiff's giant target man Leo Fortune-West spent eighty minutes grappling unsuccessfully with various defenders, was booked following a first half flare-up and finally substituted amid loud jeers and cat-calls from the home fans.

It was an afternoon to savour for the Cheltenham supporters, so often reserved in their backing for the team, yet on occasions like this one are second to none in their support for the underdog. At one stage it looked as if their team would need all the encouragement they could muster as third in the table Cardiff took an early lead and went on to control the opening twenty-five minutes. The goal arrived when Andy Legg delivered a free-kick from the right and Scott Young sent a looping header over goalkeeper Steve Book which hit the post and bounced in.

Shortly afterwards, danger man Robert Earnshaw stabbed a shot just over the crossbar and Book had to move smartly to block a close range effort from Jason Bowen. Josh Low fired high off the target from the rebound but Cheltenham, clearly fired up for the occasion having already lost to Cardiff in the League and FA Cup this season, began to chase and compete for every ball until the space started to open up for them. They were rewarded with an equaliser in the 37th minute. Chris Banks popped up on the right and laid the ball back to Michael Duff. His cross was met by Mark Yates, who had a shot blocked by Legg, but the rebound fell to Grayson who shot into the roof off the net from eight yards.

Four minutes later, Cheltenham took the lead after Charlie MacDonald had produced a superb turn and shot that was turned behind by goalkeeper Mark Walton. Russell Milton took the corner and Grayson sneaked in between a defender and the goalkeeper to send a cheeky header into the net from just inside the six-yard box. With the home support now roaring them on, Cheltenham began the second half as they ended the first and added a third goal four minutes after the break that brought the crowd to its feet. MacDonald played a ball forward that defender Rhys Weston appeared to have under control. But Grayson, ever willing, robbed him with a sliding tackle before running on to beat Walton with a low shot. Cheltenham held onto their lead with display of composed defending in the closing stages to keep their play-off pot boiling into the final weeks of the season.

I thought that Chesterfield should have been docked enough points so they couldn't have been promoted – clearly they'd broken the rules, and I think a lot of Third Division chairmen thought the decision was wrong. What they had done made a mockery of the rules.

The League table as the Robins prepared to take on Kidderminster at Whaddon Road was as follows:

	P	W	D	L	F	A	PTS
Chesterfield	42	24	14	4	74	36	86
Brighton	41	26	6	9	68	31	84
Cardiff	42	22	12	8	87	49	78
Orient	43	19	14	10	57	49	71
Hartlepool	43	18	14	11	66	53	68
Hull C	42	17	15	10	41	37	66
Scunthorpe	43	18	11	14	62	48	65
Cheltenham	43	17	13	13	56	48	64
Blackpool	42	19	6	17	65	53	63
Rochdale	40	15	16	9	52	40	61

A win was vital and with ten unbeaten games behind them, confidence was high in the home camp. However, those fans who were long-time supporters knew only too well of the Kidderminster hoodoo – the Aggborough side traditionally had a good record both home and away against Cheltenham, and this run continued as the Harriers won 3-1. In truth, the Robins made it difficult for themselves as Lee Howells was sent off for the third time in the season in the first half, and the ten men were soon 2-0 down. A second half fightback led to Neil Grayson pulling a goal back, but Drewe Broughton scored a third for the Harriers, and the unbeaten run was over. As they trooped off the pitch, that seemed to be the end of the Robins' play-off hopes, but once in the dressing room these were revived by a remarkable sequence of results – of their key rivals, Rochdale, Scunthorpe, Southend and Blackpool also lost. As a result, the play-off hopes were still alive – just – with two games still to go.

The penultimate match of the season was at Orient. Wins were now imperative and even then this might not be enough, depending on other teams' results. At Brisbane Road, Cheltenham had much the better of the game, but despite increasing pressure they couldn't deliver the required winner. The play-off dream was over, unless Chesterfield were to be taken out of the picture, and even that hope was made immaterial when the midweek results meant that not only could the Robins not finish seventh and qualify for the play-offs automatically, they also could not finish eighth with the possibility of benefiting from any Chesterfield punishment. For the second season running, it was a case of so near and yet so far for the manager.

It was a tough one that day. It was a great result, in fact – 0-0 at Orient in any season would be a good result. I went round everybody in the dressing room afterwards and told them I was full of admiration for them. We'd pushed the season this far again against all adversity and they could be really proud of what they'd achieved.

The last game of the season at home to Southend saw another sending off, this time Neil Grayson. This meant that a total of six Robins players had been given their marching orders at Whaddon Road during the season. This time the ten men prevailed, with a wonderful winning goal from Grant McCann, who was playing in his last game before returning to West Ham. The final position in Division Three was ninth.

So, what are the reflections on what, in terms of League position, was the least successful in the five years under Cotterill? Injuries and, to a lesser degree, suspensions will be the abiding memory – if one looks at the appearance records of some of the players, the magnitude of the disruptions becomes clear. John Brough made just four starts, Jamie Victory three, Neil Grayson played in under half the games, and between the Macclesfield game on 14 October and the Brighton game four months later, Cotterill could only pick the same side in successive matches on two occasions. A total of 28 players were used during the season, including the full five loan players allowed. Under the circumstances, perhaps the final position should be seen as a remarkable achievement.

Graham Allner, in his first full season at the club, is definitely of that view:

I know Steve was particularly disappointed in the end, but you can't do without key players for as long as we had to. To have finished ninth and gone so close was a fantastic achievement really.

The chairman's view was positive:

At the time you feel disappointed, but I think you look back now and feel pretty pleased, particularly given the dreadful run of injuries and remembering how you felt at Mansfield at the end of that run. So I think that season was a successful season, not in terms of winning anything, but in terms of turning it round from what was a very difficult time into just missing out in the play-offs – its far better to just miss out on the play-offs than to be hanging on to stay in the League.

Chris Banks looks back and reflects on the achievements as much as the disappointment:

To have had a season with all those injuries and still come so close was in fact a good season. Cheltenham is a small club with a small squad and for us to do so well was a good season in fairness.

Of all the chapters in the book, this was the hardest one to write in many ways, for it was a season that few people remember with much affection and really wanted to recall. There is a sense of pride, perhaps, that the club battled so well to try and overcome the appalling injuries, but no more. It was very noticeable that when we met

Steve Cotterill to interview him, this was the season that he found it hardest to talk about, as he readily admits:

This season I could have skimmed through without talking much about it really. I could sum it up by saying it was my worst season at the club. It was actually the first year that we finished with fewer points than the season before, and of course we were a place down, but when I look back at it, it was probably my biggest learning season from a managerial point of view. I think you learn to cope better with injuries and get on with things – how we managed to put a team out week in week out I still do not know, but you manage it and you get through it. When I look back, though, I could argue that that was the season that we really achieved to get to where we got because that was such a tough season.

The obvious question, which can never be answered, is whether the Robins would have been promoted without all the injuries. As the statistics show, there was a disproportionately high number of injuries – most sides get some over the season, but this was unusual. The squad simply wasn't big enough to cope, and the money wasn't there for the club to buy their way out of the injury crisis.

On reflection, the answer to the question may be that the team would have made the play-offs. They came mighty close, while Chesterfield, Brighton and Cardiff were all strong sides who comfortably gained automatic promotion (despite the off-pitch issues at the Derbyshire club) and there were a number of clubs in play-off contention. A full strength Cheltenham side were surely one of the stronger ones of that group.

In a curious way, perhaps the injuries issue did, in the end, even itself out. The following year was, as we shall see, largely free of injuries – mercifully – perhaps some evening out of what had happened in 2000/01. So, another close season beckoned, and the manager knew his summer priorities:

I needed another striker, I needed someone with that extra bit of quality who would help us unlock things. That for me was the key signing I would try and make.

We now know he was successful in his quest, but only after some ups and downs along the way.

6

The Glory Season
2001/02

After the near misses of the previous two seasons, Steve Cotterill decided to go for experience when making his signings during the summer of 2001. In came goal-keeper Carl Muggleton, signed from Stoke City, and defender Keith Hill, from Rochdale, both of whom had played consistently at a higher level during their early careers. The third signing was a familiar face to the Robins faithful – Steve Jones, who rejoined the club from Swansea City. Jones had previously played for the club in the Dr Martens years, making 111 league appearances and scoring 9 goals. All three were signed on free transfers.

Paul Baker explains the board's position, with a reminder that transfer fees are but one part of a club's outlay on a player:

Certainly Muggleton and Hill were expensive for us, not because of paying money for them, but because of wages and signing-on fees. Steve Jones wasn't as expensive, but as a board we wanted him back, because he was desperate to come back, and you want that type of desire to play for you – it's been disappointing for us and him that it hasn't worked out.

As new players arrived, one of the survivors from the start of the rise moved on. Mark Freeman, who had come to epitomise the team effort and commitment Cotterill had built at the club, moved to Boston United for a fee of £15,000. Many had doubted whether the centre-half would be able to play at Conference, let alone League level, but he had proved them wrong and left with the best wishes of everyone at the club, after 224 appearances and 16 goals.

Steve Cotterill remembers the popular defender:

I think we'd got to the stage at the back end of the previous season where Boka was struggling to get in – people like Richard Walker and John Brough were there, although Broughy was of course injured. We had Michael Duff coming through strongly, Neil Howarth was there and Boka was getting squeezed out. At the time, he felt that a move into non-League would help him, and it was a good time for him to go, because he went to Boston and his deal there was better. But of course he ended up finishing there, which was a nightmare for him – he hurt his back or hip there and never recovered. He used to regularly tweak his back in pre-season and be a little sore and to be honest when I heard he was injured again I thought it was just one of those, so it was a real shock when I heard he had to give up altogether.

Lee Howells was again optimistic about the new season:

I think we came back a lot fitter, and were mentally and physically better prepared for the season. The pre-season tour to Germany was important, because although the results weren't very good, we spent a lot of time sitting around and talking and it got people thinking about what we could achieve. The other thing was that we knew play-offs had to be the aim – a lot of people's contracts were up, and we felt that if we didn't do it this time then we might all be gone.

Of the three new signings, all of whom would ultimately play only a limited part in the season to come, only two (due to Hill's suspension) lined up for the Robins' opening game of the season on 11 August, at home to Orient, who had narrowly missed out on promotion by losing in the play-off final in the previous season. However, the name on the fans' minds as they made their way to Whaddon Road for the big kick-off was not one of the new signings but the one who appeared to have got away – Tony Naylor.

News of the possible signing of Naylor had leaked in the early part of the month, prompting a real sense of anticipation amongst the fans about the possibility of seeing a player with a proven goalscoring record in Divisions One and Two in Cheltenham colours. However, by the start of the season the deal appeared to be dead in the water, which left a sense of regret amongst fans and the manager, as Steve Cotterill recalls:

Tony had some problems at home, and just didn't feel he could commit himself to us, or to anybody else. So I said to him that I needed an answer by the Monday, to try and twist his arm a little bit, but when he still couldn't decide then I said to him, 'OK, let's leave it then'. So I called it a day, but still hoped he might call me back.

Against Orient, not even the sight of Steve Cotterill wearing a blazer and tie in a bid to end his jinx of never having won an opening day match whilst at the club could inspire Cheltenham to a win. Matt Lockwood put the visitors ahead, following up to score after Carl Muggleton, playing in place of the injured Steve Book, had saved his initial spot-kick. A point was gained from an unlikely source – subsitute Jason White, who scored his first (and as it proved only) goal for the Robins to equalise. A draw against one of the division's favourites for promotion was not a bad start, but the fans were left wondering what might have happened if the skills of Naylor had been available.

As far as those who left the ground were concerned, the signing of Tony Naylor was no longer a possibility. Little did they know of what was still going on behind the scenes, as Paul Baker explains:

Steve had been trying to get Tony as the final piece of the jigsaw, and without doubt he was the biggest gamble, in monetary terms, that this club has ever made – a quality player, a proven player and goalscorer, but to get a proven goalscorer is always going to be expensive. It was such a big signing that I wanted to make sure that all the board were supportive, because we really couldn't afford him – that season we were looking at a budget deficit of £200,000 which is no way to run a business. So he was a really, really big gamble, but Steve felt it was important, all the board were excited by it, because we're all football fans at heart, and in the end we were chuffed to bits when he signed, and I think we really thought we could do something with the season.

Steve Cotterill explained what happened:

About a week after the initial deal fell through, I was sitting in the office and I said to Mike Davis, 'Do you want to give Tony Naylor a call and ask him if the situation is the same or whether he wants to sign for us. Tell him if he wants to sign, he meets us at junction fifteen of the M6 at six o'clock tonight.' Tony said he was interested, so we drove up and he signed that night. The reason why he signed was that we offered him the same terms as we'd offered the previous week – we didn't try and change anything, and I think he felt that we were being honest and straight with him. Then, of course, we had to try and get him fit, which was another job in itself, because his problems at home meant he hadn't been able to engage himself in full-scale training – and as anybody who has played under me or watched my teams will know, my players are fit. I don't think many players from other clubs would find their fitness levels good enough, let alone somebody who hadn't done much for a month.

For the player himself, it had been a difficult time:

Steve rang me up inititally and asked me if I wanted to join. I was very interested, but at that time my wife was ill and I didn't fancy the travelling so I said no. The club then called me again and by then things had sorted themselves out at home so I was happy to sign. My first impressions were of a small, but very much family-orientated club, which appealed because I'd been at Crewe and Port Vale who were similar as clubs. You immediately sensed that everyone got on and that there was a great atmosphere.

Lee Howells saw Naylor's signing as key:

I think as a player you always look out for goalscorers in your side and Tony was clearly a proven player. You just knew after playing with him what a good player he is – you give it to him and make a run and know you're going to get it back – he's just got that extra footballing brain. He was a great signing.

The next game was a big test, away at recently relegated Luton, who were managed by Cotterill's old boss, Joe Kinnear. It was bound to be a big test, and so it proved, although there was real encouragement in the way the team battled back from a 2-0 half-time deficit against a side who, even at that early stage of the season, looked as if they would be going straight back up. In the end, despite the introduction of Naylor as a second-half subsitute and numerous chances they could only pull back one goal, via Neil Howarth, and they slipped to an unlucky defeat.

Another unlucky defeat followed the following Tuesday against Bristol City at Ashton Gate in the Worthington Cup, Neil Grayson's 35-yarder bringing their goal in a 2-1 defeat. The side had battled back well after conceding an early goal to their Second Division hosts, but given the way the team were playing, it was widely expected that the first win of the season would not be long in coming.

How wrong we were! The next four League matches brought only two points, at home to Torquay, and away at Swansea, both courtesy of last minute Mark Yates goals, whilst the other two matches – at home to Mansfield and away at Shrewsbury were both lost. Little did we know the importance of that defeat to Mansfield courtesy of a last minute goal by the Stags' Wayne Corden (which would prove to be the only home defeat of the season).

By 8 September, after six matches the table looked bleak (P6 W0 D3 L3) and the Robins were in the bottom three, with just Carlisle and Exeter below them. In five successive League matches the side had found themselves two goals down, and although on each occasion they had battled back well, it had not been a good start. Graham Allner, however, was not all that disappointed.

I remember when we lost at Shrewsbury the dressing room was really down, and I said to them, look, in my two years at the club that's probably the best footballing performance we've given. I know that sometimes makes it feel worse, but in hindsight despite the results the signs were there in the performances.

Paul Baker needed to take a deep breath:

It's a nightmare scenario, because you've already got a budget deficit of £200,000, and you're near the bottom of the table, so the next thing that's going to happen is that your crowds are going to start to go down, yet you've got players on two or three year contracts. It was a worry, but at least we were showing a lot of fight, and even when we were going 2-0 down, you were thinking that the game wasn't over. I suppose that whilst it was worrying, at least we were playing well, and at least it was early on in the season so there was plenty of time to turn it round.

Steve Cotterill's recollections are similar to those of his chairman:

Yes, we kept going 2-0 down and having to dig ourselves out of a hole, and we kept doing it and doing it and doing it. The one thing of course you can't do is to say to the players before they go out 'don't go 2-0 down' because when you send them on the pitch that's what they think and it has a definite influence on players – the whole area of positive and negative thoughts. The one thing this spell did show was the character of the players – and we did really well to keep coming back, and it just shows that the players never gave up, which of course is part of the reason for our success.

The Robins needed a win, and they got one, or to be more precise, two in quick succession. Carlisle were comfortably despatched at Whaddon Road for the first victory of the season, and this was then followed up on the following Tuesday with a 1-0 win at Hartlepool, the first away win since victory at Torquay in January a whole eight months previously. Relief abounded – the season was up and running.

The next match was one that supporters had been looking forward to since the fixtures had been released – Rushden away, the first trip to Nene Park since the 'Conference Decider' of April 1999. There was a new face for this game – Lee Williams, signed on loan from Mansfield, one half of a deal that saw Jason White go the other way, also on loan. White would soon return; Williams stayed and played a crucial role in Cheltenham's season, as Graham Allner explained:

Lee Williams was a really important signing for us – he gave us real width and a lot of quality with it. He struck up a good understanding with Tony Naylor and their combination work was critical during the season – don't underestimate his importance to our success.

Williams couldn't make a winning debut though; luck was against the Robins as a clearance from Keith Hill rebounded against home striker Jean-Michel Sigere and ended up in the net for a freak goal, the only goal of the game. The Robins cursed their luck, while the Rushden fans enjoyed their victory over their 'enemy' – a result that was to be avenged in the most dramatic fashion later in the season.

Meanwhile, as the side battled to regain ground in the League table, things were happening off the pitch. The old Wymans Road stand had been demolished during the close season and a new stand, with 2,071 seats was nearing completion – although not in time for the expected bumper gate against local rivals Bristol Rovers for a match due in late September, so the match had to be rescheduled. Once again, Colin Farmer was the man who oversaw the project:

We're obviously quite boxed in as a ground, so planning permission was always going to be tight – the first two ideas I put to the planners were rejected. The first idea was to build a stand with terracing below, but that got rejected because it would have been too tall, and then we submitted another plan which had executive boxes at the back which was again rejected. I'm really pleased with the final outcome though – there's a great view and the fans seem to like it. What you've got to try and do is to keep on top of all the regulations needed – what people don't realise is that although you can join the League with only 1,000 seats, you have to get that up to 2,000 seats within three years of membership, so basically we've done that earlier than we needed to.

(The main stand at Whaddon Road, which until the building of the new stand was the only seating at the ground, holds just over 1,000.)

At this point, it's worth paying tribute to the board – there will be more on this in due course, but on the day we met Colin, both he and Arthur Hayward were at the ground,

Progress is made on the new stand at Whaddon Road ...

... and the stand in all its glory.

helping out and supervising close-season changes such as new toilets, and (very importantly!) the construction of a new press box. Both were doing this unpaid, like all the directors, all of whom have freely given of their time and effort for the club they have supported for many years. Few supporters probably realise how much effort the directors make to the hands-on running of the club, and in an age where most boards are distrusted by the fans, Cheltenham are lucky to have such a good team at the helm of the club. The chairman saw it as further proof of the way the club was developing:

The stand cost £1.25 million, and although we got a grant for the best part of £1m, it was still a six-figure sum to find. In fact, all the way through this success we've had to plough quite large sums of money into the ground – we couldn't just put it all into the playing budget. Our playing budget has consistently been one of the lowest in whatever league we've been playing in, partly because we've had to spend a lot of money on ground improvements and pitch improvements. What the board like to think of themselves as is as custodians of this club for the time being – so when we move on, we'll leave a good legacy for our successors in terms of bricks and mortar. So the ground has been a constant drain and has also been a constant management issue in terms of managing the balance between playing and non-playing budgets.

The C&G stand was really important because it gave us an end – I think all clubs have an end don't they, but we've never had an end before, which gave the fans somewhere to keep dry and generate an atmosphere. The C&G stand gave us a great place for fans to watch the game, for families as well, and I think has had a big impact on our crowds – they know they can come and watch the game and stay dry.

The new stand was then the development that for me, completed the transition into a real football ground – fantastic views and again added to the atmosphere. It took time for the crowds to congregate there, but when it's full it's made a huge difference. We've always tried to look after the fans; we can all remember standing on the terraces in the old days with sub-standard facilities.

After the frustration of Rushden, the results started to mirror the performances. Between the end of September and the start of November the side was to be unbeaten in the League with three wins and three draws. The quality of football was some of the best ever seen at Whaddon Road according to many of the 'older fans', and at the heart of most of it was Tony Naylor.

It had taken Naylor time to gain full fitness, having missed out on pre-season training and also time for him and the team to get used to each other's style of play, but once he settled in, Naylor was inspirational. It took him nine full games to score – a scrappy goal in the home win against Lincoln – but he was soon scoring and creating goals and forming an impressive understanding with giant striker Julian Alsop in a classic 'Little and Large' combination. Steve Cotterill remembers Naylor's early games well:

As I've already said, we had to work on his fitness, and in his first few games he didn't really look like scoring – he set up other people but didn't look like putting them away himself. You think at the time 'Have I made the wrong decision?', but we stayed out every afternoon doing extras with him – simple running and the like, and then I think the first one went in off his backside from a Russell Milton shot, and then there was no looking back. He ended up being a really important member of the side, a great character and a key signing for the football club.

The team was taking on a settled look. An injury to Richard Walker in the defeat at Rushden led Steve Cotterill to move Michael Duff from right-back to centre-back to partner Chris Banks for the win at Southend on 28 September. This was to be an important move – Duff and Banks were to be crucial factors in Cheltenham's success over the coming months, with the former ending the season as the Robins' first ever full international. The move was initially against Cotterill's better judgement:

It was something that bothered me a bit, playing them together, because they're both good footballers and I envisaged them having ten passes between them every time they had the ball. I believe you need one dominant, Mark Freeman type, and in the end Michael Duff took on that role but it didn't just happen. We had to work on their partnership and get them doing what we wanted and perhaps put a bit more aggression into their play.

What it did enable us to do though was to play a little bit higher up the pitch because with them and then Antony Griffin we now had more pace and we didn't have to worry so much about the grass behind us as we had people who could cover. Of the defence who then started to play regularly, I guess Banksy is the slowest but he's no slouch and his positional play is at least as good as the other three. I thought that Michael and Chris were great. Of course, you saw Michael get his rewards with the player's player of the year and getting in the PFA Division Three side. More than anything, to get an international cap from a third division club, and indeed a small third division side, was an incredible achievement.

The six-match unbeaten run meant the team was in eleventh place by the time they made the long trip to Humberside to face Hull City on 3 November. At this stage in the season, Hull were going well under the management of former Leicester and Aston Villa boss Brian Little. Whilst a difficult game was expected, nobody was prepared for the final result – a 5-1 drubbing. This was the Robins' heaviest ever League defeat, with Julian Alsop continuing his goalscoring form with the only goal. Cotterill, however, remained defiant:

Hull was one where I got ridiculed a bit for saying that I wouldn't swap my players for theirs. I meant what I said at the time, but I guess I was talking with my heart rather than with my head but thankfully the players didn't let me down.

By the end of the season his judgement was proved right. Hull slipped out of automatic promotion, and ultimately play-off contention, and Brian Little parted company with the club. And as for Cheltenham …

For Graham Allner, the Hull game was a case of déjà vu:

Every time they went forward, they scored – it was one of those games. The funny thing is that a week or so earlier the reserves had gone to Brentford and the same thing had happened – we played really well but they scored on every attack. We got back to Cheltenham and we told Steve that we had been the better side, and he kept saying, but you lost 5-0. So on the coach home when we were discussing the Hull game we reminded him of that game and his reaction ...!

The defeat heralded a run of three games without a goal, although home points were gained in goal-less draws against Bristol Rovers (with the new stand now fully open) and Plymouth. However, the game at Oxford was to be a turning point – a 3-0 defeat and a time, according to Graham Allner for tough talking.

Oxford was a really poor performance – they scored at the right times and we had no answer to them on the day. The key though was how the lads would respond, because you've got to accept that you are going to get the odd below par performance. In fairness, they responded brilliantly.

Just how big a turning point that defeat and its aftermath were can be judged by the run that the side now went on. It was the last League defeat until 16 March – a total of sixteen games without losing, which moved the team from eleventh place to the thick of the promotion shake-up.

The run started in a somewhat stuttering fashion, with a 2-1 win over Halifax on 1 December, Alsop again providing the winner after Jamie Victory had levelled an early opening goal by the visitors. Victory at this stage was in inspired form with five goals to his name – not bad for a defender before Christmas!

Further League wins followed before the end of the year at York and at home to Shrewsbury, before a Lee Williams goal at Torquay on New Year's Day, in the only Third Division game to escape the adverse weather, made it four League wins on the trot and seventh place in the table.

As the League results picked up, the side were also making their way in the FA Cup. The first round had taken them back to old rivals in Kettering, their rivals for the Conference title in 1998/99 who were surprisingly relegated to the Dr Martens League at the end of 2000/01 (they would subsequently return at the first attempt after a close battle with Tamworth for the one automatic promotion spot). Viewed in the cold light of day, the 6-1 win looks comfortable enough, but the Robins were a goal down early on, and if Darren Collins had not missed a straightforward chance they would have gone 2-0 behind. Paul Baker remembers a nervous afternoon:

We're 1-0 down, could have been 2-0 down, Dale Watkins is convinced he's going to score against you, a pudding of a pitch – we were very relieved to get out of that one.

Steve Cotterill knew a cup run was important for the club:

We'd not had a good cup run as a League club, and all of a sudden the FA Cup starts giving you decent rewards financially, so it was even more important than usual. We had a difficult looking tie at Kettering, and everybody was a bit nervous because all of a sudden the boot is on the other foot for us and we're looking at being turned over by a non-League club. After four minutes I thought 'Hang on what's happening here?', but the lads stuck at it and I thought showed the changes between the clubs in the last three years, because don't forget that Kettering were right up with us in the Conference. In the end it could have been ten, not that I would have wanted that for Kettering's sake.

The second round jogged memories for many Robins fans of longer standing, a trip to Hinckley United, also of the Dr Martens Premier, but only recently promoted, and a club whose ground was more akin to those generally found during Cheltenham's days at that level – cramped but very hospitable. The manager was very aware of the possibility of an upset:

I remember going up there one night in midweek with Paul Godfrey and looking over the fence at their pitch to find out what we would be walking out to. I remember one night they were training, and whilst they were training I wouldn't look over the fence because I think that would be unethical but I wanted to find out what their pitch was like. Then we basically trained on the same bit of grass all week so it got very muddy and rutted, in order to make sure that nobody was going to turn their noses up at what they would play on come Saturday. I don't mean that to be in any way disrespectful to them because that was their best chance of winning the game – we'd asked them if they wanted to switch the tie and they'd declined like I would have done. So there was plenty of hype about whether they might knock us out but in the end we were very professional.

In the end the Robins won comfortably, goals from Alsop and Naylor put them into the third round for only the third time in the club's history, and to put the recent rise into perspective the second time in Cotterill's time as manager. Players, supporters and officials dreamed of the tie at Old Trafford, Highbury or Anfield…

The actual draw was somewhat different – a home draw against Oldham Athletic, founder members of the Premiership but now a side challenging for promotion to Division One. The chairman remembers his feelings on hearing the draw.

It was a big anti-climax really, with no disrespect to Oldham – people forget that they were in the Premiership, but not traditionally a popular club with a big following, so it was disappointing. Then you think, 'hang on, we've got a chance of getting a result, we are at home', so we looked forward to it.

For it to be a 'good draw', the Robins needed to win, and record their first ever victory over a side in the Second Division or higher. That's exactly what they did, thanks to two goals from Tony Naylor, the first a brilliant individual solo effort, and the second a far post header that went in off a defender. There were memorable scenes at the final whistle as the club celebrated their first ever third round win, and arguably their greatest ever FA Cup result – little did we know that this was to be surpassed three short weeks later. The manager was delighted with the result:

I thought that we thoroughly deserved it. We played well, in fact I thought both sides played some good football, but in the end I thought we got what our perfor-mance warranted.

Cheltenham v. Oldham, FA Cup third round. Tony Naylor in action in a game the Robins won 2-1.

Cheltenham Town 2 Oldham Athletic 1

Cometh the hour, cometh the man – and that man was Tony Naylor as his two goals sent Cheltenham Town into the fourth round of the FA Cup for the first time. Naylor struck after 25 and 60 minutes to send Whaddon Road wild as the Robins sunk their Second Division opponents – and now set their sights on promotion-chasing former Cup winners Burnley on 26 January.

Oldham were packed full of experience, with 37-year-olds John Sheridan and David Eyres pulling the strings, but Cheltenham turned in a committed performance which deserved a reward. Little Naylor twisted and turned the Oldham defence, which struggled to contain his large partner in crime, Julian Alsop. In midfield, Mark Yates and Lee Howells were their tigerish selves, denying John Sheridan the chance to impose himself on proceedings.

Russell Milton and Jamie Victory combined well on the left, while Lee Williams showed his value with dangerous crosses – the best of which led to Naylor's winner. At the back, Chris Banks and Mike Duff formed an impenetrable barrier for Allan Smart, a striker with Premiership experience, while Antony Griffin stuck to his task against the wily Eyres. Behind them, Steve Book was assured when he had to be and, right from the off, Cheltenham looked to impose themselves.

Alsop was a nuisance for Stuart Balmer and David Beherall at the heart of Oldham's defence – in the third minute he towered above them and flicked on a long throw, setting the pattern for the afternoon. He had the first effort of the game, a 30-yarder which fizzed wide after 13 minutes, then had a header cleared by Lee Duxbury after Naylor turned Scott McNiven inside out. The Robins then claimed a penalty after an Oldham hand seemed to deflect a Milton corner away, but the roof nearly came off after 25 minutes when the deadlock was broken.

Alsop flicked on a long Book clearance and Naylor shrugged off Balmer's challenge to drill a low shot past Gary Kelly. Oldham recovered well and forced three quick corners but Cheltenham held firm, although John Sheridan fired a free-kick into the wall, then John Eyre had a tame shot saved by Book after Paul Murray got to the by-line.

The visitors drew level two minutes before the interval when Darren Sheridan put Eyre away and his low cross was met by Eyres, whose low shot was palmed by Book, but he was unable to keep it out. Cheltenham shrugged off that setback after the break as Balmer was forced into clearances from shots by Naylor and Williams. But at the other end, Eyres was finding a lot of space on the left and fired a shot across the face of Book's goal.

On the hour though, Cheltenham conjured up a goal out of nothing. Williams got away on the right and cut back on to his left foot, swinging a cross to the far post where Naylor came in and headed home via Balmer's chest. Oldham boss

Mick Wadsworth responded with three changes in quick succession, while referee John Brandwood turned to his cards, cautioning Alsop and Darren Sheridan.

Oldham had to chase the game, and Eyres fired a shot at Book before Duxbury made a hash of a good chance after good work from substitutes Craig Dudley and Matthew Tipton. Oldham's last chance went when Darren Sheridan went in for a challenge with Alsop and referee Brandwood showed him a second yellow card. Naylor went close to a hat-trick when his 85th-minute shot was saved by Kelly but it mattered little as Cheltenham hung on for a famous victory.

Cheltenham v. Oldham, FA Cup third round. Steve Cotterill and Tony Naylor celebrate at the final whistle.

Again there was the tension of the draw. With only thirty-two clubs left, and with most of the twenty Premiership sides left in the competition, surely the Robins would find themselves playing a side from the top flight in English football in a competitive fixture for the first time. Again, it was not to be. The Robins had another home draw, this time against Burnley, a club with a great FA Cup tradition and who were now challenging for promotion to the Premiership. Paul Baker again:

Again it was a slight feeling of anti-climax, if only because of who it could have been, and because at that stage of the competition you're looking to maximise your revenue, so you're looking to be on the television – that's the big difference because if you are chosen then that's a six-figure sum. However, like the Oldham game you think we've got a chance, and then you think about Burnley, and you realise that when I was at school Burnley were a really big club, and we are Cheltenham Town, hosting them at Whaddon Road, and if we get a draw we can go up to Turf Moor.

As the cup run developed, League form continued to be strong. The weeks between the Oldham and Burnley games saw three further undefeated League games – the home game with Luton being one of the best games seen at Whaddon Road all season. Tony Naylor, who was enjoying an outstanding run of form at that stage of the season, scored a tremendous thirty yard opener before an uncharacteristic Michael Duff error let Luton, by far the best attacking side the Robins played all season, in to equalise in the second half. A comfortable win at Orient followed before Darlington goalkeeper Andy Collett played one of the best games of his life to enable his side to secure a goalless draw in the home match played just five days before the Burnley cup-tie.

   Tickets sold fast for the cup tie, which was moved to Sunday 27 January, with a 1 p.m. kick-off on police advice. At one stage it looked as if the club might benefit from the cash windfall that comes with a live television game, but that was ultimately not to be the case, to the disappointment of the chairman. Suddenly Cheltenham were big news in the media, not just the old tried and trusted favourites like *The Citizen*, *The Pink 'Un*, *The Gloucestershire Echo* and BBC Radio Gloucestershire, but in *The Times*, *The Daily Telegraph*, *The Sun*, and BBC Radio Five Live. The players took it in their stride, as Lee Howells explains:

Burnley was superb, and meant a lot to me partly because of the fact that I knew one of their players, Kevin Ball from when I was a kid at Portsmouth – I stayed in digs with him. I was really looking forward to playing against him and showing what I could do. The press build up was intense but we kept focused and at the team meeting before the game we just said that we wanted to show everybody how good we were, and that's of course what happened.

Graham Allner was delighted:

I thought we won comfortably in the end – I know 2-1 doesn't sound like it, and we were hanging on a little at the end, but I think we did look comfortable against what was a leading Division One side. It gave the lads a lot of self belief in what they could do.

This match was a real highlight for the manager:

For us to beat Burnley, who were then second or third in the First Division and going for promotion to the Premiership was just phenomenal really. I remember the after-match events as well. As soon as we got into the dressing room, I said to the lads: 'Let's enjoy it, but no shouting off at them afterwards. It's really important that you're humble, because the press are going to be looking for quotes, and if they ask you did you think you could win and you say yes, then the headlines will make you look big-headed and we don't want that'.

I saw Stan Ternent at the final whistle and asked him for a drink afterwards after we'd done the press. I actually thought Stan was quite clever because he didn't see me after I'd done the press, and he waited until the Tuesday to phone and say well done, not only on the game but how we, as a club, had been humble about our win and done the right things. So we certainly won Burnley over, and they were one of the clubs that got in touch to congratulate us at the end of the season after we got promoted.

Cheltenham v. Burnley, FA Cup fourth round. Goalscorers Russell Milton and Julian Alsop celebrate at the final whistle.

Cheltenham Town 2 Burnley 1

Manchester United, Liverpool, Aston Villa, Leeds United, Sunderland – great football clubs and FA Cup winners all, but none of them have lasted as long in this season's competition as Cheltenham Town. That was the wide-eyed boast of the boys from Whaddon Road last night after they wrote yet another amazing chapter in their recent history. Manager Steve Cotterill was presented with mementoes to mark his five years in charge of the Robins, but even he cannot have imagined that, ninety nerve-wrenching minutes later, he would have been celebrating a place in the last sixteen of the world's greatest knock-out competition.

Those five years have seen a lot of highs – promotion to the Conference, a winning trip to Wembley in the FA Trophy, and a dramatic last-minute winner against Yeovil to seal a Football League place. But this will surely rank up there alongside those triumphs as Cheltenham – with only three previous wins over Football League opposition in the cup – ousted Burnley, a club who won the trophy in 1914 and who are on the verge of a return to the big time. In striker Ian Moore, Burnley had a player who cost them £1 million, compared to the £72,000 in transfer fees it cost Cotterill to field his side, so surely Cheltenham should not have stood a chance.

However, roared on by over 7,000 people – Whaddon Road's second highest-ever attendance – dreams became reality. The princes of Burnley were always second best to Cheltenham's paupers, who started brightly and never let their grip slacken. Moore and Gareth Taylor were rarely allowed any time or space to display the talents which have seen them move for big money as the master and pupil, Chris Banks and Michael Duff, led from the back. Anthony Griffin and Jamie Victory were able to spend more time attacking down the flanks, lending vital support to wide midfielders Lee Williams and Russell Milton. In midfield, Mark Yates and Lee Howells were tigerish in the tackle and continually probed forward, while in attack, Julian Alsop and Tony Naylor ran Burnley ragged. Alsop has caused plenty of headaches for Division Three defences this season, but Artur Gnohere and Ian Cox will not quickly forget their ninety minutes in his company.

They simply did not seem to relish their aerial duel with the former hod carrier, and their cause was not helped by also having to keep an eye on the waspish Naylor, who was forever flitting around their ankles. Behind them all was Steve Book, secure in his handling and agile when he had to be, which, thanks to those in front of him, was not too often. Alsop forced a second-minute corner, winning the first of many headers against Burnley's central pairing, and that set the pattern for the afternoon. A nice passing move involving Griffin, Howells, Naylor and Milton ended with Victory's cross skimming wide off Alsop's head. Then Victory burst through after more slick inter-play from Milton and Naylor, and as things seemed to open up for him, he screwed his shot wide.

Cheltenham were on top, but Burnley soon started to get a foothold on the game. Alan Moore broke clear on the left, but Banks made a well-timed tackle to stop him.

The Robins skipper then threw himself in the way of an Ian Moore shot, and hooked out a whipped-in Lee Briscoe cross. Cheltenham had more than weathered that crucial first twenty minutes and as the half wore on, so the belief grew. Fate did them a favour on 18 minutes as Milton rasped a twenty-five-yarder which Nik Michopoulos took at the second attempt.

The Greek goalkeeper crumpled in pain as he went to clear the ball, and on came Luigi Cennamo for his debut. The change immediately had an unsettling effect on Burnley, as Gnohere and Cox seemed reluctant to pass the ball back to the new stopper. Cheltenham were eager to test the new boy, and the chance came within six minutes as a high challenge on Yates twenty yards out gave them a free-kick. As the wall lined up, Burnley manager Stan Ternent was frantically gesturing for his goal-keeper to move across the goal, as he saw the left-footed Milton lining up the chance. It was all to no avail. Naylor tapped the ball to Yates who teed up Milton, and he whipped the kick with deadly accuracy round the side of the wall into the spot where Ternent had signalled for Cennamo to stand.

Two minutes later and Cheltenham's fans, barely over celebrating the first goal, were in dreamland. Alsop and Naylor linked up on the left, and Naylor hooked the ball out to Milton, who cut back on to his right foot – usually reserved only for standing on – and the cross was on a plate for Alsop, who barely had to move his head to steer the ball past Cennamo. Five minutes of breathless action ended with a brilliant solo run from Alan Moore, who benefitted fully as Cheltenham's defence fatally stood off and allowed him to run through and score – game on again. More than once in the second half, Alsop proved his worth in his own box, helping out Duff, Banks and Co. as, for the majority of the time, Burnley were kept at arm's length.

After 67 minutes, a great trick by Alan Moore left Williams for dead and set Briscoe away down the left, but Ball sliced the cross wide, and Burnley came closer still after 72 minutes. Gareth Taylor broke into the box and fired low across Book, but the Robins' 'keeper's fingertips deflected the shot wide, and then minutes later he clutched Briscoe's 20-yard volley high to his right.

But Cheltenham always had the greater commitment, typified by some ferocious tackling, notably by Howells and Yates, and non-stop running from Alsop and Grayson, who replaced the limping Naylor on 53 minutes. The fourth official's signal of five minutes injury time annoyed the home support but revived Burnley's travel-ling hordes. However, this was to be Cheltenham's day.

So once again, records had tumbled. The club were through to the fifth round for the first time ever and again there was the tension of the draw, now with only sixteen teams. Again there was for some a sense of anti-climax when a major Premiership club evaded them – this time, the Robins would have to travel up the M5 to the West Midlands, and to West Bromwich Albion, another club with a proud history. Like the Robins' previous two cup opponents, they were currently challenging for promotion. Graham Allner wasn't too disappointed though:

I knew the area well of course, and I knew it would be close to being a sell-out and what the atmosphere might be like. Of course, you'd like to play one of the really big clubs, but as a consolation prize it was one of the best – better than going somewhere like Middlesbrough, which would have been a really long journey and a smaller crowd.

Lee Howells also looked on the bright side:

I think, yes there was a sense of anti-climax, and I must admit I thought that there would only be about 12,000 people there, but once I saw the gates they'd been getting and realised how many fans we would take, I changed my mind and thought that this was going to be good.

Between the fourth and fifth round ties the weather started to bite, helping to contribute towards a fixture backlog that would ultimately have a major impact on the season. The home game with Southend and the promotion battle at Mansfield were both called off – the former within an hour of kick-off as high winds and a torrential downpour left the referee with no choice but to postpone the match. Not that this affected the side, particularly away from home. After a two-week break following the Burnley game they warmed up for the fifth round by winning successive matches away from home – 2-0 at Exeter and 2-0 at Darlington. These results meant that going into the West Brom cup tie the Robins had won six League and Cup ties on the trot away from home, dating back to the Hinckley tie in early December. Only one goal had been conceded in these games. The manager recalls being absolutely delighted with the away form:

We were playing well, and not many teams were getting near us. I thought at York for instance we were sensational – Tony Naylor was unbelievable and it was good to put three goals past Alan Fettis because he's haunted us down the years. So I remember us playing really good football, and of course there was that mental strength again which we've already talked about.

Now a brief interlude to recognise a truly outstanding individual achievement. The win at Darlington on 12 February was achieved without Michael Duff, for a very good reason – the central defender, at Cheltenham since the age of sixteen but born in Belfast, was becoming the first Cheltenham Town player to play in a full international.

It was a massive surprise when it happened. Steve called me in one day and said that there was a game at Macclesfield for Sammy McIlroy against a Northern Ireland team and they wanted me to play in it. I hadn't really thought about playing for Northern Ireland, but I went and thought I played all right.

Then he called me in when the squad for the Poland game was announced and said I was in it, and I couldn't catch my breath for a moment – this was little Cheltenham Town and I was a Division Three player, and here I was going to play international football. Steve said that he had told Sammy McIlroy about me and that Sammy had watched me a couple of times and he must have liked what he saw.

Duff played for the last fifteen minutes against Poland – in slightly unusual circumstances, the match was played in Cyprus, perhaps slightly warmer than a February night in Belfast or Warsaw. Northern Ireland were well beaten, but never mind, Cheltenham Town now boasted a current British international on their books!

Meanwhile, the media circus descended on Cheltenham in droves ahead of the fifth round tie. The Robins were the last surviving Third Division side left in the competition, and Steve Cotterill's men found themselves in the limelight as potential giant-killers, and the possibility of becoming the first side from the bottom division of the Football League to reach the sixth round for many years. Inevitably, much of the attention was directed at the manager.

Paul Baker had a positive view on the publicity, even though much of it only raised the profile of his bright young manager.

I think if you've got a manager who's doing great things and is being linked with other clubs then that is a credit to Cheltenham Town Football Club, in much the same way as if our players are being linked elsewhere – it just means that people are linking positive things with the club which is always good.

Cheltenham Town's FA Cup Press day. Captain Chris Banks listens to manager Steve Cotterill.

West Bromwich 1 Cheltenham Town 0

They came, they saw, but although they could not conquer, Cheltenham Town did themselves proud at the Hawthorns on Saturday. The gallant Robins made West Brom, a team knocking on the door of the Premiership, scrap all the way for the last eight FA Cup place they have been looking for since 1982.

They came within a whisker of taking a shock lead when Adam Chambers' chest blocked Jamie Victory's goalbound 55th-minute header, but it was uphill all the way after Daniele Dichio headed home what proved to be the 64th-minute decider. West Brom's defence could teach Scrooge a thing or two about being miserly – only seven goals have gone past it this season and the Baggies are the masters of grinding out the 1-0 win.

At the other end, they had the game's quality performer in Jason Roberts. He was no stranger to Cheltenham's defence, who came across him in their Conference days when he was starting out at Hayes. But he was very different from the skinny, raw youngster of four years ago, having turned into a player of menace every time he gets the ball. He posted his intent from the off, a third minute charge into the box being snuffed out by Jamie Victory, and the Cheltenham defence always had their hands full with him. Antony Griffin may wake up with nightmares of Roberts twisting and turning towards him, but he deserves credit for sticking manfully to his task. He didn't allow Roberts many direct shots on goal, the one he did get was turned brilliantly away by Steve Book at his near post on the hour.

At the heart of the defence, Michael Duff oozed the confidence he has obviously gained from spending a week training alongside Premiership stars in the Northern Ireland squad. He looked at ease in this company and looked after Dichio well, with the help of his mentor and skipper Chris Banks, and Jamie Victory, who caused Albion problems when he looked to get forward.

Banks was at the centre of the game's greatest controversy after 20 minutes when Roberts snaked through and went down under the 36-year-old's challenge as he had Book in his sights. Referee Matthew Messias, whose fussiness was not conducive to helping the game flow, could have produced a red card, but opted for yellow.

Cheltenham visibly grew in confidence as the first half went on, with Mark Yates and Lee Howells giving as good as they got from Andy Johnson and Derek McInnes in midfield, while out wide, Lee Williams and Russell Milton pushed wing-backs Igor Balis and Neil Clement back. But Tony Naylor and Julian Alsop were forced to live off scraps by Darren Moore, Larus Sigurdsson and Phil Gilchrist, who protected Russell Hoult superbly.

Yates had a plausible penalty claim rejected in the first half after a foul by Gilchrist and Cheltenham forced a few corners and had a handful of long-range efforts as they showed they had not come to surrender tamely. After half-time,

Baggies boss Gary Megson had obviously asked for more from his side as they pressed Cheltenham back in the opening 10 minutes. But the Robins kept them at bay and Victory's chance fired a warning shot across the Baggies' bows.

It was credit to Cheltenham's dogged resistance that Megson felt the need to send on a third striker in Scott Dobie just after the hour mark, which forced Steve Cotterill to amend his shape with the introduction of John Brough in a three-man back line. The breakthrough finally came after 64 minutes when Johnson's quick free-kick put Balis in down the right, and he skinned Neil Grayson and whipped in a cross for Dichio to head home.

One goal has been enough for Albion on countless occasions this season and it was to prove the case again. Yates came closest to levelling matters with a 20-yard shot which Hoult – once a loan goalkeeper at Whaddon Road – tipped over. Dobie should have settled it but missed horrendously from six yards with six minutes left, and Albion only had to deal with a late flurry of Cheltenham pressure as they sent four men into attack before their masses could acclaim the win. Sportingly, they did not forget Cheltenham's part in the game, and the Robins fully deserved the standing ovation they got at the end from the 27,179 crowd, the largest ever to watch a Cheltenham Town fixture in their 106-year history.

In the event the match was narrowly lost, but Paul Baker enjoyed another big day out for the club:

We had a great day at West Brom – we were able to take loads of supporters, there was a great atmosphere and a big gate – not sure how many other cup matches in that round attracted over 28,000 spectators, and so nearly a result for us. It wasn't a great game, but we defended well, were difficult to break down and played well.

Lee Howells will never forget the game:

It was a fantastic stadium, and the noise was incredible – I was about 3-4 yards from Michael Duff during the warm-up and he couldn't hear what I was saying. I thought it was a great game, even though there wasn't much goalmouth action, and we did really well and could have got a draw.

What does Steve Cotterill remember about the day?

I remember Chambers chesting Jamie Victory's header off the line. I remember Dichio's header and that organisationally we could have done better at stopping the cross. I remember us playing very well – I thought we were unlucky not to have got a replay, and had we done so I would have really fancied us at our place. To get that far in the FA Cup, though, I don't think that will be equalled for a while.

With the cup run over, attention now was fully focused on the League. The Robins were by now in eighth place, just one point off a play-off place, which at that stage of the season appeared to be the focus of their ambitions. A combination of the cup run and inclement weather meant that they had four games in hand on some of their promotion rivals.

The first game after the cup adventure was to be a disappointment – Southend came to Whaddon Road and scrambled a draw thanks to a late goal by their player-manager Rob Newman. It was to be a familiar tale for the Robins, as a run of home draws would ultimately cost them dearly. In the final analysis, although only one home game was to be lost, no fewer that eleven of the other twenty-two home games would end all square. Graham Allner was frustrated:

It was a major disappointment because of the three points for a win system and the fact that a draw is two points lost really at home. I think some of it was down to a bit of pressure and fear because the crowd's expectation levels were getting higher, especially as we got closer to the end of the season, and I think the players felt that. However we only lost one all season at home, which is still a great achievement.

The match following the Southend game did bring a home win though. Hartlepool, starting to run into some form after a wretched start to the season, were beaten 3-0 as the unbeaten run continued. That night saw three more goals for the striking partnership – two for Naylor and one for Alsop. They had now scored a highly impressive 35 League and cup goals between them. Tony Naylor says that sometimes striking partnerships just work:

Every partnership takes time to develop, but we hit it off straight away and things just went on from there. Jules puts a lot of effort into his game and his goals were just reward for all he does for the team.

We were now into March, with the games coming thick and fast as the side began to play the backlog of games they had built up. Tuesday evening games were to be a fixture of the latter part of the season, and they had just one Tuesday off between 12 February and 26 March. Many of those Tuesday evening games were away from home, with the first two Tuesdays in March seeing the team at Bristol Rovers and Lincoln. Both games were won, extending the run of away League victories to a remarkable seven in succession, but the win at Bristol Rovers was a mixed night. Whilst a 2-1 victory, aided by Richard Walker's first goal for the club, was secured, one of the men who had been part of the rise from the beginning suffered a broken leg – Lee Howells:

I think everyone realised how much playing in Bristol would mean to me and I was really looking forward to the game. As for the injury, I just got caught, but as there was only a bit of bruising initially, I thought this might not be bad. They took me to Frenchay Hospital, which is only ten minutes from where I live and when I'd had the X-rays they said it was broken – a really frustrating time to get an injury like that.

The injury to Howells seemed at the time to be a hammer blow. Howells had formed a crucial central midfield partnership with Mark Yates, which had been instrumental in the success the Robins had achieved. In addition, central midfield was one area where there appeared to be limited cover. Inevitably Cotterill moved quickly, and by the time of the match at home to York City he had signed John Finnigan from Lincoln City to take Howells' place. Finnigan had started out at Nottingham Forest, but had played most of his football at Lincoln where he had played over 150 games for the club, scoring just 3 League goals, including one for Lincoln at Whaddon Road during Cheltenham's first season in the league.

Finnigan was to double his career goals tally in eight dramatic weeks; the first strike coming on his debut as York City were beaten 4-0 at home – the Robins' biggest ever League win, which kept the pressure on the clubs above them. Finnigan's second game though was to bring defeat – the first suffered by the side since 24 November at Oxford.

The long unbeaten run had to come to an end of course, but few expected it to finish at bottom club Halifax, and certainly not by a heavy defeat – the hosts won 4-1, even after Jamie Victory had given Cheltenham an early lead. It proved to be a false dawn for the Yorkshire side though, and at the end of the season, for the second time in under ten years, they were relegated to the Conference.

Steve Cotterill, meanwhile, was getting concerned about the tiredness factor. With the season due to finish on 20 April, the Robins faced nine matches in the final month of the campaign. Reinforcements were needed, and two loan signings were made – Nathan Tyson, a striker from Reading who was the spitting image of Thierry Henry, and midfielder Martyn Lee from Wycombe, via Cotterill's links with his old Wimbledon team-mate Lawrie Sanchez.

Four points from two home games, with Tyson scoring the winner against Kidderminster in the second of the two, kept the momentum going. However, the win was marred by an injury to Chris Banks. We weren't to know it then, but it was to finish the season for the club captain.

Easter Saturday appeared at the time to be a crucial day in the season. The Robins went to Glanford Park, Scunthorpe, one of the toughest places to go in the Third Division, and won 2-1, with goals by Alsop and Naylor. Equally importantly, Mansfield who had held third place for many weeks, but had suffered a number of recent reversals away from home, lost at home to a resurgent Rushden. Suddenly, Cheltenham were above Mansfield and were in third position – the last of the automatic promotion places. Steve Cotterill knew that Easter had often been a happy time for his sides.

I said to the lads that we'd always done well over Easter and I sent them back in time to the Rushden and Kidderminster games the year we won the Conference. I thought it was a little backs to the wall up at Scunthorpe, but we got the goals at important times and defended fantastically. I'm not sure we deserved to win it, but maybe we did – there were plenty of other games where we deserved to win and didn't, so it evens out.

On Easter Monday, Mansfield were at Luton. The match kicked off at lunchtime, so by the time that the Robins' home match against Hull City kicked off at the more traditional time of 3 p.m., we knew the score – Mansfield had lost again, 5-2 this time, and a win would mean a four-point cushion in third place. A win was exactly what was achieved, courtesy of a John Brough header in the second half. Now with five matches to go three wins would guarantee promotion. This was the situation after Easter weekend:

	P	W	D	L	F	A	PTS
Plymouth Argyle	42	28	8	6	63	27	92
Luton Town	43	28	6	9	90	48	90
Cheltenham Town	41	20	14	7	63	44	74
Mansfield Town	42	21	7	14	65	56	70
Rushden & D	43	19	12	12	64	48	69
Rochdale	42	18	14	10	56	47	68

Even allowing for the impressive away form, the one concern at this stage was the fact that of the five matches to play, four were away from home. The first of these was lost – 1-0 at Macclesfield. The unusually off-key visitors were beaten by a late Matthew Tipton goal, and with Mansfield beating Bristol Rovers on the same day the gap, was down to one point as the side prepared for the next game – at none other that Mansfield.

The away fixture at Mansfield was one that had looked important for a while, but mainly because supporters felt that in order to have any hope of automatic promotion Cheltenham would need to go there and win. The situation had changed markedly over the last couple of weeks – now it was Cheltenham holding on to the crucial third place. Paul Baker gave the board's view:

It was always going to be a huge game for us – we'd had a great run and caught up a lot of ground on them, and we were going up there to win and really put ourselves in the driving seat.

The atmosphere at Field Mill was electric. The kick-off was delayed for fifteen minutes to allow all the fans in the ground, and the large number of travelling Robins supporters was soon silenced by an early Chris Greenacre goal for the hosts. In a frenetic first half the visitors fought back well and were deservedly level by half time through Mark Yates, the new skipper due to the continued absence of Chris Banks. The second half was no less exciting but it was Mansfield who won it through a late goal by Andy White, and thus claimed a slightly fortunate victory. The manager thought his side were unlucky:

I thought at Mansfield we were as good in the first half as we had been for six weeks, so to not beat them up there was very disappointing. One of my strikers with me now at Stoke of course scored that night, and I haven't yet managed to have a five-a-side so I can give him a swift kick to remind him of that one, but I will do!

With three games to go, Mansfield were back in third place; however, Cheltenham still had their fate in their own hands, as although they were two points behind, they had a game in hand. On the penultimate Saturday of the season the table looked like this:

	P	W	D	L	F	A	PTS
Luton Town	44	29	6	9	94	48	93
Plymouth Argyle	43	28	9	6	63	27	93
Mansfield Town	44	23	7	14	69	56	76
Cheltenham Town	43	20	14	9	64	47	74
Rochdale	44	20	14	10	62	50	74

The final home League game of the season was against local rivals Oxford United, who themselves had enjoyed a dramatic climb through the League in the 1980s, but were now playing their first season in the basement division since the mid-1960s. A record League gate of 7,013 turned up to Whaddon Road to see a comfortable 2-0 win for the Robins, both goals scored in the first half. The second half of the match was fairly ordinary, but there was no shortage of atmosphere or excitement in the ground as the news came in of goals for York at home to Mansfield, as they ran out 3-1 winners. Now automatic promotion was very close – two points from the last two away games, at Carlisle in midweek and at Plymouth on the final Saturday of the season, would guarantee success.

Carlisle, as anybody who has been there will confirm, is a long way from Cheltenham (or indeed almost anywhere), yet over 400 supporters made their way up the M5 and M6 to see if a win could be secured to secure promotion. Sadly it wasn't to be, as the Cumbrian side were typically rugged and dogged in denying the Robins their three points. It finished 0-0 and is a game not fondly remembered by Graham Allner.

It was awful. Obviously they're a club with problems, and earlier in the day a youth team match had been played on the pitch, which meant the playing surface was terrible. I think the lads all thought that they had to win up there, and pressure can do some strange things to people, because it was an awful game – not one of our best.

The chairman remembered the sense of anti-climax:

We took a lot of fans because they all wanted to say they'd been there when we finally got promoted, it's a hell of a long way, and in the end it just didn't happen for us. The pitch was terrible and I suppose 0-0 was probably the right result on the night. But it was a long way home…

So, to Saturday 20 April and the final day of the full League season. The two matches that would matter for the final automatic slot were Plymouth *v.* Cheltenham and Mansfield *v.* Carlisle. The table stood as follows:

	P	W	D	L	F	A	PTS
Plymouth Argyle	45	30	9	6	69	28	99
Luton Town	45	29	7	9	94	48	94
Cheltenham T	45	21	15	9	66	47	78
Mansfield T	45	23	7	15	70	60	76

One of the things that many fans do when the fixtures come out is to look and see where the last game of the season is, and decide whether the team their side is playing is a good one to meet if points are needed, for whatever reason. When the fixtures had come out in the summer of 2001, there had always been a possibility that Plymouth away would be a very difficult match – somehow, despite two mediocre years in the Third Division, the Devon side would surely be too big a club not to make a promotion push soon.

That likelihood had turned into reality in spectacular fashion during 2001/02. The Argyle were already up, were already Champions, and had an outstanding home record, having won 19 out of 22 games since losing their opening two games at Home Park. Furthermore, they had only conceded four goals at home since the New Year started, and none at all since the end of February. The match against Cheltenham would be a huge celebration at the recently rebuilt Home Park, with a full house of 20,000 expected – all but 1,500 were there to see the Champions parading the divisional trophy.

Robins players, supporters and officials knew it would be tough. The team were tired after so many games and travelling and, despite some people hoping that the party atmosphere in Devon might cause the home side to be less focused, they were very aware that Plymouth would be going all out for three points to equal the record for the most ever points in a season in either the old Fourth Division or new Third Division.

The situation was simple. Assuming Mansfield beat Carlisle, which they were expected to do, then one point was needed. Defeat, and the play-offs loomed. Graham Allner remained optimistic:

Plymouth was always a big ask, but I had a sneaking feeling that we'd do it. We'd played some big matches during the season, and were used to a big atmosphere, and I thought that as they were already up they might get caught up in the celebrations – I really thought we'd do it.

Paul Baker adds:

You're hoping that because they're already up they won't be as focused on the game, but of course in the end, nothing could be have been further from the truth.

Steve Cotterill knew it was always going to be quite a test:

The last place you want to go to on the last day of season was Plymouth, because they were champions, and deservedly so, because they were the best side in it, and you knew there would be 20,000 screaming against you.

Home Park on 20 April brought a new meaning to the phrase 'sea of green'. Everywhere you looked there was green – flags, banners, scarves, wigs, and of course green seats in the impressive new stadium. The press had been told to arrive early, and as soon as the gates opened we were treated to an absolute cacophony of sounds from one of the loudest public address systems in the country as the party got under way. Sadly on the pitch the party was to continue.

It was very clear from an early stage that the Robins would not get any favours from Carlisle as Mansfield scored, like Plymouth, very early on, and were two up by half time, holding on for a comfortable win. The Stags were up; for the Robins it would be the play-offs.

Plymouth Argyle 2 Cheltenham 0

Cheltenham Town must pick themselves up for the play-offs after the crushing disappointment of missing out on automatic promotion on Saturday. The Robins never looked like being party-poopers at Plymouth's biggest celebration since Sir Francis Drake came back from sinking the Spanish Armada, but this was not where they lost their promotion chance. They can look back over 11 draws at Whaddon Road, away defeats at places like relegated Halifax and Macclesfield, and Tuesday's goal-less game at Carlisle, where the Robins dominated without making it count. Hartlepool now stand in the way in the two-legged semi-final on Saturday and Tuesday 30 April, but the Robins can claim their luck was out on Saturday. They had a mountain to climb anyway, with 18,000 Devonians in the impressive-looking stadium ready to acclaim the Division Three champions, but two early goals ended all hope. A draw would have been enough, had Mansfield failed to hit Carlisle for 10, but four minutes in and Cheltenham were behind. Graham Coughan picked out Ian Stonebridge down the left, he skinned John Brough and cut the ball back for the incoming Jason Bent to beat Jamie Victory to it and fire past Steve Book.

News came through immediately that Mansfield had scored an early goal, so things were looking bleak. The second goal summed up that it was not going to be Cheltenham's day. Paul Wotton's long ball was headed across goal by Lee Hodges, but it fell to Russell Milton at the far post. He tried to clear and the ball hit John Finnigan's head and spun back towards goal, where the spin made the ball like a bar of soap for Book, and he failed to gather it, with Coughlan nipping in to score. To rub it in, news came in of a second Mansfield goal. Cheltenham, with Finnigan the driving force in midfield, tried their hardest to get back into it, but they were confronted with a defence that has only let in 28 goals all season and a team hungry to put on a champion show for their fans. Michael Duff had a shot tipped round by the impressive French goalkeeper Romain Larrieu, then Victory's 30-yard shot was tipped onto the bar by Larrieu. Nathan Tyson's pace was introduced at the interval while Brough, who had a torrid first half, was replaced by Neil Howarth, but the green wall was not going to be breached. Alsop's fortune was out as he had several headed chances, with two being saved by Larrieu, who also blocked a Mark Yates effort. Cheltenham won 12 corners and had more on-target efforts than Plymouth, but it was all in vain as the final whistle sparked off Plymouth's party, but left Cheltenham to contemplate the play-off lottery.

Steve Cotterill cut a desolate figure as he tried to conduct a brief press conference after the match in a corridor. Usually an animated talker, there were long pauses, punctuated only by celebrating Plymouth fans walking past, as he tried to come to terms with the second last day disappointment in three seasons.

Going a goal down after four minutes was pretty desperate really, and then of course we were two down soon afterwards. But in the second half, after we changed our shape, we could have scored five. Larrieu pulled off three world-class saves, and we could have won the game. At the time you're driving home and you are very low.

I went in the dressing room afterwards and said: 'There are thirty-five of us in the dressing room now and thirty-four of you are waiting for me to say something, and I don't know what to say to you because whatever I say to you now you're not going to hear anyway'. So I said to them that tonight is the night to be disappointed because we've put so much into it, so be disappointed, because by this time next week we've got to make sure we're back up there.

So there we were, going back on the bus, and all the sayings go through your head. I'm depressed, the boys are depressed, but I'm paid to motivate them, not them to motivate me – so it's about who motivates the motivator, and that saying just kept going round in my head. I'm thinking, something has got to happen here, because I'm not going to wake up on Sunday and feel happy or as a fresh as a daisy, because we haven't made it. So I don't think that anyone ever motivates the motivator – I just think that the motivator is a certain type of person who is strong mentally and rehabilitates quicker than the others because he has to. So I rehabilitated on Sunday, that's what I set out to do, not to read the papers but to get ready for Hartlepool. I had to make sure that by the end of Sunday I was focused, and had let go of all the baggage and focus on the new competition – where by League table we were the best team, but on League form we were the worst team, so I had to get myself thinking about how to handle that.

The club captain can recall the day only too well. It's not a happy memory:

It was incredibly disappointing not to clinch promotion automatically. The atmosphere on the coach back home from Plymouth was shocking – nobody really said anything, and we had to somehow pick ourselves up for the play-offs. Steve deserves great credit for picking us up and getting us ready for the matches in the right frame of mind.

And so, to the play-offs – in February, not to mention early September, reaching them would have seemed a triumph. Now the team had to regroup, as Cotterill explained:

We had a chat on the Monday – they were all a little down, but I knew the first thing they would look at was how long my face was. So I went in as chirpy and bubbly as I could possibly be. The first person I saw was Neil Howarth, and he was low, so I said to him, hang on, I'm not having that. I waited for everyone to come in, and waited to see what happened. They didn't liven up straight away but after the session about Monday lunchtime things were starting to get better.

Lee Howells had of course been watching it all from the sidelines:

We'd played a lot of games and watching, you had a sense that we were limping to the end of the season. I wasn't sure how much was in the locker to be honest.

The play-offs had been a huge success since their introduction in 1987. They meant that clubs who had long ago given up on automatic promotion still had plenty to play for as the season neared its climax, bringing extra interest, excitement and revenue. By way of an example, on the last day of the Third Division season, as Cheltenham and Mansfield battled it out for automatic promotion, with the losers guaranteed a play-off place with Rochdale, who had already qualified, there were four other clubs trying to secure the last two places. Indeed, as we travelled down to Devon on that last day, we were struck not just by the number of red and white scarves going down the M5, but also the number of blue and white scarves in cars as well – Hartlepool fans going to Exeter, a round trip of around 700 miles, to see if their side could make it into a top seven finish.

In the end, those long distance fans would be smiling. Hartlepool's win, together with Shrewsbury's home defeat to Luton, meant that the Pools had made it. This was a tremendous achievement after a dismal start to the season – just 2 defeats in their last 20 League matches and five successive wins had transformed their season. They would play the Robins, while Rushden, another side who put together a great end-of-season run, would face Rochdale.

In many people's eyes, Cheltenham suddenly found themselves as underdogs for the two-legged semi-final, the first leg of which was to be played at Victoria Park, in the North East on the Saturday after the Plymouth match. The history of the play-offs is one that has often seen the 'in form' club come through – very often a club that has just squeezed into the end of season games wins through, whilst clubs who just miss out on automatic promotion miss cannot lift themselves. Paul Baker knew it would be difficult:

I thought it was a really tough draw for us – they were the form side, it was a long way to go to play a good side with a good manager, and obviously I don't think we could have been in the best state of mind given what we had been through in the previous week – you could almost feel it all going through your fingers.

So the Robins, together with around 600 of their fans, whose travel was subsidised by the board of directors as a gesture of thanks for the support during the season, got back on the road – Carlisle, Plymouth and now Hartlepool in under a fortnight. Relationships between the two clubs were very strong, driven by the close friendship Cotterill had developed with his opposite number, Chris Turner. The Robins also had a good record at Victoria Park – two wins and a draw in their three League visits, all achieved without a goal being conceded.

Hartlepool United 1 Cheltenham Town 1

Steve Cotterill won the tactical battle with his Hartlepool counterpart Chris Turner and gave Cheltenham Town a slight advantage going into Tuesday's play-off semi-final second leg at Whaddon Road. No-one – especially Turner – expected Cotterill to hand in a team sheet showing four changes from the side beaten at Plymouth last weekend.

It was a team chosen to do a specific job, and, thanks to Neil Grayson's 89th-minute equaliser, it worked. Cotterill left out John Brough, Lee Williams, Russell Milton and Tony Naylor and all four replacements were eager to make the most of their chance. At the back, Richard Walker was impressive alongside Michael Duff as he helped to make 18-goal Gordon Watson a spectator for most of the game. On the flanks, Martin Devaney had a lot of joy on the right against Mark Robinson and Martyn Lee played his part with the persistence to set up the equaliser. That goal came from Grayson, adding another crucial goal to the long list that the thirty-seven year old has contributed to Cheltenham Town's recent history came after a typical 110 per cent performance. There looked to be no danger when Chris Westwood tried to clear downfield, but Lee blocked the clearance and showed great presence of mind to find the unmarked Grayson to his left. He still had work to do, but kept his cool to fire his first goal since September past Anthony Williams and send the 600 travelling fans home happy.

The way Cheltenham lined up put the onus on Hartlepool to come out and break them down, and they were out of the blocks quickly. Watson skimmed a 2nd-minute header over from an Adam Boyd cross, but that was a rare opening for the experienced striker as he got away from Walker for once. Cheltenham settled and Grayson came close when a long ball from Antony Griffin was headed across goal by Alsop and Grayson hooked his shot over from 10 yards. Book was always commanding behind his back four except when Duff had to make a hasty clearance as he waited for Book to come out with Williams closing in. The Robins 'keeper regained his composure to field a high, dangling cross from Smith, and then came out well to cut out a dangerous Michael Barron centre after good link-up between Watson and Clarke.

Again, Cheltenham broke and came close to snatching a goal after 42 minutes. Alsop played an intelligent pass inside Robinson down the right and Devaney cut inside and got to the ball ahead of 'Pool goalkeeper Anthony Williams, but the ball rolled wide of the far post. Cheltenham fell behind on the stroke of half time as Barron crossed from the right and Eifion Williams planted his header wide of Book.

Cheltenham took the game by the scruff of the neck in the second half with Jamie Victory hitting the bar after 51 minutes when the ball spun to him as Robinson tried to clear a Duff header. A Cheltenham equaliser looked more likely than a second goal for Hartlepool, with Duff and Walker keeping Williams and Watson quiet, so much so that the latter was taken off. Midfield pair Boyd and Clarke were reduced to shots from distance with Cheltenham defenders throwing themselves bravely in the way. Devaney had a low cross palmed away by Anthony Williams, Yates sent a header wide and Grayson was denied by an Anthony Williams save, and it looked like 'Pool would hang on. But up popped Grayson, and now the equation is simple – a win on Tuesday will put the Robins into the final on 6 May at the Millennium Stadium. However, which starting eleven Cotterill will choose to look for that victory is anyone's guess.

The first shock to the Robins fans came with the team-sheet. There would be no Tony Naylor in the starting line-up as Cotterill went with a 4-5-1 formation, with Grayson and Devaney playing as the wide men in the five-man midfield alongside Lee, Finnigan and Yates. The manager explains:

I decided that I needed to change things a little bit because the 4-4-2 we had been playing had run out of steam a little bit. I suppose in my mind it wasn't just about four teams it was about four managers too, with me against Chris Turner and then, if we got to the final, me against John Hollins or Brian Talbot. At that point I decided to take Chris on, and that's what I did, because I'm sure he wouldn't have thought that there would have been no Russell Milton, no Tony Naylor and no Lee Williams on our starting team-sheet. So I thought if I can keep this under wraps, he'll have some work to do at 2 p.m. on Saturday and it would hopefully chuck a spanner in their works and throw them off track.

For most of the first 45 minutes it looked as if the record of not having conceded a goal at Hartlepool would be extended, as the Robins played well; however, just as the interval loomed the home side scored via centre forward Eiffon Williams, who signed from Torquay in March. However, the dressing room though was not despondent, as Graham Allner recalls:

It was obviously a bad time to concede a goal, but overall we as a management team were pretty upbeat and were accentuating the positives. It was a question of still believing in ourselves because we'd done OK.

The second half was again even and with the clock running down, it looked as if 1-0 would be the final score. But then, one of the most dramatic goals of the season occurred. Martyn Lee, playing in place of the injured Russell Milton, won the ball inside the Hartlepool half and sent Neil Grayson clear. The Robins striker calmly chipped the advancing goalkeeper to score the equaliser, sending the travelling contingent into raptutres – it was a great moment for the Robins legend.

Hartlepool United v. Cheltenham. Neil Grayson *(second from left)* celebrates his late equaliser.

Grayson:

I'd spent a long time on the bench during the season with Jules and Tony doing so well up front. I'd had a run in midfield but this was a more attacking role, a sort of half and half attacking and midfield role. I thought we'd done really well during the game and when the chance came, fortunately I was able to finish it off.

The chairman, Paul Baker, was equally delighted:

It was a great result for us – it meant that they had to come at us in the second leg and couldn't just sit back and defend so it set it all up for a really great game.

The final whistle soon sounded. It was a marvellous result for the visitors, who now firmly had the advantage going into the second leg the following Tuesday at Whaddon Road. Having spent much of the week lifting his players, the manager now had to try and ensure that his side kept their feet firmly on the ground.

Steve Cotterill:

I thought we played very well and to be honest that's when we won the tie. I actually thought we were the better team up there and they were the better team at our place.

The second leg was at Whaddon Road on Tuesday 30 April. The ground was, for the third time in the season, packed virtually to capacity – and full credit to the 1,000-plus Hartlepool supporters who made the trip. It was to be another roller-coaster night, and Graham Allner, for one wasn't surprised:

I think it's really difficult to play at home in the play-offs because the pressure is so great and the stakes are so high. The crowd have expectations and that transmits itself to the players, so I think we all knew that whilst the result was a great one up there, it would still be difficult.

After the game, the manager's first thoughts were for his friend Chris Turner:

I felt very sorry for Chris, because as I've already said, I thought they were the better side at our place. We'd obviously practised penalties and I'd always fancy Booky facing penalties. I thought our penalties were that night were fantastic – even the one Michael Duff missed, six inches either way and it's the best penalty of the night. So we saw off Hartlepool who were at the time the in form team.

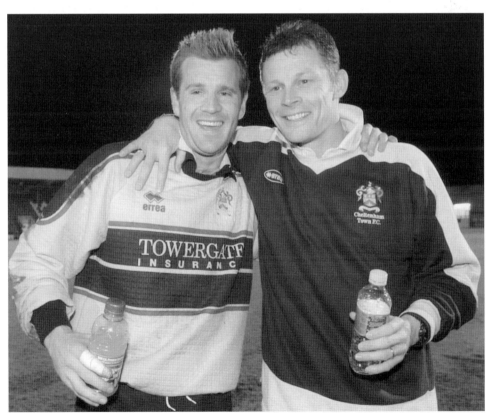

Cheltenham v. Hartlepool, Division Three play-off semi-final, second leg. Steve Book and Steve Cotterill.

The chairman found it no easier than anybody else:

We don't seem to do things the easy way, and the penalties are a lottery aren't they? When Michael Duff put his penalty wide you just think, perhaps it's not going to be our season. But then the crucial penalty of theirs – hitting the post and Steve Book – and for a moment there is just silence because nobody is quite sure about what's happened, and then we see the referee going no goal and you realise you're through.

So Cardiff it was to be, and a familiar foe awaited – Rushden & Diamonds, who had somewhat surprisingly overcome Rochdale in the other semi-final by winning 2-1 away at Spotland after a 2-2 draw in the first leg at Nene Park. The two rivals were to meet again in a match, arguably even more important than the Easter Saturday 1999 'Conference Decider'. As usual, the management team was full of respect for their opponents, as Steve Cotterill recalls:

So we've beaten the form team and now we have to play the side who are the second form team in Rushden. Everybody is thinking that we broke their hearts three years ago, now will it be their turn to beat us.

So, the town of Cheltenham geared up for a major final, for the second time in four years. This time, however, with only six days between semi-final and finall, logistics were certainly a struggle for football secretary Paul Godfrey. He recalls:

It was very difficult – we had to organise everything from tickets for disabled supporters to a police escort for the team in just six days. One of the big problems was finding a hotel for the team at such short notice, and of course everything was aimed at giving them the best possible preparation. There were also 15,000 tickets to sell for Cheltenham fans in a very short space of time, so it was very, very intense … but enjoyable!

The chairman prepared himself for another big day out:

I had a dream before the play-offs that we would get Rushden in the final, and they would get one back on us, and that Brett Angell, with all his Cheltenham connections, would get a goal. Again, going into that game Rushden were the form side, especially Lowe, what a player – he shouldn't be in the Third Division. They were scoring goals as a team left, right and centre. I personally thought that this was going to be a really difficult game – they were the favourites, they'd peaked at the right time whereas perhaps we'd overpeaked.

If there was to be one downside of the Cardiff trip, it was that two of the players who had been there from the start of the Cotterill era would miss the match because of injury – Lee Howells and Chris Banks. Lee Howells summed up the feelings:

Cheltenham Town 1 Hartlepool United 1

The Cheltenham Town fairy story will roll into Cardiff on Monday after another dramatic night at Whaddon Road. The Robins will face Rushden & Diamonds, their old non-League foes, at the Millennium Stadium with a place in Division Two up for grabs. The Robins prevailed after 210 minutes of passionate play-off fare, but Hartlepool can feel justifiably hard done by after dominating for large spells last night. Paul Arnison deservedly fired them in front after 17 minutes but Lee Williams' blockbuster nine minutes later levelled things up.

That's the way it stayed for the remaining 94 minutes, resulting in that most unsuitable way of deciding a football match, the penalty shoot-out. Neil Grayson and Paul Smith converted the first one for each side, then Martyn Lee scored for the Robins, but Paul Stephenson blasted his over for 'Pool. Mark Yates gave Cheltenham a 3-1 advantage before Arnison kept his cool to make it 3-2. Michael Duff then put his wide and Kevin Henderson squared things up at 3-3. John Finnigan and Gordon Watson traded kicks before Julian Alsop made it 5-4 for the Robins. Then came the defining moment as Richie Humphreys' kick hit the bar, struck Steve Book's leg, hit the post and bounced out. The capacity crowd held its collective breath before referee Andy Hall signalled the ball had not gone in and the celebrations began.

But it was Hartlepool who started the brighter. Graeme Lee put a header wide and Arnison and Stephenson drove just wide from distance as Chris Turner's side looked for the perfect start. They deserved it, and the goal finally came after 17 minutes when Stephenson's free-kick was headed out to Arnison, who hammered his shot under Book. Cheltenham were woken out of their slumbers and forced a brilliant equaliser. Lee Williams, back in the side after being left out of the first leg, cut in from the right and hit a scorching left-footer in off the underside of the bar. Duff had an effort deflected for a corner two minutes later after Jamie Victory touched a Russell Milton free kick to him. At the other end, a huge Anthony Williams goal kick was touched by Watson to Eifion Williams, but Richard Walker was there to deflect the shot wide.

The two sides were trading blows with Milton firing a free kick inches over and Book spilling a Stephenson drive. Hartlepool continued to take the game to Cheltenham after the break, and Darrell Clarke put a good 57th-minute chance over. Three minutes later Watson, as good last night as he had been bad in the first leg, forced Book into a save. Tony Naylor had been well shackled by 'Pool, but sent a header wide after 63 minutes. Both sides could have won it in the closing stages, Arnison driving over and Duff having a header deflected wide, but extra time beckoned. Grayson shot over in the first minute for Cheltenham, Alsop sent a header over and Martin Devaney nodded wide, but Clarke sent another shot off target as Hartlepool's threat remained. But penalties it was, and for Cheltenham there was joy, and for Hartlepool, the ultimate despair.

Cheltenham Town 3 Rushden & Diamonds 1

The adventure which started at Sittingbourne some five and a half years ago will roll into Swindon and Bristol City next season after Cheltenham hit new heights at the Millennium Stadium. The Robins will take their place in Division Two next term after brushing aside their former non-League rivals in comprehensive style. Man of the match Martin Devaney, an inspired selection ahead of the injured Russell Milton, set the ball rolling after 27 minutes, and not even the shock of conceding a goal immediately to Paul Hall could shake the Robins. They took complete control after the break, with Julian Alsop's 26th goal of the season after 49 minutes and John Finnigan's 79th-minute strike putting the gloss on another great day for the club.

The Robins came into the game reeling from the disappointment of missing out on automatic promotion, but they picked themselves up in style. Rushden, looking for their second successive promotion, started well but wilted as the game went on. In Jamaican pair Onandi Lowe and Hall, they had two dangerous attacking threats, who showed up well early on, but were anonymous after the break. That was down to Cheltenham's battling, with Michael Duff and Richard Walker solid in defence, backed up by Antony Griffin and Jamie Victory, both of whom grew in confidence as the minutes ticked by. Finnigan and Mark Yates snapped away in midfield, while Lee Williams and Devaney probed down the flanks to maximum effect.

Alsop was a colossus up front, with the terrier-like Tony Naylor never giving the Rushden back four a rest. The nerves were evident early on, and it was Rushden who opened the brighter of the two sides. Lowe, whose dazzling goal earned Rushden a draw at Whaddon Road in March, was prominent, and after ten minutes he tricked his way down the left. Victory skimmed the cross away, and Tarkan Mustafa was unable to retrieve the situation. Then Lowe was at it again two minutes later, feeding Hall, and when Victory slipped, Hall jinked into the box, beat Yates, but sliced his shot wide. That seemed to wake Cheltenham up, and they forced a couple of corners on the 15-minute mark, then Devaney skipped into the box and fired just wide after shrugging off two challenges.

Steve Book, immaculate all afternoon, came to the rescue six minutes later. Hall was again the instigator, beating the offside trap on the right and crossing into the box towards Lowe. The ball did not reach him however, as Stuart Wardley burst through and forced Book into an instinctive save. That stop was even more valuable three minutes later as Cheltenham took the lead, in slightly bizarre style. Devaney, clearly desperate to make an impact on the big stage, cut in again from the left and looked to find Alsop. Garry Butterworth got there first and touched the ball back towards goal, where Devaney was waiting to slip the ball in from a narrow angle. However, the celebrations were still rampant when Rushden levelled. From the kick-off, Hall ran through, leaving Victory, Yates and others in his wake before clipping his shot over Book.

Those goals really ignited the contest, and the sides shared chances for the remainder of the half. Billy Turley saved a Devaney header, while Book blocked a Lowe effort with his legs and Wardley and Stuart Gray tested the Robins 'keeper's handling, which was not found wanting. Cheltenham had not let losing their lead affect them, and came out with new purpose after the break. Four minutes in, they grabbed the lead again. Williams set Griffin away on the right, and the young full-back burst clear. He had the presence of mind to lay the ball back to Williams, whose cross found Alsop's head in the box. Naylor went for the loose ball with Andy Tillson, and it broke to Alsop, who was left with the simplest of tasks to tap home. With that, the confidence seemed to ooze through the Cheltenham ranks, and drain out of Rushden. Alsop headed a Williams corner wide soon afterwards, and Naylor fired a shot over. On the hour, Victory's cross was cleared to Devaney, and his dink to the far post was nearly turned in by Naylor.

Rushden boss Brian Talbot sent on former Robins striker Brett Angell and Jon Brady in an attempt to change the game, but it had little effect. Brady blasted two free kicks over, then Hall had a rare second-half run, but Book was there again to avert danger. Devaney, his work done, was replaced to a rapturous roar by Neil Grayson, and he had an instant impact by setting up the all-important third goal. Naylor found him in space on the left, and he lashed a shot against the bar. The rebound fell to Finnigan, and he still had work to do, but managed to curl his shot wide of Turley. That ensured the party could start, and it might just go on until 10 August.

It was very upsetting to miss out, but you've just got to get on with it and get behind the rest of the lads. I think I was lucky in that I'd been part of loads of other great days, so it wasn't like I'd missed out on the one big day ... but I'd have loved to have played.

Chris Banks recalls that despite having been out since late March he was close to playing:

I was nearly fit – it was actually touch and go for the play-offs as a whole, because I was almost over the knee injury. I trained perhaps a couple of days earlier than I should have done and tore my calf muscle on the opposite leg to the injured knee. Another week and I would have made it.

There were mixed views about the likely outcome amongst fans. Rushden were one of the real form sides who had had a marvellous run in the second half of the season. They were scoring plenty of goals, mainly through Jamaican World Cup star Onandi Lowe, who had scored for fun towards the end of the season, including a superb individual goal at Whaddon Road when the sides drew 1-1 in early March. They would clearly be very dangerous opponents. However, having seen one form side off in Hartlepool, some fans were confident that the team would rise to the occasion.

Cheltenham v. Rushden, Division Three play-off final. Neil Grayson's shot hits the post.

Cheltenham v. Rushden, Division Three play-off final. Martin Devaney celebrates scoring.

Cheltenham v. Rushden, Division Three play-off final. John Finnigan celebrates.

Cheltenham v. Rushden, Division Three play-off final. Steve Cotterill appears on the scoreboard shortly after Julian Alsop had restored the Robins' lead.

Cheltenham v. Rushden and Diamonds, Division Three play-off final, Michael Duff in action.

The team almost picked itself. Richard Walker had done an excellent job in central defence against Hartlepool alongside Michael Duff, and would keep his place for the final. Naylor and Alsop would link up together up front, as they had done for most of the season. John Finnigan had slotted into Lee Howell's central midfield role alongside Mark Yates, and Lee Williams would play in his regular position on the right. The only question was who would play on the left side of midfield.

Sadly it wouldn't be Russell Milton, who became another of the longer serving players to miss out through injury. That left three candidates: loan signing Martyn Lee, veteran striker Neil Grayson, who had filled in that position when Milton had been injured earlier in the season, and Martin Devaney, who had performed impressively against Hartlepool, but had played relatively little first-team football. In the end, Devaney got the nod. It was to be an inspired choice by the manager.

Says Cotterill:

I just decided to play a bit differently because the pitch was bigger – to play Lee Williams a bit wider and a bit further forward than we would have our midfield players normally and to play Martin wide as well, which I think made it a good, open game.

So all roads, and all railways made their way to Cardiff. The BBC Radio Gloucestershire team left Gloucester at 8.45 a.m. – the train was full of red and white and most peoples were having to stand. Once in Cardiff, it was evident that red and white would heavily outnumber the white, red and blue of Rushden – around the stadium, even at 12.00, when the press were admitted, Cheltenham fans were clearly there in larger numbers. In the end there were to be around 15,000 Robins supporters in a final gate of 24,368. They were to have another day to remember.

It was a magnificent afternoon, in a magnificent stadium. The atmosphere with 25,000 fans was so good, it made you wonder what 72,000 would sound like.

Afterwards the players celebrated, none more so than Neil Grayson, who had come so close to scoring:

Playing at Cardiff was a great experience. I must admit I thought I'd scored – when I hit it the ball seemed to go in slow motion and I thought it was going in, but it hit the bar. I would have loved it to have gone in, but fortunately it fell to John Finnigan, who finished it off superbly.

It was to be the last game for the Robins for the popular forward, who moved to Forest Green Rovers during the summer of 2002.

There have been just so many great memories, and I'm just grateful to have been part of it all. I got really well with supporters, although I've always got on with the fans, wherever I've played, because I think they appreciate the fact that I'll always give 100 per cent, even when I don't feel well or have a slight injury.

Tony Naylor was the one Robins player who had experienced the atmosphere before:

It was a fantastic day out, and everything about the day was great. I feel very fortunate to have been there twice now and won twice, and to go up that way was the best way possible – it's such a great stadium and experience.

Chris Banks, while disappointed not to play, still had a good day:

It was a great weekend – Steve went out of his way to make sure everybody was involved. The lads wanted me to pick up the trophy even though I hadn't played and I was really pleased about that – I thought it was a great gesture by them.

The chairman had enjoyed his afternoon:

We played out of our skins, played really good football and deserved our result – the whole day was just fantastic.

Graham Allner felt that experience gained during the season had played its part:

The performance got us the result we deserved, and I think that the games against Burnley, West Brom and Plymouth really helped because they made us able to handle the occasion better than perhaps they did.

As for the manager, who received a huge ovation from the massed banks of fans in the 'lucky' end of the ground, it was a very satisfying end to a long campaign:

I thought we scored a good goal through Martin but then they scored straight away, and I felt that was the only time, that fifteen minutes before half time, that we lost our way.

We didn't lose our way for football reasons – the grass was the same colour, the ball was the same shape, the stadium was the same – no, we lost it mentally for fifteen minutes because we were in denial. We'd worked all that time, twenty-six or twenty-seven minutes, to get in front, got our noses in front and then lost it. One thing I'll now tell any side who score at the Millennium Stadium is to stand still when you celebrate, because we went running off all over the place, and when they kicked off there were three or four of our players with their hands on their knees thinking about the goal – all of a sudden they're in behind our midfield and its like Moses parting the back four and we're all over the place. So when I look back at half time speeches or talks, the one I had at the Millennium Stadium was one of my best, and the main crux of it was that they had to let go of that equaliser and stop feeling sorry for themselves. I said to them if they had been given a half-time score of 0-0 or 1-1 they would probably have taken it, and said OK, we've got 45 minutes to play and we know we'll be fitter than most teams we play.

So it was about stopping them looking back, and getting them to move forward. To be fair, once we'd finished our chat they went back and I knew when they were going back out through the door they were going to win because their body language had completely changed from the time they came in. As I left the dressing room I felt confident and I felt a winner.

In the second half you could have cut the halfway line off, because apart from the last five or six minutes when we're 3-1 up and they had a couple of half chances, we dominated. As Brian Talbot said, to be fair to him when he congratulated us, we were deserved winners.

That is the best way to get promoted, financially and emotionally. You get nothing for finishing second or third whereas in the play-offs you get the money, the chance to play at the Millennium and the chance of a medal and have something tangible to show for your efforts.

At the end of the game, when we had the trophy and we were going round the pitch, the stewards were great because they were telling us that we could stay out for as long as we wanted to, so that we and our supporters could enjoy the day. I

Cheltenham v. Rushden, Division Three play-off final. Steve Cotterill celebrates the win.

Cheltenham v. Rushden, Division Three play-off final. Cheltenham celebrate promotion.

remember someone giving me the trophy around the halfway line, and I walked down to the end to show the fans the cup and to have some photographs taken. I realised as I did that, that it was my last game. I think it was the best time ever to leave because there were so many people to wave to and thank – it was a really special day.

It had been a great day for the press as well. We had, like the players, officials and supporters found out how the other half live – and had a great view of the match sat up high in the virtually deserted West Stand. Both of us had been trained never to show emotion in a press box; as the goals went in, we're pleased to say that we completely ignored this training and the goals were greeted with as much enthusiasm as by any fan behind the goal. The fact that one of us was on air commentating at the time merely added to the fun.

The impossible had happened. Cheltenham were in Division Two, Instead of playing Sittingbourne and Bashley, they would be playing Swindon and Barnsley.

7

A New Beginning
2002

In truth, the real interest of the many members of the National Press gathered at Steve Cotterill's post match press conference after the play-off triumph was not so much Cheltenham's promotion, but the future employment of the manager.

Speculation had been rife since the spring that Cotterill might leave at the end of the season, with Portsmouth the favoured destination. It was the latest in a long line of rumoured or actual job offers for the manager, which started shortly after he got the job at Whaddon Road. As for Cotterill he always knew that success at Cheltenham would keep others interested in him, and keep him in the limelight:

I had a number of job offers, and it was difficult to turn them down, as I'm very career-orientated and very single-minded and confident of where I want to go and what I want to do. I take my football very seriously, but the right career move was going to come along, and I just didn't think that the right club at the right time came along.

Approaches came fairly thick and fast during Cotterill's five years at the club. The man himself is a man of very strong principles and ethics and, to his enormous credit, he is reluctant to discuss individual approaches, preferring that they should remain private between him and the clubs concerned. However, it would be a safe bet to say that the number of inquiries was well into double figures by the time he did leave. The first inquiry came as early as the first Conference season. This inquiry, like a number of others, didn't make the press, but Paul Baker, by now chairman, was getting used to telephone calls about what was arguably the club's most prized asset.

We've got to where we are partly on the back of Steve Cotterill's personal ambition. I think it's fair to say that he always saw this club as a stepping stone for his career, and I think we recognised that, and weren't short-sighted enough to think that he would be here for ever – one day he was going to move on and we would thank him very much for all he's done and wish him all the best. It was always going to be a question of when, not if. The first one I remember was Hull City – we had a long chat about that and were able to persuade him to stay, and able to hold on to him.

Whilst fans were privately speculating on whether Cotterill might be approached after any number of jobs became vacant, and the press were always happy to run stories that fuelled that speculation, there was nothing concrete as far as the average fan was concerned until the second Conference season. Then, in October 1998, the Swindon Town job became vacant. Paul Baker remembers:

The Swindon approach was all done properly – I had a formal approach from their vice-chairman to ask to speak to Steve, but in the end he didn't get the job and it went to Jimmy Quinn.

The next public link was Oxford United in the autumn of 2000. This time, the job was Cotterill's if he wanted it, but again he chose to stay, as Paul Baker recalled:

I think we came very close to losing Steve then – he thought long and hard about that one, and they made him a really good offer, but in the end we persuaded him to stay.

However, as Cheltenham progressed, it became more and more likely that the manager would leave when the right job came along, and the players accepted that this was likely to be the case. Graham Allner knew that Cotterill wouldn't be around forever:

We all knew that the time was coming to move on, because he's very ambitious, and given how long he'd been at the club, the time was coming to make that next move,

Cheltenham Town manager Steve Cotterill (left) and chairman Paul Baker after announcing that the manager will not be moving to Oxford United.

which I think is very understandable really – he needed to move to another club which could help him get to where he wants to go – which is obviously the Premiership.

By the time of the cup run of 2001/02, Cotterill was one of the hottest management properties around. His network with some high profile managers was excellent, and he had been recognised by the FA as being one of the brightest young managers around when they selected him to do the UEFA Pro B coaching licence. It seemed to be not a case of whether the manager would leave but when, with the end of the season, irrespective of what happened to the team on the pitch, being the most likely time.

As the 2001/02 season moved towards a close, Portsmouth appeared to be the most likely destination, and there were a number of stories to this effect which ran in the press. Much of this was based on the manager's well-known friendship with the Portsmouth director of football, Harry Redknapp, who had taken over as manager on what appeared to be a temporary basis after the sacking of Graham Rix. Then Redknapp seemed to have been given the job on a full-time basis, which meant that any role for Cotterill would have to be as an assistant, which was perhaps less likely at this stage of his career. Paul Baker says this was all just speculation.

We never had an official approach from Portsmouth and I think it was a case of a lot of people putting two and two together, because of where he lived and Harry Redknapp and all that.

By the time of the play-off final, the interest in the manager's future was at an all-time high. Fans and press speculated whether Cardiff would be his last game in charge. Indeed, at the post-match press conference after Cheltenham's memorable win, there were more questions about the manager's future than about the game itself.

As one would expect from a man of great integrity, Cotterill was honest about the situation, telling the assembled gathering (a fair few more than the usual rabble who gathered for his post-match conferences in the tunnel at Whaddon Road) that he simply didn't know whether he would be Cheltenham's manager for their first match in Division Two.

In fact, out on the pitch earlier, as he was to subsequently realise when he reflected on the day, the decision had become clear. He would be moving on, as he now explains:

I've already said that it was as I was showing the trophy to the fans at the Millennium I think I realised I would be moving on, but I didn't know where to. I knew of Portsmouth and Wimbledon's interest, but I hadn't spoken to them during the season because that would have been unethical. At that stage I didn't know of Stoke's interest of course. Things moved quickly after the Cardiff victory, as Paul Baker recalls:

I had calls from the chairman of Stoke and the chairman of Wimbledon, both of them asking for permission to speak to Steve. We've always said that we would never stop our manager speaking to other clubs, so Steve spoke to them both and in the end chose Stoke.

So on 27 May, three weeks to the day since the play-off final triumph, came the announcement that all connected with Cheltenham knew would one day happen. The manager, one of the longest-serving managers of all 92 League clubs was leaving. After five glorious years, an era was over – it was a difficult decision for the manager, but one he is sure was right.

I just think that coming to Stoke was the right career move for me. It's a great club, a big club and the time was right for me to leave Cheltenham. The fan base here is massive – I mean we had 4,000 for a pre-season friendly with Newcastle Town and only about a dozen of them didn't have a red and white replica shirt on! It's a working-class area, similar to where I grew up in Cheltenham and yet everyone will have a replica shirt, no matter how long it takes to save up to buy one. The stadium is magnificent, when you see it close up it is just really impressive.

Whilst excited by the Stoke challenge – when we met him over the summer he was just into pre-season training – part of Steve Cotterill, Cheltenham-born and bred, will always be with the club.

There was always a risk going back to your home town – there will be people in the town who know you from school, and of say ten people, not all of them are going to like you and some of them will want you to fail. So it was always big pressure to do things in your home town and I felt that throughout the five years, and I just feel that when it's your home town it does make it more special, because I will be remembered now in my home town for what I've done, helping put Cheltenham Town on the football map.

Graham Allner found out his boss was leaving whilst on holiday:

Steve called me before I left for holiday to tell me that he was talking to Stoke, and then when I was in Spain I saw on Sky News that he had taken the job. He called me that night and we had a long chat about what had happened. I've got a lot to be thankful to Steve for – he helped me when I was low after leaving Worcester and he picked me up and gave me the opportunity to recharge my batteries.

Mike Davis was expecting Cotterill to go:

After Cardiff, I knew the time was right for him to go. I knew he would be given opportunites to go to big clubs after we won there, and I knew he would take them. I think this was because his record at Cheltenham was unblemished and now will be so for ever – no-one can take that away from him.

Chris Banks wasn't surprised:

Everyone expected him to leave sooner rather than later, and I think it was probably a good time for him to leave in terms of his career. I wasn't surprised and I'm sure he'll do well at Stoke.

Graham Allner, Cheltenham Town's new manager, trains with the team at the Eagle Star playing fields.

Jamie Victory only has good wishes for his former manager:

Division Two was another challenge for him and I thought he might stay so I was a little surprised when he went, but Stoke is a big club and no-one can begrudge him going. We all owe him a lot. For me personally, he improved my game and my stature as a person as well, and I looked up to him a lot.

Paul Baker reflects on his now ex-manager:

I think much of his success is down to his personal ambition and drive. He is totally, totally focused on the job in hand. He is a great motivator – I think he's learnt a lot from his Wimbledon days on that, and he has this personal character which means he is very committed to anything he does. He also has great attention to detail.

I think the big thing though is in the dressing room, it's like one big family – wherever we go, all the squad go, even though the board used to moan about that on away trips from time to time. He treats everyone the same – no prima donnas – and ensured they all got on together.

The relationship with Steve wasn't always easy, but the fact that we are opposite characters made it work – we never quite knew how he would be, he could be very up one moment and down the next. I shall miss him and I wish him well and hope we keep in touch.

The question was who now? The board were inundated with applications; if you consider that at any one stage only ninety-two men can manage a League club, there will always be some good managers not currrently in employment. Paul Baker recalls:

We didn't actually advertise the job at any stage, but given the rumours about the Portsmouth situation, we had been getting letters for several months from agents of out of work managers enquiring about the manager's position at Cheltenham Town. Once it was announced that Steve was going, and remember we never advertised the job, we've had thirty applications, from some very high calibre managers. I don't think it's fair to name them, but some of the quality of managers was a real eye opener about how far the club had come. When we appointed Steve I think we had a shortlist of three!

However, the board already knew the man they wanted. Paul Baker continues:

What was really important was continuity. Graham knew all the players, he had the respect of all the players, which is very important, and to a man all the players have been very supportive. I think the continuity thing is so important, because being in the Second Division is a big thing, and changing managers is a big thing, and what you don't want to be doing is bringing in someone from outside who doesn't know what he's got and wants to bring in his own backroom staff, possibly bring in some players and get rid of others – you just don't need all those changes. Graham's got the managerial ability and coaching skills to do a very good job for us.

The man himself had already been tipped off that he was in the frame:

When I spoke to Steve the night he took the Stoke job, he told me that the chairman had been trying to get hold of me, and it was all sorted out very quickly really once I got back.

So, on 30 May, just three days after Cotterill had left, Cheltenham had a new manager. Allner had been denied the chance to manage in the League when Kidderminster, having won the Conference under his management in 1994, were denied entry to the Football League because their ground wasn't up to standard. He had wondered whether he'd ever get another chance. Now, at fifty-two, he would be a manager in Division Two.

I didn't really have to think too much about whether to accept the job, because I've been here for two and a half years now – I get on well with the players and know how the club is run. A lot of people have called and told me that I deserve it after what happened at Kidderminster and us not getting into the League because of off-field problems, but I guess I don't see it like that – you can't look back in life. I'm quite philosophical about these things and I just want to be as good as I can be – and if I do that, then I'm confident I'll succeed.

So one era ends, and another begins. In 2002/03, Cheltenham's local derbies will not be against Gloucester City, or Bath City, their more traditional local rivals, but against Swindon Town and Bristol City. There is no doubt that the step up presents a major challenge for all at the club – just to remind anybody who might doubt that, when the fixture list came out for the new season, the team's opening fixture would be at home to Wigan, whose resources run to spending over £1m on a single player at the end of the 2001/02 season. However, the recent story of Cheltenham is one of triumph over adversity; we can be sure that whatever happens there is plenty more to be written about the remarkable story of the club from the Cotswolds.

Perhaps the final words should go to the three men charged with leading the Robins on the latest stage of their adventure. Firstly, Chris Banks:

I don't see why we shouldn't establish ourselves in this division – of course it's going to be tough, because we're not the biggest club, and everybody recognises that. But I do think though that we can build on what we've done and have a good season.

The new manager has clear goals:

I'd like to think that we could establish ourselves as a Division Two club, and not just survive. Look at Wycombe Wanderers – look how they've established themselves. [At this point the interviewer asks if that meant that the manager was setting his sights on an FA Cup semi-final appearance to match Wycombe's achievement, only to be reminded that the Robins were only two rounds away this season.] I think that we have to organise ourselves to keep progressing and keep getting more from players. I think what is important is that the club in general, and the board of directors in particular, have done a great job in keeping up with what's been happening on the field off the field – I know to my cost from when I was at Kidderminster how important that is. It's inevitable that the steep curve that the club has been on will flatten as we find our feet at a new level ... but then everyone said that when we got into the Third Division and look what happened.

Finally, the chairman:

I'm looking forward to the future. It is the end of era, which I think is inevitable when a manager has been there a long time – and five years is a long time. It's a new era now but it's the same bunch of players, the same board, and the same ethos at the club. Why shouldn't we continue to do well?

By the time this book is published, you will know how the latest instalment of the Robins' journey is shaping up. There is no doubt that Division Two will be another major step up, and will present huge challenges. It's a big ask, but that was what was said about the Conference and Division Three – don't bank on this remarkable story not having a few more twists to come!

Epilogue

As Cheltenham enter a new era under the management of Graham Allner, it is probably a good time to reflect on the five years under Steve Cotterill, and to try and understand what it was that led to such a remarkable run of success.

That success is arguably more significant because of the lack of major achievement at the club previously – this was no returning of a club to its 'former glories' or 'rightful place'. As a reminder, the club had previously had a highest ever league placing of eleventh in the Conference. There was little sense of football history in the town. To try and draw a parallel, this is the equivalent of, say, Rochdale regaining their position in the Second Division, winning promotion to the First Division for the first time, and then going on to win the First Division play-off final to end up in the Premiership. So why did it happen?

Let's start with Arthur Hayward, the long-serving board director who has been at the club since the early 1980s. How does he explain the last five years?

Perhaps I'm being biased, but I think it starts at the board – if you don't get it right there, then you're in trouble. We've been very selective about who we've invited to join the board – they've got to be a football fanatic, and be prepared to be hands on. No member of the board takes any money out of the club – we all pay our own way on away trips for example – so we're non-paid directors and we see ourselves as being very approachable to the fans. Getting things right off the field is really important.

Then of course, the appointment of the manager is a key task and we have been really lucky with Steve. There is no doubt in my mind that we would not have got to where we are today without him – his outstanding managerial talent and his ability to inspire others. Don't forget Lindsay Parsons from a management point of view either – he signed a lot of the players that Steve was given to start with, and then Steve really developed them. John Murphy helped us get back on our feet in the 1980s – he was a great guy, and what's not generally known is that when times were tough financially he went weeks without talking a salary.

But Steve was key – and I'd like to think it was a two-way thing in terms of the relationship. He used to tell us where he thought we were going wrong and gave us help in the off-field developments, and I think we helped him find his feet as well. At the end of the day, we were all in it together – players, management, the board, supporters. We don't have prima donnas here and we all work together.

Paul Baker joined as the rise continued. What are his thoughts?

In the early days, I think it was down to being able to spend a reasonable amount of money on some quality players which made the difference between our team and other teams. That, combined with the undoubted managerial skills of Steve Cotterill, who moulded a bunch of players into a really good working outfit made a real difference. Going forward, again it was the motivational skills of Steve, coupled with the continual backing of the manager by the board in terms of investment in players. It's been having a good backroom, having good support in terms of training facilities from the University of Gloucestershire, and good facilities at the ground. We've looked after our players in terms of pre-season tours, and in some cases mid-season tours.

Overall though, it's been about this sense of togetherness and I think being one big happy family as a club – we have had no prima donnas – a good bunch of lads, working hard, good management and good backing.

Director Colin Farmer paints an interesting perspective of the board's role in the rise:

We're all fans – I mean I've supported Cheltenham since the Southern League cup win against Gravesend in 1957/58. We work as a team though, and we try and help the players and manager as much as we can – there's no us and them mentality here and the players will even occasionally buy us a drink from the kitty! The board go to every game, home and away – I shall never forget going to one club in the League and finding out that their board didn't travel to away games – they took it turns to be the 'duty director' who was the one who went away. Why would you do that? I mean, we all love our football at the club and we want to watch it!

How about the manager – what does he think accounts for the run of success?

A good collective spirit, a good work ethic and a good team – not just the football team but everyone at the club – the chairman, the directors, the office staff, the kit-man, the tea ladies, the manager, the players, all the way to the supporters. It was just a good team – we all rowed the boat in the same direction and if someone got tired someone took over. Everybody believed in the man next to them and we all worked together.

As success developed, he was of course joined by the man who would be his successor. Graham Allner had been very successful in his own right at Kidderminster. What are his relections?

It's a combination of factors really. Steve is obviously key, but so is the contribution of Paul Baker and the board of directors. The supporters have responded so the gates have gone up which has helped. We've had a great work ethic – everyone gets on and does their bit and we all pull together, so it's impossible to say that it's down to any one thing or person … but Steve Cotterill and Paul Baker should take a lot of the credit.

Mike Davis has been at the club, on and off, as long as anybody.

It was the right people at the right time. The coming together of the right playing staff, the right management staff, the right chairman and the right board of directors meant that success happened. It was the right blend, the right chemistry and the right personalities. Everyone was totally committed to the cause, and all had a vision and a passion for the club. And Steve Cotterill and Paul Baker were the people who brought it all together.

Four current players – skipper Chris Banks, Jamie Victory, Lee Howells and Michael Duff – were there when Cotterill took over. As players, why did they think the success happened? Skipper Chris Banks also paints a picture of a united club:

I don't think you can ever say it's any one person, or factor – I think everyone has pulled their weight and made it happen. Obviously Steve has been crucial, because of his drive and passion, but don't forget Graham and Mike Davis as well – they have taken pressure off Steve at key times. It's a great club and everyone mucks in, and as a result we really achieve more than you think is possible.

Like Banks, Jamie Victory has been at the club for all of the five years.

Players were playing within themselves and Steve brought the best out of them. He also brought in players who were good enough and brought the best out of them as well. He just got the right blend together and we all learned a lot from him.

Lee Howells is the club's longest serving player, having been at Whaddon Road since 1991, so he is ideally positioned to comment on the last five years:

I think I'd pick out the team spirit really – everyone gets on really well and so we all enjoy, and have enjoyed, playing together as we've gone up the leagues. A bit like playing with your mates in many ways.

Finally Mike Duff, the first player ever to play in a full international as a Cheltenham player:

Being at Cheltenham Town over the past five years is how football should be. If I ever move, I wonder if it would be the same, and if I would adjust to it as there may be little cliques at other clubs which we have never had here. On the field we are very professional, and off the field Steve blended it very well. There were a lot of players underachieving, for instance how Chris Banks spent ten years out of the League I will never know, and the same goes for Lee Howells.

   Steve's man-management was great – don't forget that our record signing is only £25,000: people never believe me when I tell them that. What he did was to go out and get the players he wanted, not just as footballers but as characters too. Being a good player wasn't good enough for him, he also looked at their character and if they would fit in with us. If he did sign a bad egg, they didn't stay for very long.

So what is the conclusion from these discussion? Firstly, as the history of football, and indeed teams in any form of life shows, a united team, with a common purpose, will more often that not defeat a team of apparently more talented individuals. This is not to say that the Robins have not had talent; rather, it is to acknowedge the role of team spirit in making this happen, on and off the field. As some of the comments above show, everybody in the club has pulled together to make things happen. Both on and off the pitch the club has allowed no prima donnas who might seek to do things for their own, rather than the collective benefit.

It is, however, worth looking at what could be broken down into four separate factors (in alphabetical order): the directors, the management, the players and the supporters.

Let's face it, boards of directors are not really flavour of the month amongst fans, yet they are becoming ever more important in football. Sadly there are all too many cases where the directors have their own interests at heart, be it for status or financial reasons. At Cheltenham, things could hardly be further from the truth – the board are all Robins fans in their own right, often of long standing, who, as we have seen, take no money from the club, and put hours of unpaid time into off-the-field activities. This book has repeatedly stressed how important it has been for the club to keep pace off the field with what has been happening on the field – from getting the finances right to enable the financial requirements of the Conference to be met in 1997, to bringing the ground up to the latest League regulations in 2002. The board deserve great credit for that, as well as for contributing to the general atmosphere of openness and approachability by being available to fans. I can think of few chairman who would have invited your two authors round to their house for an evening to be interviewed for a book such as this, as Paul Baker did. Oh … and they appointed, and kept for five years, a certain Steve Cotterill.

This brings us on to the second factor – the management of the club. This, as Cotterill would be the first to recognise, was again a team effort, with Mike Davis and Graham Allner both playing key roles in the success. The esteem in which this duo are held within the club was evident when, despite the unsolicited applications from much bigger 'names' for the vacant manager's job after Cotterill moved to Stoke, the board decided very quickly, with the full support of the players, to confirm Allner and Davis as the 'new' management team.

However, mention 'management' in conjunction with Cheltenham Town, and the first thoughts are about Steve Cotterill. There is no doubt that Cheltenham are fortunate to have had him – he is quite simply an outstanding manager and coach who is destined to reach the very highest levels in the game, as is shown by the interest with which high-ranking officials at the FA are monitoring his progress. His contribution has been immense and it is difficult to pick out specifics out, but let's pick out two of the main ones.

Firstly, he has the ability to build teams – to take players and mould them into a side which is much greater than the sum of its parts, through coaching, through motivation, perhaps even through a bit of fear, and then to get those teams performing consistently for long periods of time. The numerous long unbeaten runs of the Cotterill era bear testimony to that, and in the 200 or so games he was in charge for, how many really poor Cheltenham performances can you remember? And he built these teams with very little money. To get the success he has achieved whilst spending nothing on transfer fees in the last three years, and working with one of the lowest wage budgets in the division is simply astonishing.

Secondly, and perhaps this is the most important legacy, he personally drove Cheltenham Town to believe in themselves more, and to aim higher. Much of what has been achieved, as Paul Baker has already remarked on, was around Cheltenham being 'carried' by Steve Cotterill's own personal drive, motivation and energy. This drove the club, both on and off the field to go for higher goals than they had previously believed possible: as an example, when they got back into the Conference most involved in the club would have been happy to have just survived, likewise once League status was achieved. Cotterill's restless energy made sure that progress rather than consolidation was the aim, and this drive affected everybody at the club – players, supporters and officials. Cheltenham Town, and indeed the town of Cheltenham, owe him a lot. Good luck at Stoke, Steve.

The third group who contributed to the rise of the club were, of course, the players. Again stating the very obvious, no matter how good the off-field or on-field management of the club, it has been to those out on the pitch to deliver the goods. The players have, of course, delivered magnificently; they have worked together as a team for the common good, and have seen the results come through. Perhaps the key factor is how many of them have consistently raised their standards, season after season, as the rise has continued. Four players – Chris Banks, Michael Duff, Lee Howells and Jamie Victory – now face a new season where they will be playing at a level three years higher than they were five years ago, and it is to their credit that after each of the previous promotion they have made the step up to be key members of the side in the new division. Others, such as Steve Book, Richard Walker, John Brough, Mark Yates and Russell Milton, have come through from Conference days and made the step up into the Football League.

What makes the rise of Cheltenham unique in recent football history is that so many of the players have stayed as the club has risen up the divisions. If one looks back at other clubs who have had similar runs of success in terms of a number of promotions in short order, the teams they have fielded have often changed markedly as players have left, unable to cope with the higher level of playing. The fact that so many of the successful Cheltenham side last year were playing at the highest level they had consistently played at in their careers is testimony to their ability to adapt and improve. Compare that with Rushden or Kidderminster, the two sides who came up from the Conference after Cheltenham – both of them have made significant changes to their teams since their non-League days.

Finally, there are the fans. The simple truth is that Cheltenham has no real history as a football town. As a result, the club has not had latent support within the area to draw on as the on-field transformation took place. This is very different from a club with a deep tradition, where though they might fall on hard times and gates suffer accordingly, at the first hint of success the fans will flock back – a Wolves, a West Brom, even a Swindon.

Accordingly, the support that has taken the average gate from 700 to just over 4,000 in six years has, in many cases, been 'new' support – people who have never previously watched the club on an ongoing basis. The trip to Wembley for the FA Trophy gave some indication of how many people had some interest in the club – some 18,000 went up from Gloucestershire that day – and with Cheltenham as a town being situated some distance from other League clubs, there has always been the possibility of gates improving.

It is, however, to the supporters' credit that the average gate has continued to rise. Of course, nothing attracts fans more than success and the real challenge will be once a more difficult time comes on the pitch. Yet the town has reacted positively to the club's success and the hard core of people who will go week in, week out has significantly increased – without this increase, the finances of the club would look a lot less healthy.

So, everyone has played their part in the rise, and for those clubs seeking the formula, hard work and teamwork, together with some outstanding individual talent, which has been harnessed for the common good, seems to be. It's easy, when written down, and sounds more like something you would find in the pages of a business book. The trick is in delivery ... and that's why the Robins have risen!

Statistics

2001/02 Nationwide League Division Three

	P	Home					Away					Pt
		W	D	L	F	A	W	D	L	F	A	
Plymouth Argyle	46	19	2	2	41	11	12	7	4	30	17	102
Luton T	46	15	5	3	50	18	15	2	6	46	30	97
Mansfield T	46	17	3	3	49	24	7	4	12	23	36	79
Cheltenham T	46	11	11	1	40	20	10	4	9	26	29	78
Rochdale	46	13	8	2	41	22	8	7	8	24	30	78
Rushden & D	46	14	5	4	40	20	6	8	9	29	33	73
Hartlepool Utd	46	12	6	5	53	23	8	5	10	21	25	71
Scunthorpe Utd	46	14	5	4	43	22	5	9	9	31	34	71
Shrewsbury T	46	13	4	6	36	19	7	6	10	28	34	70
Kidderminster H	46	13	6	4	35	17	6	3	14	21	30	66
Hull City	46	12	6	5	38	18	4	7	12	19	33	61
Southend Utd	46	12	5	6	36	22	3	8	12	15	32	58
Macclesfield T	46	7	7	9	23	25	8	6	9	18	27	58
York City	46	11	5	7	26	20	5	4	14	28	47	57
Darlington	46	11	6	6	37	25	4	5	14	23	46	56
Exeter City	46	7	9	7	25	32	7	4	12	23	41	55
Carlisle Utd	46	11	5	7	31	21	1	11	11	18	35	52
Leyton Orient	46	10	7	6	37	25	3	6	14	18	46	52
Torquay Utd	46	8	6	9	27	31	4	9	10	19	32	51
Swansea City	46	7	8	8	26	26	6	4	13	27	51	51
Oxford Utd	46	8	7	8	34	28	3	7	13	19	34	47
Lincoln City	46	8	4	11	25	27	2	12	9	19	35	46
Bristol Rovers	46	8	7	8	28	28	3	5	15	12	32	45
Halifax T	46	5	9	9	24	28	3	3	17	15	56	36

2000/01 Nationwide League Division Three

	P	Home					Away					Pt
		W	D	L	F	A	W	D	L	F	A	
Brighton & HA	46	19	2	2	52	14	9	6	8	21	21	92
Cardiff City	46	16	7	0	56	20	7	6	10	39	38	82
Chesterfield*	46	16	5	2	46	14	9	9	5	33	28	80
Hartlepool Utd	46	12	8	3	40	23	9	6	8	31	31	77
Leyton Orient	46	13	7	3	31	18	7	8	8	28	33	75
Hull City	46	12	7	4	27	18	7	10	6	20	21	74
Blackpool	46	14	4	5	50	26	8	2	13	24	32	72
Rochdale	46	11	8	4	36	25	7	9	7	23	23	71
Cheltenham T	46	12	5	6	37	27	6	9	8	22	25	68
Scunthorpe Utd	46	13	7	3	42	16	5	4	14	20	36	65
Southend Utd	46	10	8	5	29	23	5	10	8	26	30	63
Plymouth Argyle	46	13	5	5	33	17	2	8	13	21	44	58
Mansfield T	46	12	7	4	40	26	3	6	14	24	46	58
Macclesfield T	46	10	5	8	23	21	4	9	10	28	45	58
Shrewsbury T	46	12	5	6	30	26	3	5	15	19	39	55
Kidderminster H	46	10	6	7	29	27	3	8	12	18	34	53
York City	46	9	6	8	23	26	4	7	12	19	37	52
Lincoln City	46	9	9	5	36	28	3	6	14	22	38	51
Exeter City	46	8	9	6	22	20	4	5	14	18	38	50
Darlington	46	10	6	7	28	23	2	7	14	16	33	49
Torquay Utd	46	8	9	6	30	29	4	4	15	22	48	49
Carlisle Utd	46	8	8	7	26	26	3	7	13	16	39	48
Halifax Town	46	7	6	10	33	32	5	5	13	21	36	47
Barnet	46	9	8	6	44	29	3	1	19	23	52	45

*Nine points deducted, breach of rules

1999/2000 Nationwide League Division Three

	P	Home					Away					Pt
		W	D	L	F	A	W	D	L	F	A	
Swansea City	46	15	6	2	32	11	9	7	7	19	19	85
Rotherham Utd	46	13	5	5	43	17	11	7	5	29	19	84
Northampton T	46	16	2	5	36	18	9	5	9	27	27	82
Darlington	46	13	9	1	43	15	8	7	8	23	21	79
Peterborough U	46	14	4	5	39	30	8	8	7	24	24	78
Barnet	46	12	6	5	36	24	9	6	8	23	29	75
Hartlepool Utd	46	16	1	6	32	17	5	8	10	28	32	72
Cheltenham T	46	13	4	6	28	17	7	6	10	22	25	70
Torquay Utd	46	12	6	5	35	20	7	6	10	27	32	69
Rochdale	46	8	7	8	21	25	10	7	6	36	29	68
Brighton & HA	46	10	7	6	38	25	7	9	7	26	21	67
Plymouth Argyle	46	12	10	1	38	18	4	8	11	17	33	66
Macclesfield T	46	9	7	7	36	30	9	4	10	30	31	65
Hull City	46	7	8	8	26	23	8	6	9	17	20	59
Lincoln City	46	11	6	6	38	23	4	8	11	29	46	59
Southend Utd	46	11	5	7	37	31	4	6	13	16	30	56
Mansfield T	46	9	6	8	33	26	7	2	14	17	39	56
Halifax T	46	7	5	11	22	24	8	4	11	22	34	54
Leyton Orient	46	7	7	9	22	22	6	6	11	25	30	52
York City	46	7	10	6	21	21	5	6	12	18	32	52
Exeter City	46	8	6	9	27	30	3	5	15	15	42	44
Shrewsbury T	46	5	6	12	20	27	4	7	12	20	40	40
Carlisle Utd	46	6	8	9	23	27	3	4	16	19	48	39
Chester City	46	5	5	13	20	36	5	4	14	24	43	39

1998/99 Nationwide Conference

	P	Home					Away					Pt
		W	D	L	F	A	W	D	L	F	A	
Cheltenham T	42	11	9	1	35	14	11	5	5	36	22	80
Kettering T	42	11	5	5	31	16	11	5	5	27	21	76
Hayes	42	12	3	6	34	25	10	5	6	29	25	74
Rushden & D	42	11	4	6	41	22	9	8	4	30	20	72
Yeovil T	42	8	4	9	35	32	12	7	2	33	22	71
Stevenage Boro	42	9	9	3	37	23	8	8	5	25	22	68
Northwich Vics	42	11	3	7	29	21	8	6	7	31	30	66
Kingstonian	42	9	7	5	25	19	8	6	7	25	30	64
Woking	42	9	5	7	27	20	9	4	8	24	25	63
Hednesford T	42	9	8	4	30	24	6	8	7	19	20	61
Dover Athletic	42	9	5	7	27	21	6	4	9	27	27	58
Forest Green Rov	42	9	5	7	28	22	6	8	7	28	28	58
Hereford Utd	42	9	5	7	25	17	6	5	10	24	29	55
Morecambe	42	9	5	7	31	29	6	3	12	29	47	53
Kidderminster H	42	9	4	8	32	22	5	5	11	24	30	51
Doncaster R	42	7	5	9	26	25	5	7	9	25	29	48
Telford Utd	42	7	8	6	24	24	3	8	10	20	36	46
Southport	42	6	9	6	29	28	4	6	11	18	31	45
Barrow	42	7	5	9	17	23	4	5	12	23	40	43
Welling Utd	42	4	7	10	18	30	5	7	9	26	35	41
Leek T	42	5	5	11	34	42	3	3	15	14	34	32
Farnborough T	42	6	5	10	29	48	1	6	14	12	41	32

1997/98 Vauxhall Conference

	P	Home					Away					Pt
		W	D	L	F	A	W	D	L	F	A	
Halifax T	42	17	4	0	51	15	8	8	5	23	28	87
Cheltenham T	42	15	4	2	39	15	8	5	8	24	28	78
Woking	42	14	3	4	47	22	8	5	8	25	24	74
Rushden & D	42	12	4	5	44	26	11	1	9	35	31	74
Morecambe	42	11	4	6	35	30	10	6	5	42	34	73
Hereford Utd	42	11	7	3	30	19	7	6	8	26	30	67
Hednesford T	42	14	4	3	28	12	4	8	9	31	38	66
Slough T	42	10	6	5	34	21	8	4	9	24	28	64
Northwich Vics	42	8	9	4	34	24	7	6	8	29	35	60
Welling Utd	42	11	5	5	39	27	6	4	11	25	35	60
Yeovil T	42	14	3	4	45	24	3	5	13	28	39	59
Dover Athletic	42	10	4	7	34	29	5	6	10	26	41	55
Kettering T	42	8	6	7	29	29	5	7	9	24	31	52
Stevenage Boro	42	8	8	5	35	27	5	4	12	24	36	51
Southport	42	9	5	7	32	26	4	6	11	24	32	50
Kidderminster H	42	6	8	7	32	31	5	6	10	24	32	47
Farnborough T	42	10	3	8	37	27	2	5	14	19	43	44
Leek T	42	8	8	5	34	26	2	6	13	18	41	44
Telford Utd	42	6	7	8	25	31	4	5	12	28	45	42
Gateshead	42	7	6	8	32	35	1	5	15	19	52	35
Stalybridge Celtic	42	6	5	10	33	38	1	3	17	15	55	29

1996/97 Dr Martens League Premier Division

	P	Home					Away					Pt
		W	D	L	F	A	W	D	L	F	A	
Gresley Rovers	42	12	5	4	38	20	13	5	3	37	20	85
Cheltenham T	42	11	5	5	33	19	10	6	5	43	25	74
Gloucester C	42	13	4	4	45	28	8	6	7	36	28	73
Halesowen T	42	11	5	5	40	27	10	5	6	37	27	73
King's Lynn	42	12	2	7	36	28	8	6	7	29	33	68
Burton Albion	42	10	7	4	37	22	8	5	8	33	31	66
Nuneaton Boro	42	15	2	4	44	20	4	7	10	17	32	66
Sittingbourne	42	10	3	8	38	33	9	4	8	38	32	64
Merthyr Tydfil	42	11	3	7	42	27	6	6	9	27	34	60
Worcester C	42	10	6	5	32	23	5	8	8	20	27	59
Atherstone Utd	42	8	9	4	24	21	7	4	10	22	26	58
Salisbury C	42	6	8	7	26	28	9	5	7	31	38	58
Sudbury T	42	8	3	9	34	33	7	4	10	38	39	55
Gravesend & N	42	10	4	7	34	27	6	3	12	29	46	55
Dorchester T	42	10	6	5	36	29	4	5	12	26	37	51
Hastings T	42	7	9	5	28	27	6	5	10	21	33	51
Crawley T	42	6	6	9	23	30	7	2	12	26	37	47
Cambridge C	42	6	6	10	31	37	6	5	7	28	28	46
Ashford T	42	8	4	9	30	32	5	6	10	23	47	45
Baldock T	42	6	4	11	24	41	5	4	12	28	49	41
Newport AFC	42	6	5	10	26	33	3	8	10	14	27	40
Chelmsford C	42	5	7	9	31	34	1	7	13	18	36	32